NEW SOCIOLOGIES OF SEX WORK

New Sociologies of Sex Work

Edited by

KATE HARDY
University of Leeds, UK

SARAH KINGSTON
Leeds Metropolitan University, UK

TEELA SANDERS
University of Leeds, UK

LONDON AND NEW YORK

First published 2010 by Ashgate Publishing

2 Park Square, Milton Park, Abingdon, Oxfordshire OX14 4RN
52 Vanderbilt Avenue, New York, NY 10017

Routledge is an imprint of the Taylor & Francis Group, an informa business

First issued in paperback 2020

Copyright © Kate Hardy, Sarah Kingston and Teela Sanders 2010

Kate Hardy, Sarah Kingston and Teela Sanders have asserted their right under the Copyright, Designs and Patents Act, 1988, to be identified as the editors of this work.

All rights reserved. No part of this book may be reprinted or reproduced or utilised in any form or by any electronic, mechanical, or other means, now known or hereafter invented, including photocopying and recording, or in any information storage or retrieval system, without permission in writing from the publishers.

Notice:
Product or corporate names may be trademarks or registered trademarks, and are used only for identification and explanation without intent to infringe.

British Library Cataloguing in Publication Data
New sociologies of sex work.
  1. Prostitution. 2. Prostitutes--Social conditions.
  3. Prostitutes' customers. 4. Sex-oriented businesses.
  5. Prostitution--Research.
  I. Hardy, Kate. II. Kingston, Sarah. III. Sanders, Teela.
  306.7'4-dc22

Library of Congress Cataloging-in-Publication Data
New sociologies of sex work / [edited] by Kate Hardy, Sarah Kingston and Teela Sanders.
    p. cm.
  Includes index.
  ISBN 978-0-7546-7986-8 (hbk) -- ISBN 978-0-7546-9968-2 1. Prostitution. 2. Sex-oriented businesses. 3. Sex. I. Hardy, Kate, 1983- II. Kingston, Sarah. III. Sanders, Teela.

  HQ118.N49 2010
  306.74--dc22

2010028779

ISBN 13: 978-0-7546-7986-8 (hbk)
ISBN 13: 978-0-367-60249-9 (pbk)

Contents

List of Tables	*vii*
Notes on Contributors	*ix*

Introduction: New Sociologies of Sex Work in Perspective *Sarah Kingston and Teela Sanders*	1

PART I   PROSTITUTION POLICY: THEN AND NOW

1	Flappers, Amateurs and Professionals: The Spectrum of Promiscuity in 1920s Britain *Samantha Caslin*	11
2	Intent to Criminalize: Men who Buy Sex and Prostitution Policy in the UK *Sarah Kingston*	23
3	Out of the Shadows (and Into a Bit of Light): Decriminalization, Human Rights and Street-based Sex Work in New Zealand *Lynzi Armstrong*	39

PART II   METHODOLOGY: DOING SEX WORK RESEARCH

4	Tackling Taboos: Men who Pay for Sex and the Emotional Researcher *Natalie Hammond*	59
5	Walking the Beat: Doing Outreach with Male Sex Workers *Mary Whowell*	75
6	New Technologies, New Territories: Using the Internet to Connect with Sex Workers and Sex Industry Organizers *Suzanne Jenkins*	91

PART III MOBILITY, SEX WORK AND CONSUMPTION

7 Situating the Female Gaze:
Understanding (Sex) Tourism Practices in Thailand 109
Erin Sanders

8 The Place of the Gringo Gulch:
Space, Gender, and Nation in Sex Tourism 123
Megan Rivers-Moore

9 Taxi Dancers:
Tango Labour and Commercialized Intimacy in Buenos Aires 137
Maria Törnqvist and Kate Hardy

10 Temporal Dimensions of Cabaret Dancers' Circular Migration
to Switzerland 149
Romaric Thiévent

PART IV SEX WORK: ORGANIZING, RESISTANCE AND CULTURE

11 'If you shut up, they kill you':
Sex Worker Resistance in Argentina 167
Kate Hardy

12 'Just get pissed and enjoy yourself':
Understanding Lap-dancing as 'Anti-work' 181
Rachela Colosi

13 The Diverse Vulnerabilities of Lesbian, Gay, Bisexual
and Trans Sex Workers in the UK 197
Kath Browne, Mark Cull and Phil Hubbard

14 Repackaging Sex:
Class, Crass, and the Good Vibrations Model of Sexual Retail 213
Lynn Comella

Index 227

List of Tables

6.1	Number of interviews by methods and gender	99
10.1	Origin and number of cabaret dancers holding an 'L' permit in December 2008	152
13.1	When you sold or exchanged sex who did you have sex with? – Men by gender (*Count Me In Too*, missing data excluded)	202
13.2	When you sold or exchanged sex who did you have sex with? – Women by gender (*Count Me In Too*, missing data excluded)	202
13.3	Payment for sexual acts by sexual identity (*Count Me In Too*, missing data excluded)	202
13.4	Frequency of selling or exchanging sex (*Count Me In Too*, missing data excluded)	203
13.5	What have you ever exchanged sex for? (Multiple responses allowed, *Count Me In Too*)	204
13.6	What were/are your reasons for selling sex? (Multiple responses allowed, *Count Me In Too*)	207
13.7	Major categories from qualitative data: What were/are your reasons for selling sex?	207

Notes on Contributors

Lynzi Armstrong is a PhD student in the Institute of Criminology at Victoria University of Wellington. Her research interests include prostitution law reform, feminist criminology, and sexual violence. She is currently completing a thesis on strategies to manage the risks of violence, amongst female street-based sex workers in New Zealand.

Kath Browne is a Senior Lecturer in Human Geography at the University of Brighton. She is the lead researcher in the *Count Me In Too* research project (www.countmeintoo.co.uk), which she has been working on since 2005. She co-wrote *Queer Spiritual Spaces* and has co-edited two key texts, *Queer Methods and Methodologies* and *Geographies of Sexualities: Theory, Practices and Politics*. She has written over 40 publications across a range of disciplines, using diverse formats. She is currently writing the Count Me In Too book with Leela Bakshi.

Samantha Caslin is a postgraduate research student at the University of Manchester where she is studying for a PhD in History. Having completed her undergraduate degree in History and Sociology from the University of Liverpool in 2006 she is very interested in conducting interdisciplinary research and exploring the historical dimensions to contemporary moral issues. Her PhD examines the influence of moral purity on Liverpool's streets during the early and mid-twentieth century and considers how cultural anxieties about prostitution have impacted upon women's use of public space. Sam's research interests extend into the areas of gender and sexuality, consumerism and social theory.

Rachela Colosi is a Lecturer in Social Policy at the University of Lincoln. Before joining the University of Lincoln, Rachela was a Lecturer in Youth Studies at Teesside University, where she worked for a year after completing her PhD in 2008. Before working in academia she worked as a lap-dancer and agency stripper, a set of experiences which has shaped her current academic interests. Rachela is author of *Dirty Dancing? An Ethnography of Lap-dancing*, based on her PhD, and is currently conducting a study about lap-dancing club customers. Her research interests are in the area of sex-work, particularly erotic dance. She is also interested in youth cultures and the night-time economy.

Lynn Comella is an Assistant Professor in the Women's Studies Department at the University of Nevada, Las Vegas. She received her PhD in Communication from the University of Massachusetts, Amherst in 2004. Her research and teaching interests include media and popular culture, sexuality studies, and consumer culture and citizenship, with a particular focus on sexual commerce and the adult industry. She has written extensively about the emergence of the women's market for sex toys and pornography, and is currently completing a book-length manuscript on the history and retail culture of feminist sex toy stores in the United States.

Mark Cull has worked in the voluntary sector for the past eight years. For Hove YMCA, in partnership with the University of Brighton, he researched the experiences and needs of homeless Lesbian, Gay, Bisexual and Transgender young people in Brighton and Hove. More recently, he was employed as a Health Promotion Coordinator for the Terrence Higgins Trust, where he provided sexual health and HIV-related services to male sex workers, and took a strategic lead around the local male sex work industry. Mark is again working for the YMCA as the Right Here Project Leader, a young people's resilience building project to prevent mental health issues.

Natalie Hammond is in the final stages of her ESRC-funded PhD in the department of Sociological Studies at the University of Sheffield. Her doctoral thesis focuses on men who pay for sex. In exploring the commercial and non-commercial experiences of men who engage in sexual commerce through the lens of sexuality and relationships, men's attraction towards and involvement in commercial sex is located in part of the broader landscape of male heterosexualities. Her research interests are in the areas of men and masculinities; heterosexuality; and the wider aspects of the commercial sex industry.

Kate Hardy is a researcher in the School of Sociology and Social Policy at the University of Leeds. She is currently working on an ESRC project 'The Regulatory Dance', which is investigating the rise of lap dancing in the night time economy, particularly focusing on labour conditions in the industry. Her PhD thesis is entitled 'Proletaria de la vida: sex worker organising in Argentina', which explores strategies for sex worker resistance and union organization. She has published pieces in *International Labour and Working Class, Journal of International Development, The Guardian* and *Developments* and presented papers at conferences on labour, geography and sexualities. Her research interests include informal, irregular and 'atypical' labour, ethical and responsible methodologies, feminism, gender, agency and resistance.

Phil Hubbard is Professor in Urban Social Geography. He has published widely on geographies of commercial sex and is author of the forthcoming text *Cities and Sexualities*.

Suzanne Jenkins is an independent social researcher. Her main research interests are in the legal regulation of off-street sex work. Suzanne's PhD research, completed at Keele University in 2009, was entitled 'Beyond gender: an examination of exploitation in sex work'. This was an empirical study which built upon feminist theories of prostitution by comparing the experiences of female prostitutes with male and transgendered escort sex workers. Suzanne is also interested in research methodology, especially in the context of hard-to-reach populations and sensitive topic matters. Most recently, she has contributed to various research projects on topics such as male circumcision, the history and purpose of birth registration and conscientious objection in public life. She is a member of the Keele Gender, Sexuality and Law Research Group and the AHRC Research Centre for Law, Gender and Sexuality at the University of Kent.

Sarah Kingston is a researcher affiliated with Leeds Metropolitan University. She also works as an associate lecturer for the Open University and teaches at Leeds University. Sarah is Co-founder and Coordinator of the Sex Work Research Postgraduate Conference. She recently completed her PhD at Leeds University in 2009 in which she explored community perceptions of prostitution. She is currently undertaking research into young people's perceptions of religion, funded by the ESRC and EHRC in conjunction with colleagues from Leeds Metropolitan University, Brunel University and Middlesex University. Sarah is also a member of the UKNSWP. Her recent publications include 'Demonizing desire: Men who buy sex and prostitution policy', Research for *Sex Work Journal* and is currently working on publishing from her PhD.

Megan Rivers-Moore is a postdoctoral fellow at the Women and Gender Studies Institute, University of Toronto, and a research fellow at the Instituto de Investigaciones Sociales, Universidad de Costa Rica.

Erin Sanders is a Research Fellow in the Social Policy Research Centre at Middlesex University in London. Her ESRC-funded PhD research was conducted at the University Nottingham in the School of Sociology and Social Policy. This ethnographic study explored western women's interactions with sexualized tourist spaces in Thailand.

Teela Sanders is a Reader in Sociology in the School of Sociology and Social Policy at the University of Leeds. Sitting on the borders of criminology and sociology, Teela explores the inter-relationship between human sexuality and socio-legal structures. She has published on the indoor sex markets, *Sex Work: A Risky Business* (Willan, 2005); *Paying for Pleasure: Men Who Buy Sex* (Willan, 2008) and was principal author for the path-breaking textbook *Prostitution: Sex Work, Policy and Politics* with Maggie O'Neill and Jane Pitcher (Sage, 2009). She is currently working on an ESRC funded project, *The Regulatory Dance: Investigating the Structural Integration of Sexual Consumption into the Night Time Economy.*

Romaric Thiévent is a final year PhD candidate at the Institute of Geography of the University of Neuchâtel, Switzerland. In his PhD entitled 'Circulatory migration: the case of cabaret dancers', he analyses the trajectories and the logics of circulation of foreign strippers who come to work in Switzerland. Broadly, his research interests bear on circular migration, the gendered aspects of mobility, sex work and the spatial dimensions of asylum policies.

Maria Törnqvist received her PhD in Sociology from Stockholm University, Sweden. She is currently conducting research on tango tourism in Buenos Aires. She has also published on Swedish gender equality politics in *Könspolitik på gränsen* (*Gender Politics at the Border*) (2006) and has published a prize winning teaching book in feminist theory, *Feministisk teori i rörliga bilder* (*Feminist Theory in Motion*), with Katharina Tollin in 2005. For the 2006 academic year she was a visiting scholar at the Sociology department at UC Berkeley, and from Fall 2007 she has been a postdoctoral fellow at GEXcel (Centre for Gender Excellence) Örebro University and Stockholm University, Sweden.

Mary Whowell completed her PhD on the practice, performance and regulation of male sex work at Loughborough University in August 2009. Following this, she moved to Simon Fraser University in Vancouver to pursue a post-doctoral project, funded by a prestigious Commonwealth Scholarship, on the regulation of adult entertainment through licensing and municipal by-law in 13 cities across Canada. Mary has experience as a volunteer outreach worker, and has delivered harm minimization services to male and female sex workers, operating in both on and off street environments in the UK and Canada. She is a member of the UK Network of Sex Work Projects, and has publications in *Geoforum* and the *Journal of Law and Society*. In September 2010 she will join the School of Arts and Social Sciences at Northumbria University as a Lecturer in Criminology

Introduction
New Sociologies of Sex Work in Perspective

Sarah Kingston and Teela Sanders

The area of sex work studies, which is now established into the emerging discipline of 'the sociology of sex work' (Sanders, O'Neill and Pitcher 2009), has seen an expansion in publications over the past decade, drawing together disciplines from across the social sciences (namely sociology, criminology and social policy) and humanities, as well as other disciplines such as health, medicine and social care, geography, psychology and theology. Much has been published on this topic from the Western world, with different theories, insights and empirical research exposing the diverse nature of the sex industry alongside the social issues connected to commercial sex. However, there has still been a tendency for research and writing to focus on the more obvious parts of the sex industry – that is the visible elements of female street prostitution and those topics which attract media attention such as the criminalized aspects of prostitution, drugs, and health issues.

In order to immediately move away from the traditional focus on 'prostitution', this edited collection, *New Sociologies of Sex Work*, will demonstrate some of the breadth of sociological inquiry that is taking place by researchers new to the field. One criticism of the current literature is that the same topics are reproduced and over-concentrated on, which stifles attention to activities which are on the margins. The sex industry is diverse in its nature, organization, presentation, who takes part, responses to it and how it sits in the broader context of globalization and regulation (see Agustin 2007). In order to reflect this reality, this edited collection seeks to promote an interdisciplinary approach to understanding the sex industry. It is our aim to promote this objective by addressing several issues in terms of what is a 'new' contribution to the sociology of sex work.

New Sociologies of Sex Work will be of interest to anyone concerned with this topic, especially those in the fields of criminology, sociology, social policy, and gender studies. More broadly those interested in research methodologies and those involved in developing policy and service responses to sex work will equally find these contributions useful. This book will be of use to researchers, undergraduates and postgraduates who are interested in the area, studying such modules or writing dissertations. The book will also appeal to a wide audience who want to gain an understanding of the diversity and dynamics of the sex industry in a number of international contexts.

What's New?

The area of 'sex work research' has witnessed an explosion in recent years: new technologies, changing social relations and shifting social and sexual boundaries have shaped and informed the sex industry in many ways. For example, the mass expansion of the Internet has opened up avenues to sex sell all over the globe (see Bernstein 2007). Technological advances have enabled instant access and communication. With over 400 million users of 'Facebook' and other social networking sites, technology has enabled the development of global networks across borders and physical social boundaries. Furthermore, sex workers have gained independence through the Internet and one argument is that sex workers have more control over their work and clientele (Veena 2007).

With new technologies and avenues of communication we can also see the mixing of cultures. The mixing of ideas, beliefs, and cultural practices can inform national and international politics, and social norms. For example, mainstream publications are now accessible online, such as the US magazine *Playboy* which went online in 1994 and became the 11th most visited site on the web in 1996. In 1995 live video conference, technologies which enable live person to person video and audio transmission was introduced on the internet. This new video technology enables strip shows and live sex shows to be viewed over the internet. Thus consumption is no longer just limited to place and consumption patterns are neither solely locally nor nationally based. With changing social norms such as an increasing recognition of gay rights and growing significance of sex as leisure, the social world remains in constant flux with new ideas, new sexual practices, sexual aids and sexual relations emerging.

Current economic times also bring social and political changes. According to Leheny (1995) sex tourism in Thailand was adopted as a means of economic development in the 1970s and flourishes because of the number of male tourists from Europe, America and Japan. Lim (1999: 7) argues that 1.5 per cent of the female population in the Philippines, Malaysia, Thailand and Indonesia work as prostitutes, demonstrating the size of the sex industry and influence of foreign visitors. Demanding economies across the globe mean there is an equation of more people (particularly impoverished women) who need to make money to survive, with fewer skilled jobs. It is here that the informal economies, such as sex work, become mainstream employment for many.

New national policy developments have also shaped the sex industry in recent years. Since editing this book, for instance, the UK has witnessed significant changes in UK law with new legislation which criminalizes the purchase of sex from those forced into prostitution; harsher penalties for those apprehended for kerb-crawling, and orders to exit and change behaviour for 'persistent' street prostitutes under the Policing and Crime Act 2009 (Home Office 2009). Significant changes can also be seen in China where an anti-porn drive has led to the closure of over 90 websites (Branigan and Kiss 2009). Such shifts and changes have significant impacts for the sex industry in terms of how it is organized, how sex workers manage their work, how the sex industry is responded to and how it is viewed by politicians, policy makers and the public.

Global changes in migration, public policy, health and employment are having a major impact on the sex industry. For instance, with advancements in aviation technology people are able to travel extensively for their sexual pleasure (Soothill and Sanders 2004). The industrialization of the sex trade and its globalization are fundamental factors which make the contemporary sex industry different from previous times. In this context, the sex industry has grown and diversified on many spatial and functional levels. It is now more specialized, diversified and sophisticated (Hausbeck and Brents 2002). No longer confined by national borders the sex industry has developed in new forms. This book is testament to these developments, not only in sex work but also in research practice.

Why Sex Work?

The title of this book reflects a growing appreciation within the literature that the sale of sexual services can be a form of work (Bindman and Doezema 1997, Brewis and Linstead 2000). This collection recognizes that 'sex work' is more diverse and varied than prostitution, limited not to the act of 'sex', but also to various forms of direct and indirect sexual activities. From lap dancing to phone sex, dominatrix to prostitution, this collection will examine the sex industry in some of its many forms, rather than focusing upon the most commonly identified aspect of the sex industry, street sex work. It will also consider the role of those who are integrated in the 'sex as leisure' industry such as phone sex worker, maids, managers, lap dancers and sex shop assistants.

Although we acknowledge there are those men, women and children who do not exercise choice in their participation in the sex industry, due to trafficking, exploitation or abuse, this collection focuses exclusively on 'sex as work'. Given this focus, the use of the term 'sex work' pays appreciation to the men and women who identify themselves as 'sex workers'. Viewing sex as a form of work has lead to heated debates, both theoretically and politically. Put crudely, radical feminists for example, see prostitution, in all its forms, as a form of violence against all women as it reduces women to sexual objects for men's pleasure. Liberal feminists on the other hand recognize that some men and women make a rational choice to sell sex given their circumstances and that rather than being socialized into a subordinate position; they recognize that power is not one-dimensional and that not all sex workers are women.

New Sociologies

The sociological gaze is the lens through which these chapters have been researched and written. Drawing on the cultural context of the setting in which sex work takes place, and the wider context where by commercial sex is part of a wider story of leisure, work, and movement across borders, these chapters offer sociological insight into the contemporary organization of the sex industries. Whilst drawing from expected disciplines such as criminology and social policy, these chapters keep in focus the relationships between structure and agency which are at the heart of the sex-work nexus. In this sense, the social relations which are embedded in the sex industries are explored beyond issues of criminalization, 'deviance' or other judgements about the morality of the sex industry. Therefore these chapters bring to the reader a fresh and critical look at the diversity of contemporary sex work and draws attention to aspects which are seldom reflected upon.

Book Outline

The collection explores theoretical, policy, methodological and empirical ideas as each chapter pushes the boundaries of a specific area by offering new, critical research and commentary. We were particularly concerned that the collection is diverse and speaks to a range of audiences who are interested in the diversity of the global sex markets, methodology and policy. Equally it was essential that the topics covered are not Eurocentric but reflect the global nature of the sex industry as several pieces reflect wider cultural contexts in which sex work occurs. The contents of this book are divided into four themes: policy; methodologies; mobility; and sex worker resistance. We have pulled together these themes because they map onto general areas of research and current debates.

Part I – Prostitution Policy: Then and Now

We begin the collection examining how policy and legal regimes influence the organization and experience of sex work. This first section will examine historical and contemporary policy which surrounds the sex industry in the UK and then moves on to explore prostitution policy in New Zealand. Samantha Caslin begins this collection by exploring prostitution in the 1920s. As this chapter demonstrates, female prostitutes were the focus of contention both socially and politically, a focus which has characterized prostitution policy for many decades thereafter in the UK. This chapter illustrates how the law has been used to distinguish between good women and prostitutes and that debates around the use of the term 'common prostitute' have historical roots.

Although the history of prostitution policy in the UK has been characterized by a focus on the criminalization and stigmatization of female sex workers, recent shifts in policy in the UK has witnessed a focus on men who buy sex. In Chapter 2, Sarah Kingston explores recent legislation which criminalizes the purchase of sex under the Policing and Crime Act, 2009. This chapter will explore the process through which this new legislation was developed, arguing that the consultation process which preceded the act was biased and the evidence upon which this law was based was unreliable.

In contrast, New Zealand witnessed the decriminalization of prostitution in 2003. Lynzi Armstrong explores the rationale behind this shift in prostitution policy in Chapter 3. In this chapter she considers some impacts of decriminalization, such as changes in sex workers working practices, sexual health, the extent of violence and exploitation, the numbers and visibility of sex workers and their clients, sex worker-police relations and stigma.

Part II – Methodology: Doing Sex Work Research

Natalie Hammond begins the second part of the book by examining the role that emotions can play in researching men who buy sex. In Chapter 4 of this collection Natalie considers how emotional responses and feelings experienced by the researcher can sometimes inhibit the research process and may impact upon research findings. In her very truthful account of her own emotional responses to sex work research, Natalie gives researchers' food for thought, as although she argues research is meant to be unbiased and objective, it can sometimes be difficult for researchers to remain completely impartial. It is argued that by being aware that sometimes emotions can inform sex work research, researchers may be in a better position to prepare themselves to overcome methodological barriers and obstacles.

Mary Whowell explores the realm of outreach work and offers her accounts of acting both as a researcher and an outreach worker in Chapter 5. In this chapter she considers some of the issues which arise from doing outreach, such as the potentially dangerous nature of outreach. This chapter will be of use to researchers who may consider using sex work support agencies to gain access for research purposes. As Mary shows, there are many factors in being a support worker which should be considered before embarking on this type of research.

In Chapter 6, Suzanne Jenkins explores how new technologies, such as the Internet, can offer exciting opportunities for sex work researchers. Drawing upon empirical research with escort sex workers, she illustrates how the Internet is useful in providing access to hidden populations, facilitating the administration of surveys and by providing a sensitive means of communication for interview purposes. Suzanne's work demonstrates how the use of such techniques can produce both insightful and rich data which potentially may be unobtainable by the use of many traditional methodological approaches.

Part III – Mobility, Sex Work and Consumption

Erin Sanders begins this section of the book in Chapter 7 exploring her own PhD research of female tourists experiences in Thailand, a country characterized and constructed as a male sexual space. In this chapter however, Erin uses empirical data to suggest that western women engage within these sexualized spaces as part of what they see as their cultural experience, something that, as tourists they

6   *New Sociologies of Sex Work*

engage in on their visit to Thailand. Whilst most women that Erin met did not participate in overt sexual encounters (i.e. not buying sex from sex workers), they actively explored these sexualized spaces in ways that they would not normally do in their own countries.

In Chapter 8 Megan Rivers-Moore explores how the Costa Rican state attempts to define the sex tourist area of 'Gringo Gulch' as a foreign space, plagued by immorality. In doing so, Gringo Gulch is represented as a sex tourism trade dominated by foreigners whom the state seeks to remove. Yet, rather than evicting both foreign sex workers and their clients Megan demonstrates that the removal of otherness is exclusively linked to the female body, as sex workers and not their male clients are considered as foreign. State discourses about sex workers as 'foreign' and the state's immigration raids seek to distinguish Gringo Gulch as foreign, thereby protecting the nation's morality, yet simultaneously benefiting from money being spent by sex tourists. It is argued that 'State discourses and migration controls therefore play a central role in determining precisely which foreign bodies are welcome and which are intolerable'.

Chapter 9 moves the focus to Latin America, where Maria Törnqvist and Kate Hardy explore the concept of 'transnational intimacy' drawing from an ethnographic study of tango tourism in Buenos Aires. For visitors from far away looking for 'authentic tango' there are Argentine men who make a living out of selling dance companies to foreign women at the tango venues. The aim of this contribution is not only to show how such a sensual economy of emotions is put to work, but also to challenge the notion of romance tourism by looking at the intimate relationships between the male dancers and the female western tourists.

In Chapter 10, Romaric Thiévent examines the migration of cabaret dancers to Switzerland based upon his empirical research with 21 current and former cabaret dancers, 11 agents, seven cabaret owners and two waiters. Here is it argued that rather than dancers migrating in one direction, from their country of origin to Switzerland; many migrate in a circular fashion, migrating from their home country to Switzerland and then back home. In this chapter, Romaric explores this circulatory migration whilst documenting the many reasons why dancers migrate in this manner, such as family commitments, work permits limitations, availability of employment and education.

Part IV – Sex Work: Organizing, Resistance and Culture

Kate Hardy explores the successes of sex worker organization in Argentina in Chapter 11. In this chapter, the author examines the history of the sex work organization AMMAR, charting its emergence and lobbying successes. In doing so, she contextualizes its success by considering the many barriers and challenges sex worker organizations may face, and in particular the barriers which the sex work organization AMMAR has faced. Yet despite these challenges Kate demonstrates how the organization has been successful in producing solidarity amongst sex workers in the harshest conditions of disempowerment.

Continuing the theme of labour, Rachela Colosi develops the concept of 'anti-work' in relation to the motivations and experiences of women who work as lap-dancers in the UK. From her 'dancer-ethnography' of 'Starlets', these insider observations provide the reader with challenging ideas regarding why women work as dancers, the resistance tactics that collectively create and implement as a means of resisting management, and having 'fun' at work.

In Chapter 13, Kath Browne, Mark Cull and Phil Hubbard provide an overview of data gained from the *Count Me In Too* and *Out On My Own* research projects based in Brighton which sought to explore sex working in the LGBT community. In doing so this chapter adds to limited research on selling sex within the LGBT community. Through contextualizing the experiences of LGBT sex workers within Brighton's specific geographical context; this chapter considers how engagement in theses spaces may encourage routes into sex work. The chapter considers how issues of identity, vulnerabilities and empowerment may inform entry into sex work, and thereby argue that sex work is not always best understood as an issue of gendered exploitation which considers that only women can be exploited.

In Chapter 14 Lynn Comella explores how the Good Vibrations model of sex retailing, an educationally based and quasi-therapeutic approach to selling sex toys, has become a prototype for many feminist sex toy businesses across the United States. Drawing on over a decade of ethnographic research, including over 70 interviews with feminist retailers, sex toy manufacturers, and porn producers, Lynn examines the underlying philosophies and retail strategies that comprise the Good Vibrations model of sexual retail. As Lynn shows retailers worked hard to differentiate their businesses from the stereotype of sex toy stores as sleazy, sexist places through the design of their retail environments, the products they sell, and the type of customer service they provide.

References

Agustin, L.M. (2007). *Sex at the Margins: Migration, Labour Markets and the Rescue Industry*. London: Zed Books.

Bernstein, E. (2007). *Temporarily Yours: Intimacy, Authenticity and the Commerce of Sex*. Chicago: University of Chicago Press.

Bindman, J. and Doezema, J. (1997). 'Redefining Prostitution as Sex Work on the International Agenda', Anti-Slavery International, London (UK), Network of Sex Work Projects (UK).

Branigan, T. and Kiss, J. (2009). 'China closes 90 websites as internet crackdown intensifies: Nervous Beijing "determined to quell online dissent" as economic gloom deepens and sensitive anniversaries loom', *The Guardian* [online 12 January 2009], available at: http://www.guardian.co.uk/media/2009/jan/13/china-internet-censorship [accessed 20 January 2010].

Brewis, J. and Linstead, S. (2000). *Sex, Work and Sex Work: Eroticizing Organization*. London: Routledge.

Hausbeck, K. and Brents, B.G. (2002). 'McDonaldization of the Sex Industries? The Business of Sex', in G. Ritzer (ed.) *McDonaldization: The Reader*, pp. 91–106. Thousand Oaks, CA: Pine Forge Press.

Home Office (2009). 'Policing and Crime Act 2009'. London: HMSO.

Leheny, D. (1995). 'A political economy of Asian sex tourism', *Annals of Tourism Research*, 22(2): 367–84.

Lim, L.L. (1998). *The Sex Sector: The Economic and Social Bases of Prostitution in Southeast Asia*. Geneva: International Labour Office.

Sanders, T., O'Neill, M. and Pitcher, J. (2009). *Prostitution: Sex Work, Policy and Politics*. London: Sage.

Soothill, K. and Sanders, T. (2004) 'Parlour Games: The value of an internet site providing punters' views of massage parlours', *Police Journal*, 77(1): 43–53.

Veena, N. (2007). 'Revisiting the Prostitution Debate in the Technology Age: Women Who Use the Internet for Sex Work in Bangkok', *Gender, Technology and Development*, 11(1): 97–107.

PART I
Prostitution Policy: Then and Now

Chapter 1

Flappers, Amateurs and Professionals: The Spectrum of Promiscuity in 1920s Britain

Samantha Caslin

In this chapter I argue that in the early part of the twentieth century, female prostitution in England and Wales was treated, often conflictingly, as both a social problem and a criminal practice. Legally and socially, prostitutes were *defined* as 'others', as a separate and lower class of women. They represented a threat to gender norms and were understood to be a danger to the moral order. A repository for wider fears about social dislocation and the changing position of women, the female prostitute, as she emerges in the historical record, was a highly politicized and much contested figure. She featured in distinct yet overlapping debates about issues of class, gender and popular culture. Indeed, during the 1920s, conceptions of prostitution as 'criminal' or 'deviant' were reinforced by contemporary anxieties surrounding female sexuality generally. Fears about prostitution as a social contagion appeared alongside a perceived rise in promiscuity amongst young women.

This chapter argues that during the 1920s the boundaries used to define 'professional' prostitute women from the 'amateurs' (girls who would occasionally engage in sexual acts with men for money or some other form of payment) became volatile, causing significant concern about what was to be done about the sexual habits of young women. In fact, though it may be possible to provide a general definition of what was meant by a 'professional' or 'amateur' prostitute in 1920s Britain, there was by no means consensus as to the boundaries separating these two forms of deviance. It is suggested that the very labelling and categorization of women in this way was illustrative of Britain's struggle to make sense of a spectrum of sexual practices and femininities. This spectrum ranged from the respected domesticated female, through the flapper and the amateur, to the more transgressive professional prostitute. Official concerns about how the prostitute could or should be distinguished from other women, as reflected in evidence put to the Departmental Committee on the issue of solicitation in 1927 and 1928, were interrelated with wider fears about the degree of influence prostitutes might have over other younger women. Consequently, a historical approach to sexual morality has the potential to draw out how the criminalization of the prostitute has been used as part of wider cultural discourses which seek to regulate which types of sexual practice are respectable and thus acceptable.

Although prostitution[1] has in fact already been the subject of considerable historical investigation much of this work has concentrated on the Victorian era. In particular, the seminal work of Judith Walkowitz (1982, 1992) on Victorian London has been very influential in women's and gender history.[2] However, less is known about prostitution during the early-mid twentieth century. With academic interest in contemporary prostitution, or sex work, increasing, it is pertinent that this gap in the academic literature is addressed. The way in which prostitution is understood and legislated is very much a product of the history of the discourses and anxieties that surround it. To this end, I offer a reading of the prostitute as a constructed subject rather than an objective, *a priori* agent whom the law merely intervenes to control.[3] I work from the assumption that the ways in which prostitution is defined and understood are products of their social contexts.

Although other historians have begun to address early twentieth century prostitution in Britain much remains to be explored in terms of the cultural history of prostitution. Recently, Julia Laite (2008a, 2008b) has done useful work on the policing of prostitution in the early twentieth century as well as examining the role of pressure groups such as the Association for Moral and Social Hygiene in provoking a review of prostitution laws. At the same time Helen Self's (2003) work has provided us with a detailed account of prostitution law in the mid-twentieth century. Focusing on the proceedings of the Wolfenden Committee (1954–1957), she offers a feminist interpretation of prostitution law and argues that it has been morally shaped. This work seeks to add to these studies on the law and prostitution in this period by providing a cultural analysis of the subject. I draw on a wide range of sources, from books by noted social commentators such as Mrs Cecil Chesterton to accounts provided by senior officials within the police service. I argue that much of the anxiety that surrounded prostitution and the debates about how prostitution should be dealt with was the result of the widespread cultural practice of using prostitution to define how women should not behave. For many cultural commentators and officials, responses to prostitution were intended to send out a message to all women about how to behave. However, this is not to say that there was by any means consensus about the specifics of such a message. This chapter illustrates that, during the 1920s, there was a great deal of concern about

---

1   Throughout this chapter I refer to 'prostitution', and occasionally 'vice', rather than 'sex work' as these were the terms used most often during the era being examined.

2   For more on Victorian prostitution see, for example, Trevor Fisher (2001) *Prostitution and the Victorians*, Stroud: Sutton Publishing; Paula Bartley (2000) *Prostitution: Prevention and Reform in England, 1860–1914*, London: Routledge; Paul McHugh (1980) *Prostitution and Victorian Social Reform*, London: Croom Helm.

3   Carol Smart (1995) also advocates this poststructuralist approach to the relationship between the subject and the law in her work *Law, Crime and Sexuality: Essays in Feminism*, London: Sage, see p. 8 in particular.

female respectability. I propose here that a discursive spectrum of promiscuity was invoked by law-makers and commentators in a bid to make sense of prostitution as a form of transgression requiring legal control.

Prostitution as Part of a Spectrum of Promiscuity

During the early part of the twentieth century, the symbolic figure of the female prostitute was often invoked by cultural commentators and journalists seeking to make statements about the sexual morality of Britain as a whole. Motivated particularly by concerns about the perceived promiscuity of Britain's young women, especially in the aftermath of the First World War, the female prostitute acted as a 'nefarious "other"' in the process of post-war reconstruction (Hubbard 1999: 1). Following the war, domesticity, 'an ideal for which [Britain's men] might risk their lives', assumed primacy as the peacetime idyll and the focus of post-war reconstruction (Bourke 1999: 162–3). Yet against this vision of what Britain could and should be there was fear that the war had challenged and changed Britain's sexual mores and practices. Uncertainties about gender roles created an unsettled view of social order. Judy Giles (1995: 102) has argued that the war broke down gendered geographies of urban space in Britain with women's increased social and financial independence making them more visible in urban life. The idea that a woman's 'respectability' could be ascertained by her patronization, or lack thereof, of particular city spaces had been disrupted. Moreover, war itself was linked to heightened sexual awareness amongst women. For example, in 1934 Magnus Hirschfeld believed the war to have 'confirmed' the theory that 'war atrocities and bloody deeds have an erotic effect on women' (in Kohn 1992: 47). Beneath this sentiment was a belief that the war had somehow sexualized women. In some instances the eroticization of women came to represent war itself. In 1929 Mary Borden invoked images of female prostitution to personify 'pain' as 'a harlot in the pay of War', a creature who could be seen 'plying her trade here any day' (in Kingsley Kent 1993: 71). Unsurprisingly then, the 'modern young woman', 'the flapper', that iconic mix of 1920s androgyny and hedonistic debauchery, received an 'exceptional' amount of attention in contemporary press and literature (Bingham 2004: 47). Fresh, fashionable and sexually provocative, the flapper was invoked alongside the 'amateur' prostitute as an 'eternal Eve' (Melman 1988: 1).

With considerable overlap in terms of how 'flappers' and 'amateurs' were defined, discourses about the lifestyles of 'modern' women were implicitly and sometimes explicitly conflated with those about prostitution. The amateur, just like the flapper, was said to frequent 'Bohemia' and the 'underworld'; both were considered to be influenced by literature and cinema and spend their days idly shopping or visiting the cinema whilst earning their 'keep by going for joy rides with young men' (Chesterton 1928: 158). This meant that the boundaries between who was defined as a 'flapper' and who was defined as an 'amateur' prostitute were blurred. According to one cultural commentator, the amateur was simply a girl who was 'ready to have promiscuous relations for gifts or pleasures, or even for no external reward' (Hall 1933: 19). Sometimes a girl did not even have to engage in 'promiscuous relations' to be labelled an amateur: Unlike the 'professional' or the 'part-time' prostitutes, this girl would, it was suggested, 'make a habit of "teasing"' (Chesterton 1928: 158). In this way, prostitution was understood to be one aspect of sexual deviance on a spectrum of promiscuity. There was a degree of fluidity in and uncertainty about definitions of promiscuity, amateurism and professional prostitution. In fact, from time to time a woman could be classed as moving between these categories. Mrs Cecil Chesterton argued that some amateurs would settle into jobs, others would mix this lifestyle with occasional work and some would become part-time prostitutes (Chesterton 1928: 159). Consequently, promiscuity was rendered synonymous with amateur prostitution and the deviancy of females who engaged in pre-marital sex was viewed increasingly as a derivative form of prostitution. The belief that women could fall into various categories at different points in their young lives meant that the lifestyles of all young women came under close scrutiny.[4]

The growing consumer market was seen by many at the time as linked to the sex lives of young women. In 1920 Hubert Stringer (1920: 180) conducted an investigation into the causes of prostitution. Amongst the causes he identified were 'bad literature', 'sensational – but not necessarily immoral – cinema films' and 'unpleasant shops', each encouraging 'vicious thoughts' in those of such a predisposition and stirring 'such thoughts in others'. This suggests that Stringer believed there to be a link between people's past times and their sense of morality. He implies that the viewing, reading and shopping habits of women could encourage them to engage in prostitution. At the same time, new consumerism and new leisure patterns added to anxieties that traditional courtship rituals were being eradicated in favour of new geographies of sex. It was feared that greater economic freedom amongst the young was allowing them to take ownership of certain public spaces. One commentator, Mrs Neville-Rolfe (1935: 295), worried that economic changes provided the modern youth with the money to enjoy 'their own amusements', such as the cinema, whilst 'entirely independent' of the supervision of the family. Moreover, the cinema and the dance hall were presented by her as sites of moral disorder, as places where 'girls' might 'drift for a time into a life of promiscuity or even prostitution' should they begin to meet 'casual acquaintances' there (Neville-Rolfe 1935: 295). Thus anxieties about changes in women's lifestyles came to be discussed with reference to the opportunities for promiscuity now available to young women through new forms of consumerism.

For anxious moral commentators new patterns of female consumerism intensified their fear that it was becoming increasingly difficult to tell on which part of the spectrum of promiscuity a woman sat simply by judging her appearance.

---

4   Mrs Cecil Chesterton argued that some amateurs would settle into jobs, others would mix this lifestyle with occasional work, and some would become part-time prostitutes. See Chesterton (1928: 158).

Indeed, by the late 1920s it was 'difficult to tell some of the professionals from the amateurs' (Chesterton 1928: 161).[5] Central to this ambiguity was the proliferation of girls purchasing and wearing make-up, with the young female body itself becoming a source for anxieties about promiscuity and prostitution (see Chesterton 1928: 161). Kohn (1992: 6) has suggested that within West End society there 'was no border between prostitutes and socially acceptable women'; 'wearing make-up' and patronizing the streets were 'no longer the sole prerogative of prostitutes'.

That any young woman was a potential 'amateur' became a source of great anxiety. Mrs Cecil Chesterton's work *Women of the Underworld* (1928: 163) warned of the dangers that the amateur presented to all who encountered her: 'Externally...sweet mannered', she appears as a 'flower that has been taken out of water and only needs kindness and shelter to blossom again'. Yet for Chesterton this was supposedly part of the amateur's ploy to con men into taking pity on her; thus she emerged crueller and more morally reprehensible than her professional counterpart. Describing her as an 'incubus', the amateur was presented by Chesterton as being of a lower moral standard than the professional prostitute who, in Chesterton's words, 'is not a vicious product' (Chesterton 1928: 163 and 153). Indeed, Chesterton considered professional prostitution far more sympathetically; it was suggested that this category of women were usually found 'drifting' into their trade as 'victims of circumstance' (Chesterton 1928: 153 and 1926: 79). According to Chesterton (1926: 80), it was unsettlingly plausible that a naïve young woman might 'in sheer high spirits and love of fun...go to lengths she never contemplated and wake up the next morning in a man's bed'. With a premium placed upon the respectability of women, it was difficult for a 'fallen' woman to regain her social status. At the same time Chesterton (1926: 84) emphasized the poverty experienced by younger professional prostitutes, recalling how one girl she saw had holes in her stockings and wore a 'cheap coat'. In this sense an appreciation of the economic causes of professional prostitution was not absent from debates about the issue during the 1920s.

Prostitution and the Law

With the prostitute functioning as a key figure in discourses about promiscuity and sexual morality, it is no surprise that the laws which surrounded prostitution became a matter of debate and interest. By the 1920s, the legal status of prostitution was considered by many to be unclear. Though prostitution was not in itself illegal, convictions were possible because of acts associated with the trade. The Vagrancy Act, which had been passed in 1824, punished prostitutes who wandered in public in a 'riotous or indecent manner' with either a fine or imprisonment. In addition, the Metropolitan Police Act of 1839 stated that prostitutes who lead to

---

5   The work of historian Julia Laite suggests that this was also the case during the First World War. See Julia A. Laite (2008:103).

16 *New Sociologies of Sex Work*

the annoyance of passers-by in London would be fined, whilst the Town Police Clauses Act of 1847 meant that elsewhere solicitation was punishable by a fine or up to fourteen days imprisonment. Significantly, arrests made under the 1839 and the 1847 Acts only needed to have been witnessed by one constable. Without corroborative evidence, the application of these laws was consequently open to interpretation and exploitation by the police.

Following a number of scandals, such as the 1922 overturning of Sir Almeric Fitzroy's conviction for 'annoying' two women in Hyde Park 'on the ground that one of the women, Mrs Turner, was a "notorious prostitute"', the Association for Moral and Social Hygiene (AMSH) called for changes to the 'solicitation laws' (Self 2003: 5). As with the British branch of the International Abolitionist Federation, the AMSH was opposed to the state regulation of prostitution (Jeffreys 1997: 19). Though the organization wanted a reduction in promiscuity, it did not support the notion that the law should intervene in the private activities of consenting adults. It is not surprising then that Lesley Hall (2000: 101) has described the AMSH as 'perhaps the most feminist and libertarian of the social purity organizations'. They argued that women were prosecuted for soliciting men when, in fact, men solicited women (Self 2003: 5). However, proposals that the solicitation laws should be relaxed or significantly altered proved to be controversial. The National Vigilance Association was opposed to the AMSH's campaign. In 1928 they argued that prostitution had moved from the streets and into entertainment venues such as cafes, music-halls and cinemas (Letter from the NVA to the AMSH, 10th May 1928). So, while 'vigilance, refuge and reformatory organisations' simultaneously campaigned to get the solicitation laws strengthened (Self 2003: 6), between 1923 and 1926 the AMSH supported a Public Places (Order) Bill (Laite 2008a: 217) which called for the removal of the term 'common prostitute' and proposed to replace the 'solicitation laws' with 'a simple provision, which substantially covers the same ground as the existing law, but applies to all persons alike'. It was also proposed that 'proceedings shall only be taken on complaint by or on behalf of the party aggrieved' (Public Places (Order) Bill Memorandum, November 1926). Though the Bill was not passed, the criticisms that it raised did not go unnoticed.

As a result of these debates and campaigns, the Street Offences Committee was appointed by the Home Office to examine the legalities of the law surrounding solicitation. Known, after its chairman, as the Macmillan Committee, it met between 1927 and 1928. During the course of their inquiry, the Macmillan Committee outlined what it regarded as the two main opposing positions on the legal status of the 'common prostitute'. Outlining what was essentially the AMSH's argument in favour of changing the law, the Committee noted: '[s]ome people take the view that it is undesirable to create an offence which can only be committed by a common prostitute and that the law should be expressed in general terms, saying "any person" who does these things' (see Horwood 1927: 20). The counter argument to this, as the committee understood it, was that the 'requirement of the person being a common prostitute is a protection to the ordinary woman, which may outweigh the disadvantage to the common prostitute of being so labelled' (see Horwood 1927: 20).

When giving his evidence to the Committee, the Police Commissioner of the Metropolis, Sir William Horwood, concurred with the latter argument. He suggested to the Committee that the legal category of 'common prostitute' was 'a very great protection to the ordinary woman' (Horwood 1927: 20). Rather than acting as a label which could potentially stigmatize any woman who frequented urban public spaces, Horwood's argument proposed that respectable women would not be affected by the term. He explained that though a policeman may be 'suspicious' at the sight of, in the committee's words, 'an ordinary lady' talking to a man in the street, the policeman would 'not presume she was a common prostitute' (Horwood 1927: 20). For this reason Horwood suggested that the term 'common prostitute' should remain in law. He argued that to dispense with the term in favour of prosecuting *any* persons who committed solicitation offences would make the powers of the police 'very much wider,' a prospect that he did not support (Horwood 1927: 21). In this way, the Commissioner of the Metropolitan Police was confident that it was possible to distinguish between the civil liberties of the 'ordinary' woman and those of prostitute women. In targeting the common prostitute specifically, Horwood, and indeed the law, presented prostitute women, rather than their efforts to solicit, as the main problem. Her perceived difference from other, respectable women meant that the prostitute unsettled accepted gender codes about female conduct. Thus she was legally and culturally fashioned as an 'other' because she was thought of as a moral danger and a threat to the social order of the nation's urban spaces. The law was influenced by a desire to maintain gender codes and by doing so, social stability.

Specifically, the visibility of professional prostitutes in urban spaces undermined the notion that women were to be chaste and morally pure. Though some commentators stressed the economic circumstances that drove these women onto the streets (see aforementioned Chesterton 1926: 84), others were far less compassionate in their attitudes. Gladys Mary Hall (1933: 84) argued that poverty was a 'diminishing factor' in the causes of prostitution. She suggested that it was 'impossible to know…whether [the professional prostitute's poverty] is the cause of her way of life, or the accompaniment', an argument which effectively presented the professional prostitute as deserving of judgement rather than compassion (Hall 1933: 84). Other writers offered a similarly damning assessment of the morality of the professional prostitute; factors such as 'choice' or 'laziness' and a desire to work as a prostitute were thought to be significant in attracting women into vice (Croft 1934: 29). Within these discourses, the prostitute represented a form of disreputable womanhood, with her chosen profession making her 'essentially unfeminine' (Croft 1934: 30). As a result, officials such as the Metropolitan Police Commissioner were more interested in policing this form of disreputable womanhood than dealing with solicitation per se. The only evidence Horwood required to be sure that a woman was a prostitute was that she was seen 'continually and persistently speaking to men' (Horwood 1927: 23). That the act of repeatedly talking to men in public spaces was deemed to be a transgressive enough offence to warrant the attention of the law illustrates the extent to which gendered codes of respectability informed the policing of women.

There was significant concern that the visibility of prostitutes in urban centres could have a disastrous effect upon the morality of young women in general. Stuart Deacon, the Stipendiary Magistrate of Liverpool, told the committee that it was necessary for law enforcement to focus on 'habitual offenders' as these were the individuals most likely to 'turn [...] other young girls into prostitutes' (Deacon 1928: 30). In particular, he was concerned that the mere presence of prostitutes on the streets of Liverpool would lead to a lowering of moral standards. He argued: 'There are certain lodging houses and certain streets which get known as the places where these women live, and young girls going away from home, and so on, will drift into these places and come under the influence of these older women' (Deacon 1928: 30). In this way Deacon's evidence reflects the wider cultural fears that the boundaries between prostitute women and ordinary women were increasingly being broken down by changing sexual practices. However, unlike the Met Police Commissioner in London who attempted to reassert the usefulness of the category of the common prostitute as a means for differentiating between women, the Stipendiary Magistrate in Liverpool did not believe such terminology was helpful. He argued that he wanted to see the term 'eliminated from the statute book' because it conveyed legitimacy unto the actions of these women (Deacon 1928: 5): 'I have often been struck', he told the Committee, 'by the fact that many of the women seem to regard their trade as a recognized trade.' He claimed:

> I have often heard a woman in effect say to me, apparently in good faith as far as she is concerned, "my occupation is selling my body; that is my trade"; and to a certain extent the law recognises it when it speaks of a common prostitute, as you may speak of a bookmaker; it is her trade, her occupation. (Deacon 1928: 6)

As Deacon's evidence indicates, the act of questioning the efficacy of the law should not be interpreted as the preserve of those sympathetic towards prostitutes or their freedom. Though Deacon was in agreement with organizations such as the AMSH in wanting to eradicate the term 'common prostitute', his argument was based on very different reasons. Unlike the AMSH, he does not appear to have been at all concerned with the gender bias that this legal category supported. Indeed, Deacon's summation of prostitutes as a 'danger to the community from a health point of view' depended upon a gender-biased reading of the prostitute as a carrier and transmitter of sexual disease (Deacon 1928: 6). In this respect, Deacon's argument has much in common with Victorian attitudes towards prostitution which where enshrined in the notorious Contagious Diseases Acts of the 1860s.

Moreover, the evidence of other individuals who addressed the Macmillan Committee showed a similar keenness to discuss prostitution in relation to the sexual activities of women in general. That is to say that even within the realms of official legal debate uncertainty about what might be defined as prostitution and what might be defined as promiscuity was clearly evident. For example, in evidence given to the Committee, Miss F. L. Langton, a Missionary for Bow Street Police Court, proposed four classes of prostitute (Langton 1927–28: 1). The first of these was the professional prostitute, who, she said, 'would not work' and was 'not above robbing the man'. Secondly she suggested that there existed a category of girls who come out 'during weekends' for their 'love of excitement, company, dress, or extra gaiety' (though she did not label these girls 'amateur' prostitutes her description certainly evokes this concept). Thirdly, she referred to the 'class of woman or girl who comes out only when in financial need'. According to her own estimations, such women 'often found that their greatest help has arisen from their forced appearance in a Court, and been grateful accordingly'. Lastly, Langton proposed that there was a 'younger careless class of girl' who had 'drifted onto the streets'; but, she cautioned, these girls were 'by no means always willing to give up their present life' (Langton 1927–28: 1). Once again then, a spectrum of sexual deviance was evoked in order to try to make sense of prostitution, its impact on society and what should be done about it. The evidence of Mrs Bramwell Booth of the Salvation Army clearly reflected contemporary concern about the apparent fluidity between the respectable woman and the professional prostitute. She wholeheartedly concurred with concerns about women who wore cosmetics when arguing that changes in the 'habits of women as a whole' meant that prostitutes 'are no longer clearly distinguished' (Bramwell Booth 1927–28: Part 1 of Summary of Evidence).

In an effort to clearly demark the boundaries between the legal and moral arguments about the issue of solicitation, the Macmillan Committee ultimately recommended that the legal category of the common prostitute should be abolished. If solicitation was the offence being prosecuted, then, it was argued, it should not matter who committed the act. However, as Helen Self (2003: 6–7) has noted, the Committee's final report was ultimately contradictory in its argument that the law should not attempt to police individual morality. She argues that despite the report's claim that the law should deal only with 'the way in which the individual woman conducted herself in public and not with her private morality' there were actually over thirty references to morality in the report itself (Self 2003: 6–7). Certainly the evidence presented to the Committee that has been explored in this chapter indicates that the morality of prostitution was very much present in discussions about the nature of the offence being prosecuted. Concerns about how the prostitute should be defined in relation to other women, the degree of influence her presence had over other women and her supposed impact upon urban morality were key features in the discussions that took place. The pressing nature of these cultural concerns meant that they defined the parameters of the debate that the committee engaged in. Testimonies from members of organizations such as the Salvation Army, members of the police and from cultural commentators suggest that during the 1920s there was a significant amount of concern about the sexual and social habits of young women. Much of the debate that this concern engendered centred upon trying to decide where the boundary should lay between promiscuity and prostitution. With young women going to new entertainment venues such as the cinema and enjoying increased participation in consumer culture it was believed that it was harder to tell prostitute women apart from 'ordinary' women. Moreover, discourses about amateur prostitution meant that it was even harder to judge just what constituted an act of prostitution, throwing ambiguity over existing laws used to prosecute prostitutes. Though questions were raised about the appropriateness of the term 'common prostitute', these questions proved problematic in a society where the prostitute woman acquired great cultural significance as an example to other women of how not to behave. With the boundaries being supposedly broken down between 'ordinary women' and prostitute women, it is unsurprising that perhaps the most progressive option for redressing the quagmire of laws that were used to police solicitation, the removal of the term 'common prostitute', was ignored.

The legal use of the term 'common prostitute' continues to be an issue in the present day. The application of the term 'common prostitute' to convicted women can limit their access to certain public spaces, such as particular areas, and it means that they can be prosecuted on the evidence of just one police officer (Day 2007: 83). In fact, official responses to prostitution have remained surprisingly static over the centuries. For example, Laite's (2006) work charts the stagnation in the solicitation laws since the nineteenth century. She notes that, despite greater understanding of the women who become prostitutes and changes in the legal status of women, the legal use of the term common prostitute remains a double standard. Similarly, a recent study on failed proposals to create a prostitution 'tolerance' zone in Liverpool has suggested that such a policy would have replicated nineteenth and early twentieth-century practices of 'containment' in terms of the spatial policing of prostitutes (Howell et al. 2008: 235).

As a result of these historical continuities, we must be aware of the extent to which past debates about and strategies for dealing with prostitution shape contemporary policy. Laite (www.historyandpolicy.org 2006) has argued that using an historical approach 'may help to increase awareness of the arguments for fairer and more gender-neutral laws which consider the rights of prostitute women'. Certainly this work shows that we must pay attention to the ways in which previous debates about prostitution have been constructed if we are to fully understand the levels of gender prejudice that have shaped our approach to the issue. By identifying the existence and prominence of a discursive spectrum of promiscuity during the 1920s, this work illustrates the close relationship between cultural ideas about respectable women and policy debate on prostitution. It shows that during the 1920s the notion that the law could be used to distinguish between ordinary women and prostitute women was not abandoned despite such distinctions becoming increasingly problematic. Consequently, there are a number of key questions that future research into the history of responses to prostitution must address. Firstly, how has the stagnation in the law used to police prostitution been rationalized over time? How is it that, despite widespread social, economic and cultural change these laws have not been significantly altered since the nineteenth century? By continuing to explore these questions in more detail we may learn more about the moral and social problems involved in the criminalization of prostitution. It is also hoped that using history to critique the criminalization of prostitute women may help policy makers to find new ways of understanding and discussing the issue.

References

Bingham, A. (2004). *Gender, Modernity, and the Popular Press in Inter-War Britain*. Oxford: Clarendon Press.

Booth, B.J.P. Summary of Evidence given to the Macmillan Committee (1927–1928), HO326/8 (National Archives).

Bourke, J. (1999). *Dismembering the Male: Men's Bodies, Britain and the Great War*. London: Reaktion Books.

Chesterton, Mrs C. (1926). *In Darkest London*. London: Stanley Paul.

Chesterton, Mrs C. (1928). *Women of the Underworld*. London: Stanley Paul.

Croft, T. (1934). *The Cloven Hoof: A Study of Contemporary London Vices*. London: D. Archer.

Day, S. (2007). *On the Game: Women and Sex Work*. London: Pluto Press.

Giles, J. (1995). *Women, Identity and Private Life in Britain, 1900–50*. London: Macmillan.

Hall, G.M. (1933). *Prostitution: A Survey and a Challenge*. London: Williams and Norgate.

Hall, L.A. (2000). *Sex, Gender and Social Change in Britain since 1800*. Basingstoke: Macmillan.

Horwood, Sir W. Evidence given to the Macmillan Committee (20th December 1927). HO45.12663 (National Archives).

Howell, P., Beckingham, D. and Moore, F. (2008). 'Managed zones for sex workers in Liverpool: contemporary proposals, Victorian parallels', *Transactions of the Institute of British Geographers*, Vol. 33, 233–50.

Hubbard, P. (1999). *Sex and the City: Geographies of Prostitution in the Urban West*. Aldershot: Ashgate.

Jeffreys, S. (1997). *The Idea of Prostitution*. North Melbourne: Spinifex Press.

Kingsley Kent, S. (1993). *Making Peace: The Reconstruction of Gender in Interwar Britain*. Chichester: Princeton University Press.

Kohn, M. (1992). *Dope Girls: The Birth of the British Drug Underground*. London: Lawrence and Wishart.

Laite, J.A. (2006). 'Paying the price again: prostitution policy in historical perspective', *History and Policy* [online], available at: http://www.historyandpolicy.org/papers/policy-paper-46.html [accessed: March 2010].

Laite, J.A. (2008a). 'The Association for Moral and Social Hygiene: abolitionism and prostitution law in Britain (1915–1959)', *Women's History Review*, Vol. 17, No. 2, 207–23

Laite, J.A. (2008b). 'Taking Nellie Johnson's Fingerprints: Prostitutes and Legal Identity in Early Twentieth-Century London', *History Workshop Journal*, 65(1): 96–116.

Langton, F.L. Summary of Evidence given to the Street Offences Committee (1927–1928), HO326/8 (National Archives).

Letter from the NVA to the AMSH, 10 May 1928, 3AMS/B/04/10 (Women's Library Archive).

Melman, B. (1988). *Women and the Popular Imagination in the Twenties: Flappers and Nymphs*. London: Macmillan.

Neville-Rolfe, S. (1935). 'Sex Delinquency', in Sir H. Llewellyn Smith (ed.) *The New Survey of London Life and Labour: Volume IX – Life and Leisure*. London: P.S. King and Son.

Public Places (Order) Bill Memorandum, November 1926, HO45/12663 (National Archives).

Self, H.J. (2003). *Prostitution, Women and Misuse of the Law: The Fallen Daughters of Eve*. London: Frank Cass.

Stringer, H. (1920). *Moral Evil in London*. London: Chapman and Hall.

Walkowitz, J.R. (1982). *Prostitution and Victorian Society: Women, Class, and the State*. Cambridge: Cambridge University Press.

Walkowitz, J.R. (1992). *City of Dreadful Delight: Narratives of Sexual Danger in Late-Victorian London*. London: Virago Press.

Chapter 2

Intent to Criminalize: Men who Buy Sex and Prostitution Policy in the UK

Sarah Kingston

On 1 April 2010, the Policing and Crime Act 2009 (PCA) introduced the first piece of legislation to criminalize the purchase of sex in the United Kingdom (UK).[1] Section 14 of the Act made the purchase of sex from a person who is subject to force, threats or any other form of coercion an offence, regardless of whether the purchaser knew the person was being exploited or not (Home Office 2009). In such cases, a lack of knowledge or ignorance is no justification, excuse or defence, as the offence falls under the remit of 'strict liability'. This significant shift in legislation, which followed the first review of prostitution policy in over fifty years, demonstrates the severity by which the UK government views those who buy sex, as it could be assumed that such important and historic legislative changes could not have been made without considerable reasoning, consultation and justification. However, this chapter will demonstrate that the arguments upon which the legislation has been based are founded upon insubstantial evidence, a neglect of robust bodies of data and research and an ideological argument influenced by a particular strand of feminism.

This chapter will argue that the extent of trafficking and sexual exploitation, which underpins the reasoning behind the new strict liability offence, is far lower than the government predicted, and evidence for it cannot be found in peer reviewed research. Furthermore, although the lengthy review of prostitution policy, which preceded the Act and consisted of a number of reports and strategies, was initiated with the intention of consulting wider society, this chapter will demonstrate that despite a 'consultation' occurring, from the outset the government fully intended to further criminalize those who it deemed are the purchasers of commercial sex, *men* who buy sex. Rather than based on a nuanced view of prostitution and a consideration of the voices, opinions and experiences of a variety of people, men who buy sex from women have become a focus of prostitution policy without a thorough consultation. New Labour's renewed 'criminalization' agenda in recent years has meant that more broadly 'the problem of men' and masculinity has crept up the social and political agenda (Scourfield and Drakeford 2002: 619).

---

1 The Policing and Crime Act 2009 also removed the requirement of persistence from the offence of kerb-crawling so that men who buy sex on the street can be arrested for a first offence.

In order to examine the journey which has been taken to arrive at S14 of the PCA, this chapter will first examine the beginnings of New Labour's review of prostitution policy. By considering the initial aims of the review the chapter will demonstrate that the government's intentions of undergoing a real consultation on prostitution, grounded in solid and robust evidence and public and expert opinion were half-hearted. It is demonstrated that the language contained within consultation documents and statements made by government officials indicate a clear intention to penalize men who buy sex despite the review seeking to ascertain the views of the general public. The chapter will then go on to examine the evidence upon which the Policing and Crime Act 2009 is based, in order to show that the extent of abuse and exploitation of women within the sex industry, used as a basis for justifying the new law, is not sustained by available evidence.

This chapter aims to examine the origins of the new law and to argue that, despite undertaking a number of 'reviews' and 'consultations', the intention to introduce the new law was pre-determined. This chapter will also demonstrate that the evidence upon which the law is based is somewhat limited and misleading. Rather than 'evidence based policy', the law was guided more by ideology than a thorough review of research, literature or advice from experts in the area.

New Labour and Prostitution Policy: The Review

In May 1997, New Labour won the general election. One year later the Home Office's intention to review sex offences was announced by Alun Michael, then Deputy Home Secretary (Lord Williams of Mostyn 1999) following advice from a cross-party Parliamentary Group on Prostitution, chaired by Labour MP Diane Abbott (Lord Williams of Mostyn 1999). This group was established in 1993 and published a report based on evidence from a number of statutory and voluntary agencies and sex workers in July 1996. The report concluded that the current legislation relating to prostitution was not working, in particular because it is fragmented rather than coherent and integrated (Broadbridge 2009). It therefore recommended that the Home Secretary carry out a comprehensive review of the existing legislation relating to prostitution (Broadbridge 2009).

Initially, the Home Office (1999: 1) published a leaflet *A Review of Sex Offences* informing the public of its forthcoming review, stating that:

> A review of the criminal law on sex offences is long overdue. The structure of the law is complex and made more difficult by changes and amendments over time. Much of the law dates from a hundred years ago and more, when society was very different... Sex offences, more than any other part of the criminal law, mirror the attitude of society to sexual roles, sexual behaviour, sexual orientation and sexual exploitation... In carrying out a review of this kind it is vital that the views of ordinary people, and those with relevant expertise, are sort

and considered. We welcome all contributions which will help the Government develop the law in an open and fair way.

Such a review of prostitution policy was initiated in 2000 when the Home Office published *Setting the Boundaries* (Home Office 2000c). The review did not consider how or whether prostitution should be legal or illegal since that, they argued, was beyond its remit. However, it acknowledged the intensity of the debate and the diversity of views, and recommended that a further review examine this issue. The review was welcomed by lawyers, politicians and faith groups as it would provide the opportunity to clarify the existing law surrounding sex offences and to discuss legislation surrounding prostitution (Power 2000; Stevenson 1999; The Christian Institute 2001).

The intention to undertake this review was significant, as prostitution policy was last officially reviewed in 1957 by the Right Honorable John Wolfendon. The report of the Departmental Committee on Homosexual Offences and Prostitution focused on female street sex workers, rather than their clients and this approach has characterized prostitution policy, public opinion and police responses to the sex industry for many years. For example, the Street Offences Act, 1959 made it an offence for a *woman* to loiter or solicit for prostitution in a street or public place (Home Office 1959: S.1.1). In this sense, how the recent review of prostitution policy deals with those who buy and sell sex is therefore important. The official review of prostitution policy began in July 2004, when the Home Office (2004) published a consultation paper *Paying the Price*. As the then Home Secretary, David Blunkett stated, the review was initiated because it was believed that 'many of the laws relating to prostitution are outdated, confusing and ineffective' (2004: 5).

In January 2006, the Home Office published *A Coordinated Prostitution Strategy* devised as guidance for dealing with street prostitution in England and Wales. The *Coordinated Prostitution Strategy* sets out action to be taken by central government and local partnerships to tackle prostitution. The strategy was informed by *Paying the Price* and responses from numerous public and voluntary agencies, members of the public and an evaluation of eleven projects funded by the Crime Reduction Programme, such as the Awaken project in Blackpool which deals with the sexual exploitation of children and young people, and Hampshire Change Programme which offered arrested 'kerb-crawlers'[2] with an option to attend a re-education day as a alternative to court.

The *Coordinated Prostitution Strategy* includes five key aims prevention, tackling demand, developing routes out, ensuring justice and tackling off street prostitution, although at this stage the focus was to target commercial sexual

---

2   The offence of kerb-crawling is committed when a person 'solicits a women for the purposes of prostitution from or near a motor vehicle, persistently ... or in such a manner likely to cause annoyance to the woman solicited, or nuisance to other persons in the neighbourhood' (s.1); or, in a street or public place 'persistently solicits a woman for the purpose of prostitution' (s.2) (Home Office 1985).

exploitation, in particular where victims are young or have been trafficked. The second aim, tackling demand, included responding to community concerns by deterring those who create the demand for prostitution and removing the opportunity for street prostitution to take place. This was to be achieved through a new focus on the enforcement of the law on kerb-crawling and by introducing a new staged approach to deter kerb-crawling which included informal warnings, kerb-crawler re-education programmes and finally prosecution. The public nature of street prostitution therefore continued to be the focus of official concerns, but rather than focusing on the needs of street sex workers, at this stage it was the kerb-crawler who was the focus of New Labour's attempt to deal with prostitution. The kerb-crawler was deemed a problem for the community and links between kerb-crawlers and their impact upon local communities were highlighted throughout the document. It was by 'tackling demand' that the government responded to community concerns about men who buy sex on the street.

In order to tackle demand and assess what further measures could be taken to reduce the demand for prostitution the government launched a further six months review which commenced on 14 January 2008, the *Tackling Demand For Prostitution: A Review* (Home Office 2008b). This review included an assessment of academic research on the purchasers of sex, an audit of enforcement and prosecution practice in England and Wales to identify best practice, an evaluation of approaches to tackle demand in nine other countries and Ministerial visits to Sweden and the Netherlands to see how differing approaches have been taken. The review began with a visit to Sweden, which criminalized the purchase of sex in 1999. This was then followed by a visit to the Netherlands which operates a licensing scheme for brothels, meaning that the organization by consenting adults is not considered to be a criminal offence (Home Office 2008a).

The Tackling Demand review ended in September and was published in November, 2008 (Home Office 2008b). Six recommendations were made which included the introduction of a strict liability offence for paying for sex with someone who is 'controlled for another person's gain'; a specific marketing campaign to raise awareness amongst sex buyers about sex trafficking; an amendment to the offence of kerb-crawling and soliciting to remove the requirements of persistence, thereby allowing prosecution for a first offence; a re-run of a national anti-kerb-crawling campaign; giving powers to police to close premises linked to sexual exploitation and the encouragement of further multi-agency partnerships (Home Office 2008b: 4). One month later these recommendations were then incorporated into the Policing and Crime Bill 2008[3] which proposed the introduction of the new strict liability offence. Following consultation on the proposed bill, changes were made to the terms of the strict liability offence. Section 14 of the Policing and Crime Act 2009 thereby created a new strict liability offence which is committed if a person pays or promises payment for the sexual services of a prostitute who

---

3   A Bill is a proposal for a new law, or a proposal to change an existing law, presented for debate before Parliament (www.ukparliment.ac.uk).

has been subject to force, deception, coercion or threats. This is not therefore equivalent to full criminalization such as that associated with the Swedish model.

Identifying the reasons why the UK government would not follow the Swedish model, the Home Office concluded in its review on tackling demand that 'it would be a step too far at this time, given the relative size of the UK sex industry compared to that in Sweden and current public attitudes in the UK' (Home Office 2008a: 13). The findings of the Sex and Exploitation Survey conducted in January 2008 for the government indicated that attitudes towards making paying for sex a criminal offence were divided (Wintour 2008). Similarly Pitcher et al. (2006) and Kingston's (2009) research into community attitudes has also demonstrated a division in public perceptions towards prostitution and men who buy sex. However, rather than conducting further research, undertaking consultations or a referendum, the government argued that 'it need[ed] to work to challenge the attitudes of the sex buyers and the public as a whole before criminalizing the purchase of sex' (Home Office 2008a: 13). In the hope that as with Sweden 'over time the… public grew to support the proposed legislation' (Home Office, 2008b: 13). Given that the review of prostitution policy which preceded the act was initiated to determine and mirror the views of the public, challenging public attitudes clearly goes against this intention. Rather, as the next section will show, the willingness to engage in a consultation was never fully present.

Intent to Criminalize

The government's intention to criminalize men who buy sex from women can be seen throughout the review of prostitution policy. It is evident through legislation enacted before beginning the consultation with *Paying the Price*, within the language used in policy documents, and in suggestions made by senior government officials. This evidence questions any purported desire by the government of engaging in a true consultation.

From the start it is clear there was little intention to engage in a full consultation. Despite the government suggesting that the original intention was to consult the general public and experts in the area during the review of prostitution policy, the Home Office (1999: 1) announced that although it aimed to:

> provide coherent and clear sex offences which protect individuals, especially children and the more vulnerable from abuse and exploitation; enable abusers to be appropriately punished; and be fair and non-discriminatory in accordance with the ECHR and Human Rights Act [1998] … [it] *would not be looking at decriminalising prostitution* or pornography (my emphasis)

This suggestion is confusing, not least because the sale or purchase of sex is not, and never has been, a criminal offence. The purchase of sex was never made an offence, although the act of 'kerb-crawling' became illegal in 1985 by the Street

Offences Act. Also, it would appear that not all contributions to help develop the law in an 'open and fair' way were welcome. Thus a review of sex offences which seeks to *mirror* public attitudes, yet does so by excluding other possibilities from the outset, seems flawed from the start.

This bias in the government's approach to the consultation process was called into question before the consultation process began in 2004 with *Paying the Price*, as an underlying intention to further criminalize the purchasers of commercial sex was evident in the Criminal Justice and Police Act 2001. The Act made kerb-crawling an arrestable indictable offence where it is likely to cause annoyance to women or to other people in the neighbourhood or where it is persistent behaviour (Home Office 2001). The fact that legislation was enacted before a review of prostitution policy began questions the reasoning and will behind a review.

The openness and fairness of the consultation process is made further questionable by comments made by government officials one month before the Coordinated Strategy document was released. A policy of zero tolerance against men who buy sex and sex workers was announced in December 2005 (Travis 2005). According to the Home Office minister Fiona MacTaggart:

> Prostitution blights communities. We will take a zero tolerance approach to kerb crawling. Men who choose to use prostitutes are indirectly supporting drug dealers and abusers. The power to confiscate driving licenses already exists. We want the police to use that power (cited in Travis, 2005: 1).

Thus, before the strategy had even been released, the government made it clear that it would be taking a hard-line approach to men who buy sex, in particular the kerb-crawler.

The government's predetermined intentions were also made apparent before the *Tackling Demand* review was initiated in 2008. Despite visiting the Netherlands as part of the review, indications that the government was already considering following the Swedish model was made apparent in December 2007, when the Commons Leader, Solicitor General Harriet Harman QC held that a Swedish-style law against the purchase of sex is necessary to tackle demand for sex workers trafficked into Britain (Woodward 2007). This announcement was made despite the official review beginning in January 2008. This also introduced a shift towards viewing men who buy sex as the 'fuellers' of human trafficking for the purposes of sexual exploitation. According to Harman 'unless you tackle the demand side of human trafficking which is fuelling this trade, we will not be able to protect women from it' (Harman 2007).

Links between trafficking and men who buy sex was also evident in 2007 in the Home Office's (2007c: 31) UK Action Plan on Tackling Human Trafficking which stated that:

> A key element of this new approach to prostitution is to focus not only on those who exploit individuals through prostitution, including the traffickers, but also

to address the demand side ... to target men who might use massage parlours, saunas or other kinds of brothel, through men's magazines, websites or other targeted media using advertisements which raise awareness of trafficking for sexual exploitation and warn of the risks involved.

All of this suggests that even before the *Tackling Demand* review began, that the government had already finalized their strategy against men who buy sex.

Four months after the *Tackling Demand* review began and five months before its findings were published, the government's intentions to further criminalize men who buy sex were once again made apparent when the poster 'walk in a punter walk out a rapist' emerged, which clearly conflated all men who buy sex with potential rapists (Crime Stoppers 2008). The release of this poster one month before the visit to the Netherlands even took place further questions the process by which the Labour government undertook the legislative review. Despite undertaking a review which considered the regulation of the industry and the penalization of clients it is apparent that the government clearly intended to criminalize men who buy sex well before the review began.

Ideological Bias

The reasons that the government were so set on penalizing the purchasers of sex lie in its ideological beliefs about prostitution. These beliefs can be observed in the language used in policy documents which lead to the Policing and Crime Act 2009. For example within the consultation document *Paying the Price* no attempt is made to enter into a debate as to whether it is legitimate for someone to buy or sell sex; rather the problem of 'offenders' is continually stated. These 'offenders' are explicitly identified as 'pimps', 'drug dealers' and 'kerb-crawlers' who coerce, exploit and abuse women and children involved in prostitution (Home Office 2004: 5, 8). The exploitation, abuse and coercion is however, perceived as limited to those individuals who are categorized as 'victims'. The very limited notions of 'consent' and 'coercion' allows official discourse to appear to be doing something about the 'problem of men' whilst neglecting the material and social conditions such as poverty, and lack of choices which often condition involvement in prostitution (Phoenix and Oerton 2005). Rather, the consultation paper seeks solutions to the perceived problems of street prostitution at the individual rather than a structural level (Cusick and Berney 2005). Thus the problems are attributed to the perceived perpetrators who are thereby labelled as such. *Men* who buy sex from women on the street are identified as 'prostitute users' who 'harass women', 'fuel exploitation and problematic drug use' (Home Office 2004: 1–97). Kerb-crawlers are deemed as 'victimizers' of sex workers and communities who live in areas of street sex work.

30   *New Sociologies of Sex Work*

The language observed in *Paying the Price* shows clear similarities between radical feminist perceptions of 'prostitution user' (Jeffreys 1997: 4). Within *Paying the Price* a 'key issues' section of the document is significantly titled 'The User' and also describes them to be 'a man of around 30 years of age, married, in full time employment, and with no criminal convictions' based upon two pieces of research (Home Office 2004: 17). This gendered assumption, that men are the purchasers of sex and women the victims of sexual exploitation mirrors radical feminist beliefs which sees prostitution as implicitly gendered. Radical feminists see prostitution as the 'absolute embodiment of patriarchal privilege' (Kesler 2002: 219), a view which mirrors comments made by Harriet Harman's in her speech at a Labour Party Conference in 2009, in which she describes prostitution as 'the ultimate commodification of *women* and puts *women* at risk. It is truly degrading' (cited in Taylor 2009: 1, my emphasis).

The impact of Radical feminist thinking on prostitution is not limited to the UK. Arthur Gould's (2001) article which explored the criminalization of the purchase of sex by the Swedish government in 1999, similarly revealed the impact of Radical feminists in mobilizing support for the penalization of clients. Gould (2001) argues that the women's movement of the 1980s and 1990s played a major role in passing legislation which criminalized the client in Sweden. As with Sweden it seems the insistence that prostitution is degrading women, a form of violence again women, is the most powerful argument. The power of this argument has led to, it will be shown, a prostitution policy which lacks supportive evidence. Blinded by a particular ideological vision, the government has ignored vast amounts of data, research and academic literature to produce policy which lacks a coherent evidence base.

Ignored Evidence

In developing its policy towards men who buy sex the government ignored a wide body of evidence that seemed to contradict the path they were seeking to pursue. The evidence used throughout the consultation period, from *Paying the Price* to *Tackling Demand* was somewhat lacking. A thorough exploration of the literature, research and data surrounding men who buy sex and the extent of abuse and exploitation was not undertaken.

In *Paying the Price*, the official construction of the purchasers of commercial sex as 'user', 'abuser' and violent offender are founded upon an inadequate review of empirical research. There is no systematic review of research and literature on men who buy sex. A large amount of research and literature is ignored by the Home Office (2004). Instead, the government could have reviewed national and international research on the purchasers of commercial sex, such as Kinnell (1989; 2001), Campbell (1998; 1997), Campbell and Storr (2001), Monto (2000; 2001; 2004), Monto and Hotaling (2001), Monto and Garcia (2001) to name a

Intent to Criminalize 31

few. However, the review was limited to six pieces of literature,[4] one of which the Home Office commissioned (Hester and Westmarland 2004). Thus, this limited review did little to resolve the existing confusions and stereotypes in the media, parliamentary debates and policy as to who the clients of sex workers are, and the nature of their custom (Carpenter 2000).

Evidence which has suggested that trafficking was not a significant problem in the UK was also ignored by the government. For instance, only 13 per cent of women in one study of migrant sex workers had experienced some form of exploitation, ranging from extreme cases of trafficking to relatively more consensual arrangements (Mai 2009: 32). According to the report, only a minority (6 per cent) felt that they had been deceived and forced into selling sex in circumstances within which they had no control (Mai 2009: 32).

Findings of the government's own national police operations Operation Pentameter and Operation Pentameter 2,[5] also revealed that the extent of abuse, sexual exploitation and trafficking is nowhere near at the level originally quoted by former Foreign Office minister, Denis MacShane, of 25,000 sex slaves in the UK (Davies 2009a). Following the UK draft report from the UK Human Trafficking Centre many criticisms were raised about previous estimations made and the extent of trafficking assumed to be taking place in the UK (Davies 2009b). For example, following a crackdown on 515 premises Operation Pentameter found 84 women to be trafficked victims and 188 women were 'rescued' (Gloucestershire Constabulary 2006). It could be suggested however, that all 188 women rescued were trafficked victims but were too fearful to identify themselves as such for fear of repercussions. If so, this demonstrates that even the Police can not determine whether women are the victims of sexual exploitation, questioning the workability of the new strict liability offence.

Similarly, raids on 822 brothels, flats and massage parlours during Operation Pentameter 2 found only 167 'victims' from the national police force operation. Furthermore, of the 528 arrests made, 122 people (23 per cent) of those arrests did not take place but were recorded incorrectly, deliberately or by accident. Only 22 people (4 per cent) were finally prosecuted for trafficking, seven of which were eventually acquitted. After suggesting that 'Operation Pentameter is the mere tip of the iceberg' the results of Operation Pentameter 2 undermines this assertion and demonstrates the belief that 'several thousand more victims remain to be found' following the first operation was unfounded (Gloucestershire Constabulary 2006).

---

4   Barnard et al. (2002), Hester and Westmarland (2004), Johnson et al. (2001), Kinnell (2001), Matthews (1997), McKeganey and Barnard (1996).

5   Operation Pentameter and Pentameter 2 were nationwide campaigns launched in 2006 and 2007 to tackle sex trafficking. The UK wide policing operations involved the police, the travel industry, Government and partner agencies across the UK and Europe.

Davies (2009b) argues that this is evidence of a moral panic, as after all these efforts a total of only 15 men and women were prosecuted of trafficking offences.[6]

Given that trafficking has been cited as the reasoning behind the law it does not appear to make sense to introduce legislation which has the potential to criminalize a large proportion of men when evidence suggests that it is not as endemic as previously thought. Rather than reducing the extent of exploitation and abuse, critics such as Janni Wintherbauer, leader of the Organisation for the Interests of Prostitutes and a sex worker herself, have argued that the criminalization of the purchase of sex in Sweden has made sex workers more vulnerable to exploitation (Fouche 2007). Even the police in Sweden have commented that the law has driven women into the hands of pimps and made it harder for the police to prosecute violent men, including traffickers (Fouche 2007). Thus, as with Sweden there has been no investigation of the consequences of the new strict liability offence for women's safety.

Unworkable in Practice

During the parliamentary approval stages of the Policing and Crime Bill 2008, the terms of the strict liability offence of paying for sex with someone who is 'controlled for another person's gain' was amended following concerns raised by the Bar Council[7] and Liberty[8] about the workability and fairness of the offence. The Bar council suggested to the Public Bill Committee in its briefings on the Policing and Crime Bill, that the terms of the offence could mean that 'a defendant may be found guilty in circumstances where he could have no idea at the time that he was committing the offence' and that in their view 'the proposed clause as currently drafted is unworkable, wrong in principle and will create unfairness' (cited in Politics.co.uk 2009). Similarly, Shami Chakrabarti, the director of Liberty, made clear in her evidence to the committee that:

> Strict liability offences should be used very sparingly and should only apply to minor offences where it seems obvious in the circumstances that an offence has been committed. It should not apply when a person is unable to ascertain whether what they are doing is unlawful. Given it is not an offence to pay for sexual services of a person who is not controlled for gain, it would be unfair to impose a strict liability offence on someone who pays for the sexual services of a person who is controlled for gain but whom the offender does not know is controlled (cited in House of Commons 2009: column 1425).

---

6   Weitzer (2005) also suggests that the United States has witnessed as similar moral panic over sex trafficking.

7   The Bar Council is a professional body for barristers in England and Wales.

8   Liberty is the UK's National Council for Civil Liberties.

The unfairness of the strict liability offence lies in its onus on the client. Under this offence it does not matter whether the client knew whether the person was sexually exploited or not. The Human Rights Joints Committee concluded, from its legislative scrutiny of the Policing and Crime Bill, that it is difficult for a man to know how they should regulate their behaviour, given that a lack of knowledge that the person is being sexually exploited is no defence (Human Rights Joint Committee 2009). In this sense, the Joint Committee stated that they have grave concerns about the extent to which this offence will apply and believe that the offence could extent to people beyond who the government seeks to target. This crackdown on the purchasers of sex, they argue has the potential to place women in more exploitative and unsafe situations as the industry goes underground. They argue further that the crackdown on sex buyers may also discourage the reporting of sexual exploitation (cited in House of Commons 2009: column 1425), a knock on effect which goes against the government's intentions of reducing exploitation and abuse.

There were also concerns raised about difficulties in determining whether a person is the victim of sexual exploitation, such as those voiced by Chief Constable Tim Brain. He suggested that although he supported the new strict liability offence in principle he had concerns about the police's ability in 'gaining sufficiency of evidence to merit a suitable number of prosecutions to act as a deterrent' (cited in Whitehead 2009: 1). This may be very difficult if a person who has been trafficked or coerced may be fearful of their captors or facilitators. This is significant as these practical difficulties have implications for the justification and fairness of the offence and even the Home Office (2008a: 14) acknowledges 'the practical difficulties in proving whether a defendant knew if a woman was controlled or not'. If the government is unable to determine whether a woman is being controlled or not, how can they then expect a client to know that a woman is controlled or subject to exploitative conduct? This appears to be double standards on the government's part.

As a result of these criticisms the government proposed an amendment to the wording of the offence, replacing 'controlled for gain' with 'force, threats (whether or not relating to violence) or any other form of coercion practises ... [or] deception' (Home Office 2009), suggesting that this would prevent the offence from 'applying more widely than intended' (Jacqui Smith cited in BBC News 2009). Yet despite the original working of the strict liability offence becoming more explicit in its definition of exploitation, the current definition is still ambiguous and may be interpreted in many ways. Given that many relationships between sex workers and their boyfriends/pimps may involve 'exploitative conduct' it seems feasible that a man may be convicted of buying sex from a woman who is, for example, supporting a partners drug habit, working alongside a maid or is managed. It may be argued that such ambiguity and potentially broad application may be fully intended considering the government dis-belief that women freely choose to sell sex: 'some men and women argue vociferously that it is their occupation of choice... and they don't want to leave through a combination of fear, the process

34 *New Sociologies of Sex Work*

of normalisation or in an effort to maintain their dignity' (Home Office 2004b: 39). Rather than appreciating that some men and women may in fact choose to sell sex, the relationship is automatically seen as coercive, men who buy sex are therefore sexual abusers and rapists, again sitting neatly with a radical feminist understanding of prostitution (Jeffreys 1997).

Conclusion: An Empty Consultation and Flawed Rationale

After examining the consultation process which led to the prostitution strategy and the amendments to the Policing and Crime bill, this chapter has demonstrated that the review of prostitution policy and the consultation process was empty and biased from the start. Rather than being based upon evidence, research or the vast amounts of literature around the topic this chapter has shown that the UK government's review and legislative shifts are based upon radical feminist inspired logic which views all men who buy sex as sexual exploiters and abusers of women who sell sex. In this sense, the only means of dealing with prostitution is to eradicate the industry, hence why decriminalization has never been an option for consideration.

Furthermore this chapter has demonstrated that flawed rationale has been used to justify the introduction of a new strict liability offence which may criminalize a large amount of men. The terms of the offence have been found to be both unworkable in practice and ambiguous in principle. Given the wide ranging applicability of the offence this chapter has questioned the fairness of the strict liability offence that even the government believes is difficult to ascertain and an offence the police potentially cannot prove.

As a result of concerns over the introduction of a strict liability offence which should have been based upon a systematic review of the evidence, the Human Rights Joint Committee (2009) has stated that:

> We are disappointed that the Government has failed to provide the evidence which, in its view, demonstrates the necessity for the new strict liability offence. As we have said on a number of previous occasions, legislation should be firmly based on evidence. We consider this to be particularly important when new criminal offences are proposed, to show why the existing criminal law is inadequate to deal with the targeted conduct and how the proposed new offence tackles the behaviour in a proportionate way. In our view, it is even more imperative when the proposed new offence is one of strict liability. We recommend that the evidence be published without further delay so that Parliament can be properly informed when debating the need for this new strict liability offence (Paragraph 1.28)

This evidence has yet to be published and its use to be justified in informing the introduction of the new strict liability offence. As with the Human Rights committee many have been disappointed by the government's lack of consultation and ignorance of advice. It seems that as with recent drugs policy debates in the UK, the government consults experts but then ignores their advice. Thus any evidence to support the introduction of the new strict liability offence is not available, as evidence which exists challenges the justification of the offence. Rather than evidence based policy, prostitution policy in the UK has been developed with a specific ideological vision.

Acknowledgements

I would like to thank Kate Hardy for her helpful comments on an earlier draft of this chapter.

References

BBC News (2009). 'Smith accused over prostitute law' *BBC News* [online 19 May 2009], available at: http://news.bbc.co.uk/1/hi/uk/8056767.stm [accessed 3 June 2009].

Blunkett, D. (2004). 'Foreword', in *Paying the Price: A Consultation Paper*. London: HMSO.

Broadbridge, S. (2009). 'Prostitution', House of Commons Library.

Campbell, C. (1998). 'Invisible men: Making visible male clients of female prostitutes in Merseyside', in J. Elias, V. Bullough, V. Elis, G. Brewer and J. Elders (eds) *Prostitution: On Whores, Hustlers and Johns*. New York: Prometheus Books, 155–71.

Campbell, R. (1997). '"It's just business, it's just sex": Male clients of female prostitutes in Merseyside', *Journal of Contemporary Health*, 5: 47–51.

Campbell, R. and Storr, M. (2001). 'Challenging the kerb crawler rehabilitation programme', *Feminist Review*, 67(1): 94–108.

Carpenter, B.J. (2000). *Re-Thinking Prostitution: Feminism, Sex and the Self*. New York: Peter Lang Publishing.

Committee on Homosexual Offences and Prostitution (1957). 'Report of the Committee on Homosexual Offences and Prostitution' London: Her Majesty's Stationery Office.

Cusick, L. and Berney, L. (2005). 'Prioritizing punitive responses over public health: commentary on the Home Office consultation document Paying the Price', *Critical Social Policy*, 25(4): 596–606.

Davies, N. (2009a). 'Inquiry fails to find single trafficker who forced anybody into prostitution', *The Guardian*, Tuesday 20 October 2009.

Davies, N. (2009b). 'Prostitution and trafficking – the anatomy of a moral panic', *The Guardian*, Tuesday 20 October 2009.

Fouche, G. (2007). 'Prostitutes fume as Norway bids to criminalise sex purchases' *The Sunday Times Online* [online Sunday, July 22, 2007], available at: http://sundaytimes.lk/070722/International/i511.html [accessed 3 December 2009].

Gloucestershire Constabulary (2006). 'Pentameter Operational Overview: A Reflex Multi-agency Operation' [online], available at: http://www.pentameter.police.uk/ [accessed 27 June 2008].

Gould, A. (2001). 'The criminalisation of buying sex: The politics of prostitution in Sweden', *Journal of Social Policy*, 30(3): 437–56.

Harman, H. (2007). 'Harman on outlawing sex trade' *BBC News, Radio Four*, Thursday 20 December 2007.

Hester, M. and Westmarland, N. (2004). 'Tackling Street Prostitution: Towards an holistic approach', Home Office Research Study. London: Home Office.

Home Office (1959). 'Street Offences Act 1959', c.57. London: HMSO [online], available at: http://www.opsi.gov.uk/RevisedStatutes/Acts/ukpga/1959/cukpga_19590057_en_1 [accessed 12 May 2006].

Home Office (1985). 'Sexual Offences Act 1985'. London: HMSO [online], available at: http://www.together.gov.uk/article.asp?aid=1812&c=121 [accessed 17 June 2006].

Home Office (1999). *Home Office Leaflet, A Review of Sex Offences*. London: HMSO, The Stationery Office Group Ltd.

Home Office (2000c). 'Setting The Boundaries: Reforming the Law on Sex Offences'. London: HMSO.

Home Office (2001). 'Criminal Justice and Police Act 2001'. London: HMSO [online], available at: http://opsi.gov.uk/acts/acts2001/20010016.html [accessed 4 May 2006].

Home Office (2004). 'Paying the Price: A Consultation Paper on Prostitution', Home Office Communication Directorate, July 2004. London: HMSO.

Home Office (2006). 'A Coordinated Prostitution Strategy and a summary of responses to Paying the Price'. London: HMSO.

Home Office (2007c). 'UK Action Plan on Tackling Human Trafficking'. London: HMSO, March 2007.

Home Office (2008a). 'Tackling Demand For Prostitution Review Begins With Sweden Visit' [online 14 January], available at: http://press.homeoffice.gov.uk/press-releases/Tackling-Demand-For-Prostitution [accessed 30 September 2008].

Home Office (2008b). 'Tackling Demand for Prostitution: A Review'. London: HMSO, November 2008.

Home Office (2009). 'Policing and Crime Act 2009'. London: HMSO.

House of Commons (2009). 'House of Commons Hansard Debates for 19 May (pt 0016)' [online 19 May], available at: http://www.publications.parliament.uk/pa/cm200809/cmhansrd/cm090519/debtext/90519-0016.htm [accessed 3 June, 2009].

Human Rights Joint Committee (2009). 'Legislative Scrutiny: Policing and Crime Bill – Human Rights Joint Committee Contents' [online], available at: http://

www.publications.parliament.uk/pa/jt200809/jtselect/jtrights/68/6805.htm [accessed 20 December 2009].

Jeffreys, S. (1997). *The Idea of Prostitution*. Melbourne: Sphinifex Press.

Kesler, K. (2002). 'Is a feminist stance in support of prostitution possible? An exploration of current trends', *Sexualities*, 5(2): 219–35.

Kingston, S. (2009). 'Community perceptions of men who buy sex from women', unpublished PhD Thesis, University of Leeds.

Kinnell, H. (1989). *Prostitutes, Their Clients and Risks of HIV Infection in Birmingham*, Department of Public Health Medicine: Central Birmingham Health Authority.

Kinnell, H. (2001). 'Murderous clients and indifferent justice: Violence against sex workers in the UK', *Research for Sex Work*, 4: 22–4 [online June], available at: http://www.nswp.org/pdf/R4SW-04.PDF [accessed 5 May 2007].

Lord Williams of Mostyn (1999). 'Sex Offences: Review', *Hansard, House of Lords Debates, 25 January 1999, volume 596, cc127-8WA* [online], available at: http://hansard.millbanksystems.com/written_answers/1999/jan/25/sex-offences-review [accessed 4 April 2008].

Monto, M. (2000). 'Why men seek out prostitutes', in R. Weitzer (ed.) *Sex for Sale: Prostitution, Pornography and the Sex Industry*. London: Routledge, 67–84.

Monto, M. (2001). 'Prostitution and fellatio', *The Journal of Sex Research*, 38(2): 140–5.

Monto, M. (2004). 'Female Prostitution, Customers, and Violence', *Violence Against Women*, 10(2): 160–88.

Monto, M. and Hotaling, N. (2001). 'Predictors of rape myth acceptance among male clients of female street prostitutes', *Violence Against Women*, 7(3): 275–93.

Monto, M.A. and Garcia, S. (2001). 'Recidivism among the customers of female street prostitutes: Do intervention programs help?', *Western Criminology Review*, 3(2).

Phoenix, J. and Oerton, S. (2005). *Illicit and Illegal: Sex, Regulation and Social Control*. Cullompton: Willan Publishing.

Pitcher, J., Campbell, R., Hubbard, P., O'Neill, M. and Scoular, J. (2006). *Living and Working in Areas of Street Sex Work: From Conflict to Coexistence*. York: Joseph Rowntree Foundation.

Politics.co.uk (2009). 'Policing and Crime Bill', *Politics.co.uk* [online 17 May], available at: http://www.politics.co.uk/legislation/policing-and-crime-bill-$1296338.htm [accessed 3 June 2009].

Power, H. (2000). 'Sexual offences, strict liability and mistaken belief: B v DPP in the House of Lords', *Web Journal of Current Legal Issues* [online], available at: http://webjcli.ncl.ac.uk/2000/issue2/power2.html [accessed 21 November 2009].

Scourfield, J. and Drakeford, M. (2002). 'New Labour and the "problem of men"', *Critical Social Policy*, 22(4): 619–40.

Stevenson, K. (1999). 'Observations on the Law Relating to Sexual Offences: the Historic Scandal of Women's Silence', *Web Journal of Current Legal Issues* [online], available at: http://webjcli.ncl.ac.uk/1999/issue4/stevenson4.html [accessed 21 November 2009].

Taylor, J. (2009). 'Harriet Harman urges Arnold Schwarzenneger to "terminate" prostitute website', *The Independent*, 30 September 2009.

The Christian Institute (2001). 'Sex Offences Review: Response by The Christian Institute' [online], available at: www.christian.org.uk/downloads/sex-offences-review.doc [accessed 21 November 2009].

Travis, A. (2005). 'New crackdown on prostitution: Plan for licensed "red light" zones ditched in favour of zero-tolerance strategy', *The Guardian* [online 28 December], available at: http://www.guardian.co.uk/uk/2005/dec/28/ukcrime.immigrationpolicy [accessed 4 January 2006].

Weitzer, R. (2005). 'A growing moral panic over prostitution and sex trafficking', *The Criminologist: The Official Newsletter of the American Society of Criminology*, 30(5): 2–5.

Whitehead, T. (2009). 'Police fear laws to criminalise men who pay for sex will be "unworkable"', *The Telegraph* [online 5 April], available at: http://www.telegraph.co.uk/news/newstopics/politics/lawandorder/5109815/Police-fear-laws-to-criminalise-men-who-pay-for-sex-will-be-unworkable.html [accessed 3 June 2009].

Wintour, P. (2008). 'Harman: poll shows public support for ban on buying sex', *The Guardian* [online 4 September 2008], available at: http://www.guardian.co.uk/politics/2008/sep/04/harrietharman.socialcare?gusrc=rss&feed=networkfront [accessed 9 September 2008].

Woodward, W. (2007). 'Harman calls for prostitution ban to tackle trafficking' *The Guardian* [online 21 December], available at: http://www.guardian.co.uk/politics/2007/dec/21/uk.ukcrime [accessed 21 December 2007].

Chapter 3

Out of the Shadows (and Into a Bit of Light): Decriminalization, Human Rights and Street-based Sex Work in New Zealand

Lynzi Armstrong

Introduction

On 25 June 2003, prostitution was decriminalized in New Zealand. The passing of the Prostitution Reform Act (PRA) made New Zealand the world's first country to decriminalize indoor and outdoor sex work on a national scale. The decriminalization of sex work in New Zealand has global significance since, as prostitution is often criminalized, little is known about the potential impacts of decriminalizing sex work.

This chapter contributes to the currently available research on the impacts of decriminalization. I begin by outlining the rationale behind decriminalization, and thereafter provide an overview of the observed and documented impacts since the passing of the PRA in 2003. The remainder of the chapter has a specific focus on street-based sex work, drawing from the findings of research I carried out with street-based sex workers during 2008–2009. Twenty-eight women were interviewed about their experiences of working on the street in the context of decriminalization. Exploring the contradictions and challenges of working on the street in the context of decriminalization, this chapter will add to the debate on street-based sex work by providing a more nuanced account of how the law change has been experienced by street-based sex workers. I argue that that decriminalization of sex work in New Zealand provided a platform for change in societal understandings of sex work, but also that a broader paradigm shift is necessary to promote the human rights of sex workers globally.

A Brief History

To understand the eventual decriminalization of prostitution, it is useful to first explore the contemporary social history of New Zealand (Jordan 2010). Historically, prostitution policy in New Zealand was modelled on legislation passed in Britain (Eldred-Grigg 1984). This legislation was punitive in nature, underpinned by a public nuisance discourse in which sex workers were considered a risk to social order and public health. There was also a relatively widespread culture of tolerance for indoor, 'discreet' prostitution and sex workers were not, overall, a highly criminalized group (Robinson 1983, Jordan 2010). As a country with a relatively progressive liberal history, where women had not been 'corseted' to the same extent as their sisters in Victorian England, it is therefore perhaps not surprising that it was in New Zealand that this historic change took place in 2003 (Jordan 2010). The eventual legal change did not emerge organically, but was the result of relentless work by the New Zealand Prostitutes Collective (NZPC) and supporters. Despite New Zealand's relatively liberal history, the PRA still attracted opposition. Those most vocal in opposition were typically fundamentalist Christian groups such as the Maxim Institute and radical feminists, who argued that decriminalization would lead to higher numbers of sex workers, more frequent violence, coercion, and child abuse (Barnett et al. 2010).

Research which reviews the PRA indicates that a wide range of positive impacts have been achieved for sex workers (Abel et al. 2007, Mossman and Mayhew 2008, PLRC 2008). Broadly, these impacts include enabling sex workers to work without the constant fear of arrest, more freedom to choose the location of work, and more scope to challenge exploitation. The findings that are currently available emerged from research carried out primarily by researchers from the Christchurch School of Medicine (CSOM) in partnership with NZPC five years after the Act was passed (Abel et al. 2007).

This following section provides a brief outline of the PRA, in order that the impacts discussed later may be better understood in the wider context of politics and debates around sex work.

The Prostitution Reform Act: The Basics

Different rationales produce different approaches to all forms of legislation. In the case of sex work, concerns about social order tend to underscore legislation. This is particularly true in countries where prostitution is legalized and subject to strict state regulation (Mossman 2008). Where the rationale of legislation on sex work is underpinned by a public nuisance discourse, such as in the UK, the intended beneficiaries are often members of 'communities', rather than sex workers themselves (O'Neill et al. 2008, Boynton and Cusick 2006). In Sweden, the exclusion of the voices of sex workers from the process of policy making was characteristic of the radical feminist rationale which drove the introduction of the 1998 law, which prohibited the purchase of sexual services, defining prostitution as a form of violence and criminalizing clients as a result (Östergren 2004). What is unique about the PRA in New Zealand is that it was written with the input of sex workers themselves and put sex workers' rights and well-being at the centre of the policy. As such, the PRA can be understood as a human rights based approach that was underpinned by the principle of harm minimization (Abel and Fitzgerald 2010b).

The purpose of the Act was to decriminalize prostitution (while not endorsing or morally sanctioning prostitution or its use) and to create a framework that:

a. safeguards the human rights of sex workers and protects them from exploitation;
b. promotes the welfare and occupational health and safety of sex workers;
c. is conducive to public health;
d. prohibits the use in prostitution of persons under 18 years of age;[1]
e. implements certain other related reforms (2003).

Decriminalization and legalization are often talked about interchangeably in relation to the sex industry and it is important to stress that the PRA *decriminalized* sex work as opposed to legalizing it. This is significant in that it repealed legislation which criminalized sex workers, and provided rights to sex workers as conducive to their health and wellbeing. The PRA did not *legalize* sex work which would involve the industry being controlled by the government and only permitted under specific conditions (Mossman 2008).

The repeal of the existing legislation is perhaps the most important change affected by the PRA, since this removed the constant threat of arrest for sex workers. This was hugely significant since prostitution related convictions had a serious impact in limiting future employment and travel plans for sex workers (Healy et al. 2010). As well as removing the threat of conviction, the PRA had several impacts on sex workers.

The Impacts: What Do We Know So Far?

Challenging Exploitation

The PRA impacted positively on sex workers by increasing their legal capacity to challenge exploitative practices in the sex industry. They had greater flexibility over where they could work, increased scope to say 'no' to clients and to enforce safer sex practices (Abel et al. 2007, PLRC 2008).

The rights provided under the PRA were intended to empower sex workers and included provisions allowing up to four sex workers to work together without the presence of someone in a management role (Abel et al. 2010). One of the subsequent impacts of the PRA was the movement of some sex workers working in the managed indoor sector to work independently. This suggests that the PRA has allowed more freedom for sex workers to choose where they work, supported independence amongst sex workers to work without the involvement of a third party and, as such, potentially decreased the scope for exploitation.

---

1 Young people who become involved in the sex industry are not criminalized. The use of a young person in prostitution attracts a prison sentence of up to seven years.

Contrary to the belief that decriminalization of sex work justifies exploitation; the PRA includes provisions to decrease exploitative practices in the sex industry. Under the PRA it is an offence to induce or compel another person to provide or continue to provide sexual services. This prohibits others from threatening or blackmailing an individual to begin sex work, or to continue working (Abel et al. 2010).

As well as management, there were also stipulations with regards to workers' rights with clients. The Act states that consent to the sexual act can be withdrawn at any time, emphasizing the right to refuse clients at any stage and for any reason (Abel et al. 2010). Reflecting this, some findings have shown that over 60 per cent of workers report feeling more able to refuse clients since the law change (Abel et al. 2007). The findings also suggest high levels of awareness amongst sex workers regarding their rights under the PRA, at least 95 per cent of sex worker respondents reported feeling they had rights under the Act (Abel et al. 2007). This remarkable level of awareness is perhaps a consequence of the Act being developed by and for sex workers, with significant involvement of the NZPC.

Sexual Health

The PRA does not 'police' the sexual health of sex workers through mandatory testing for STI's, as is the case in some legalized contexts (Guy 1991, Mossman 2008, Sullivan 2007). This was recognition of the fact that sex workers could be in control of their own sexual health. Importantly, this prevents clients from making demands for unprotected sex under the pretext of positive test results (Abel et al. 2010). The Act requires that sex workers and clients attempt to protect themselves from sexually transmitted infections through the use of condoms and dental dams. It has been reported that the rights provided under the PRA have given sex workers more power to negotiate condom use with clients (Abel and Fitzgerald 2010b). Sex workers can now refer to 'the law' when enforcing condom use with clients. If a client ignores this advice and covertly removes the condom, they can be prosecuted. To date there has been one prosecution for this offence, attracting a fine of $400 (*New Zealand Herald* 2005).

The Limitations

Despite these important positive impacts, some challenges persist. The first of these relates to violence experienced by sex workers, as the Act appears limited in its capacity to reduce it (Mossman and Mayhew 2008). When prostitution was decriminalized it was hoped this would facilitate more reporting of violence towards sex workers. It was hoped that those who wish to harm sex workers would realize that they would be held accountable for their actions (PLRC 2008). Although some findings showed that more than half of those working since the enactment of the PRA felt there had been an improvement in police attitudes towards them, few workers reported violence to the police in the past twelve months. This suggests that sex workers are still reluctant to report adverse experiences to the police (Abel et al. 2007). This will be explored in more detail later in this chapter, offering some suggestions as to why some sex workers do not report violence.

Some findings also suggest that although there have been positive impacts for sex workers overall, street-based sex workers still face considerable challenges. Whilst most street-based sex workers felt they had rights under the Act, they were more likely than those from the indoor sectors to report feeling as though they had no rights. Street-based sex workers were also more likely than indoor workers to have experienced violence from clients in the last 12 months. Finally, it was also more common for those working from the street to report requests from clients for unprotected sex (Abel et al. 2007).

The continued challenges for street-based sex workers forms the basis of the rest of this chapter. Before moving on to explore these individual experiences, I provide some background to contextualize why the street sector is still fraught with these challenges.

The Significance of Street-based Sex Work

Historically New Zealand had a relative tolerance for discreet forms of sex work (Jordan 2010). However, this tolerance did not extend to street-based sex workers who formed an outcast group due to their defiance of the middle class expectation that sex work should remain in the shadows (Eldred-Grigg 2008). This intolerance of street-based sex work continues in the contemporary context. This is evident in the public scrutiny that the more visible outdoor sector has attracted since prostitution was decriminalized (Barnett et al. 2010). Street-based sex workers have continued to experience abuse and resentment from local communities (Tapaleao 2009a), and the media have continued to promote claims that the PRA is not working for those involved in this sector of the industry (Garrett 2006, Tapaleao 2009b, *The Press* 2008). The intolerance towards street-based sex work was reflected in the efforts of a vigilante group in South Auckland which aimed to drive sex workers out of the area (Buckley 2009, *New Zealand Herald* 2009). This vigilante action against street-based sex workers was supported by the Manukau City Council's attempts to re-criminalize street-based sex work in response to these community concerns (Manukau City Council 2009, Ministry of Justice 2009). Further, there have been frequent claims made about the perceived rise in the numbers of youth working on the streets (*The Dominion Post* 2004). Although the change in law brought street-based sex workers out of the shadows, their presence on the street remains cloaked in hostility.

Although the voices of street-based sex workers post-decriminalization have been captured in previous research amongst sex workers working across all sectors of the industry (Abel et al. 2007), there has been no research with a specific focus on their experiences since the law change. Whilst there is therefore some representation of their voices and experiences, the intensity of the debate makes it important to ensure space is dedicated to hearing their voices.

Challenges and Contradictions: Voices from the Street in Wellington and Christchurch

Decriminalization and Demand: Perception versus Reality

Since the PRA was passed some authors and commentators have claimed that decriminalization has led to an increase in the numbers of workers on the streets (Farley 2008, Espiner 2005). However, quantitative data suggests that there has been very little change in the numbers of sex workers on the street (Abel et al. 2009). One possible explanation suggested in this research is that since the law change demand has decreased, and thus there are more sex workers standing on the street *at one time* waiting for clients, creating a false impression of an increased sex worker population overall. Discerning the reality of the relationship between supply and demand on the street is, however, complex. As such, the perception of an increase in the street-working population is worthy of further attention. One possibility is that street-workers have emerged 'out of the shadows' since the law change, creating the impression of more people working (PLRC 2008). This view was supported by sex workers who recounted being able to be more visible on the street after the law change:

> It changed cause a lot of us had to hide before then so we were in like the darkest corners, you know? Real shady. (Claire)

> You can stand out there a lot more freely. (Laura)

> [There are] more people just walking up to you, and cars just pulling up... not like you'd have to watch where they'd go so you could see where they'd pulled up, you know? [It is] feeling a bit more freer I reckon. (Vixen)

These women reported benefiting from the decriminalization in being able to be more overt about their work, but there was an overall feeling amongst those interviewed that there was now less money to be made on the street since the law had changed. Previous research has highlighted that the prime motivation for entering sex work in New Zealand is for the financial benefits (Jordan 1991, Abel et al. 2007). This was also true for the women interviewed for this research. The importance of earning sufficient amounts of money was evident in the women's accounts of how they had experienced work after the law change. In contrast to the radical feminist argument that decriminalization inevitably increases demand for services by normalizing sex work, some of those interviewed felt strongly that there was now less demand for their services since the law had changed (Farley

2004, Raymond 2004). Lisa Lou felt that there were far fewer clients since the law change. She explained, 'actually, it has changed since they've done that (decriminalization)...the clientele's just gone dead'. The women felt strongly that decriminalization had a negative impact on their work in this way. Amy, for instance, felt that the change in law had 'ruined it'. She suggested that this did not simply mean clients were instead favouring the indoor industry noting 'look at how many parlours have closed down even ... It's amazing'. Deltah also felt this way, and said that it was as though clients were now fearful of approaching street-workers:

> I think now that it's legal they're more scared of picking us up than back in the days when I first started out. It was, you know, every man for his money or whatever. (Deltah)

Amy had a different view suggesting that the decrease in clientele related to street sex work having been normalized. Some previous findings suggest that a key motivation for clients is the thrill of the encounter (McKegany and Barnard 1996, Sanders 2008). Amy felt that the law change had normalized street-based sex work and that by removing part of the thrill, it had made it less exciting for clients. She perceived there to be less clients since the law change 'because it's not taboo anymore, it's not a "oooh" sort of thing'.

That these sex workers considered the decriminalization of sex work to have had a negative impact on the availability of clients is particularly interesting in the context of debates about decriminalization and demand. It is important to consider the complex issue of visibility in the sex industry and the difficulty in discerning the reality amongst contrasting perceptions. Less demand for services may reflect the economic downturn with fewer potential clients having sufficient money to see sex workers. It could also reflect a decreased interest amongst clients as Amy argued. Thus, the reduced demand could reflect a complex interplay of these factors.

The Economics of Safety

The importance to women of generating income through sex work was also evident in the contradictory ways that changing relationships with the police were viewed by sex workers. For some, the change in law had served to 'close a gap' with the police, meaning they felt more able to approach them for assistance if necessary:

> It builds a relationship, I think, with the Police, um, in the fact that I feel confident enough now to go to them if need be if anything, you know, went down. Whereas before you wouldn't, you know? You would not because chances are you're going to be arrested ... so I guess it's closed a bridge there, you know what I mean? (Shania)

46 *New Sociologies of Sex Work*

> ... it's just that they are actually more caring for you now. Like asking 'are you alright' and stuff like that. You know, back then, that's like when they looked at you like you were a piece of shit. But now I think that they just more fear for your safety. (Lisa-Lou)

Although these women valued the change in their relationship with some police, feelings were mixed. In Christchurch concerns were raised by the women about the frequency of police contact on the street. It was felt that the police presence on the street deterred potential clients from making contact and therefore decreased money making opportunities. For instance, Catherine noted '... we don't like seeing the cops because they drive away business when they pull over to talk, you know? The clients drive right by'. Similarly, Jane felt that the Police were now too present on the street:

> Now they're out here more often that we need them to be. When we need them they're not here, when we don't need them they're here scaring off the clients. Yeah, so we see more cop cars going past us than clients, and that scares the clients.

These women therefore experienced the change in law in contradictory ways. The decriminalization of street-based sex work had provided greater freedom for them to work in the open space without the fear of arrest and women now had greater scope to approach the police if they were attacked or hassled at work. Whilst they valued these benefits, they perceived the change to have had a negative impact on them economically. The women felt this was further exacerbated by a more frequent police presence which whilst usually well meaning, was considered to interfere with business.

Decriminalization and Stigma

The women also described continued challenges with regards the experience of stigma. This may partially be attributed to media reporting, which reinforced stereotypes of sex workers. Most reporting after the PRA remained neutral (Pascoe 2007). However, a study showed that sex workers most often remembered the small amount of morally focused articles within which sex workers were constructed as victims and links were inferred between drugs, crime and the sex industry (Fitzgerald 2010).

The perception that sex work is still considered to exist at the margins of society was frequently expressed by sex workers in this research. Overall there was a feeling that the wider population would rather not think about it, or as Jackie put it, 'I just think society are more like "we should have just left it in the cupboard"'. The continued experience of stigmatization highlights the limitation of decriminalizing sex work. The women all identified themselves as targets for verbal abuse based on stereotypes of female sexual behaviour. For instance, many women were subjected to name calling labelling them 'sluts' and 'whores', reflecting distaste for their selling of sexual services. In their study of women's experiences of sexual harassment in a red light area, Koskela and Tani found that women sometimes used humour as a resistance strategy to sexual harassment (Koskela and Tani 2005). In line with this, the sex workers in this research did not passively accept this harassment and used 'identities of resistance' to challenge these attempts to label them (Mullins 2008: 79). Vixen responded to the yelling out of 'whore', by sarcastically replying 'oh thanks for telling me, I forgot'. Catherine replied to the calling out of 'you fucking slut' with the defiant come back of 'prostitute, actually'.

Yet despite the ongoing challenge of resisting acts of stigma some of the women suggested that the law change had at least made them *feel* less vilified. Shania described feeling that the decriminalization of sex work had not made sex work 'acceptable' but had brought it out of the shadows:

> … it is allowed now, there's no hiding you know? It's out there so therefore people are more … aware of it and it's not so scary and you're not such a freak … Now that they changed the law it's taken away that shame … out of the darkness and into a bit of light … I'm not breaking the law and it's definitely made me feel that I matter, that I'm not in the darkness, a secret or like 'just forget about them and hope they'll go away'. Yeah definitely made me feel that I matter, that I am a human and that I have rights, even in the industry that I choose to work in, just like every other person. (Shania)

Decriminalization may not prevent verbal abuse which reinforces stereotypes, however there is potential for it to decrease the stigma felt amongst sex workers. Shania noted that she felt 'not so scary… not such a freak', and linked this to having rights in her work. The rights afforded to street-based sex workers, at least for some women, represented an important recognition that street workers 'matter'.

The limited extent to which the law change has been able to reduce stigma and stereotypes about street-based sex work is to be expected. Stereotypical images of sex workers are connected to deeply entrenched norms about female sexual behaviour. Though the stigma surrounding street-based sex work is partially about unease with the public act of selling sexual services, there are a number of additional issues. Street work is typically conflated with the use of drugs, which has its own stigma associated with both moral depravity and a lack of individual agency (Renzetti 2008). The conflation of street-based sex work and drug use serves to attach a 'double stigma' to those working from the street (Efthimiou-Mordaunt 2002).

The women in this research referred to the links between the stigmatization of drug use and that of street-based sex work, and the impact of this was clear for drug using and non-drug using women. For some, this stigma was more influential or damaging than the stigma associated with selling sex. Pania felt that passersby perceived her negatively as a street worker who used drugs, explaining 'it's like everyone else looks down on us... They just judge us as scum and I think that sucks'. Women interviewed for this research who were not drug users were often keen to distance themselves from the 'junkie whore' stereotype, emphasizing their abstinence from drug use. It was clear that the popular fixation with the links between street-based sex work and drug use in mainstream society left those working on the street feeling excluded and judged.

Whilst decriminalization of sex work is an important first step, potential benefits are limited by the stigma still associated with the sex workers. Public education is necessary to raise awareness of the realities of sex work and raise the profile and status of *all* sex workers. Acknowledging agency amongst street-based sex workers, regardless of moral judgements about the decisions they make and their lifestyles, is critical in reducing stigma. This is particularly relevant in the context of violence against street-based sex workers. This chapter will now move on to discuss the issue of violence against street-based sex workers, in relation to existing stigma and the decriminalization of sex work.

No Bad Women: Challenging Violence and the Disposability Myth

The negative imagery accompanying the 'junkie whore' stereotype forms part of what has been described as a 'discourse of disposal' (Lowman 2000: 1003, Wright 2006). Within this, those working from the streets are considered 'rubbish' easily disposed of in an effort to 'clean the streets' of their presence (Kinnell 2008). Women who work on the streets as sex workers have been constructed as dirty, lacking in agency and controlled by addictions (Sanders and Campbell 2007, Hubbard 1998, Kantola and Squires 2004, Hallgrimsdotir et al. 2006). More specifically, as mentioned above, it is commonly assumed that female street-based sex workers are all users of Class A drugs. As such, women working on the streets are labelled 'polluted', and may be considered 'low on the hierarchy of women' (Lees 1997: 82). The stigma associated with street-based sex work suggests that those working on the street are not full citizens and would not be missed should they disappear from the streets entirely (Sanders and Campbell 2007). Whilst the decriminalization of sex work offers some protection through the provision of rights, discourses of disposability continue to threaten the wellbeing of street-based sex workers.

The incidence of violence in street-based sex work is considered to be related to these tropes of disposability, as well as to criminalization which creates additional pressures in order to manage risk (Kinnell 2006, Shannon et al. 2009). The risk of violence is exacerbated for those working from the street in a criminalized context by having to manage the threat of violence as part of a hierarchy of risks (Sanders 2004). In criminalized contexts, sex workers must work quickly to avoid the gaze of authorities, leaving them minimal time to 'size up' potential clients (Kinnell 2006). It could therefore be assumed that decriminalization assists street-based sex workers to manage the risk of violence more effectively through bringing their work out of the darkest corners, and eliminating the risk of prosecution. The next section considers this assumption and demonstrates that whilst the change in law can assist sex workers seeking redress for violence, barriers continue to hinder the ending of violence against sex workers.

The importance of removing the threat of arrest was emphasized by a number of women interviewed, with some sex workers feeling more able to approach the police about disputes with clients which had the potential to spiral into violence. For example, Jackie felt this was particularly true in disputes over payment. She explained, 'Now that it's legal we sort of have the right to do that. When it was illegal it would have been difficult'. Kay expressed similar feelings: 'because prostitution is now, you know, legal so you can go there. As long as, you know, you're not in the wrong (laughs)'.Others felt more able to report violent incidents, reflecting on how difficult it had previously been. One sex worker reflected on being beaten and raped before the enactment of the PRA noting:

> If it happened now I would report it. I would definitely do that now. But back then it was more out of fear of what they were going to do to me, what the police were going to do. What was going to happen to me and how I was going to be exposed. (Shania)

Women also said that decriminalization had shifted power relations in negotiations with clients. Lisa-Lou described the ways in which women could work together and also warn clients not to cause any trouble. She said that she would talk to new clients while out working with her friend telling them, 'you make sure you look after my friend, and you be good to her because I've got your number plate and the colour of your car, so don't try and even think of doing anything because I'll ring the police on you'. It also made it easier to 'stand your ground'. That is, it gave them the power and confidence to resist third party exploitation. As Claire explained, 'now you can go out there and stand your ground without someone telling you "this is my corner and you have to work for me"'.

In removing the threat of arrest, the law change therefore allowed greater scope for the women to challenge exploitation and violence directly. However, although some women felt confident reporting violence and exploitative practices to the police, there was still some reluctance to do this amongst others. This may be partially attributable to the impact of the stigma of sex work (Abel and Fitzgerald 2010b). There are however other influential factors. One is the influence of codes and patterns of behaviour on the street. Another relates to previous experiences reporting violence, and ongoing distrust of the police as a consequence of earlier socialization.

Firstly then, underpinning the reluctance to not report violence was a commitment to adhere to the street cultural norm not to 'nark' on others. For some, the reluctance to report violence had little to do with sex work and the stigma attached to it, and more to do with proving to others they were not, as Licious put it, a 'snitch'. This was noted particularly amongst younger sex workers interviewed and was typically accompanied by particular feelings about the police – as Holly

50   *New Sociologies of Sex Work*

noted, 'they've always given me nothing but shit my whole life'. The reluctance to report violence amongst those working from the street is therefore underpinned not only by the stigma related to sex work, but by individual perceptions of the police as shaped by wider life experiences. Some of the women had grown up in environments in which the police were perceived as a threat to social and economic survival. For instance some had been returned to abusive and neglectful guardians as 'runaway' children. Others had witnessed family members being arrested. Not all of the women expressed distrust for the police, but amongst those who did their previous experiences of the police before they were sex workers appeared to have at least partly shaped their perceptions.

A lack of trust in the police was also expressed by some women who had previous experiences reporting sexual violence. Shannon had lost faith in the police when she reported being raped by a client several years earlier:

> I said to the Police "I want to take this further". But then they turned around and says to me "well because of what you are"... Because I am a prostitute and if they did get him it would be very hard to prove in court that he did that, you know? ... so I just turned around and said "well fuck the lot of you" and just walked out. You know, I thought they were there to help.

These examples reflect a wider set of issues and highlight the reality that the sex industry does not exist in social and legal isolation. Whilst relationship building between police and sex workers on the street is very important; this cannot be expected to entirely address these issues. For some women, a reluctance to report violence to the police related to their status as working class women as well as their identity as sex workers. Tackling the reluctance to report violence amongst these women is therefore complex, when this relates not only to their perceptions of the police but to broader systems of oppression and discourses surrounding violence against women.

Discussion and Conclusions

The introduction of the PRA in 2003 was significant in making New Zealand the first country in the world to completely decriminalize adult sex work. The current evidence available suggests that the change in law has overall impacted positively on sex workers. Although it represented a positive move forward, the legislative change cannot be expected to dramatically increase rights since the law operates in a social and political arena. It should therefore be considered an important first step, not an end point in itself in improving the well being of sex workers in New Zealand and elsewhere.

The post-2003 experiences of street-based sex workers were characterized by contradictions and continued challenges. These included questions around economic sustainability, relations with the police and violence. First, while there was a general agreement that since decriminalization they had had more freedom to work in public space, there was also a perception that since the law change there were fewer street clients, thus threatening its status as a viable economic strategy. Second, there were also contradictions in perceptions of a changing relationship with the police since decriminalization. From one perspective the police had become more approachable, and more caring. However from another perspective, the caring approach was perceived to interfere with business, and an increased police presence was thought to scare away clients, creating missed opportunities to make money.

The continued challenges faced by street-based sex workers highlight the limitations of the decriminalization of sex work. The change in law has not, for instance, removed the stigma attached to sex work. Removing the criminality of street-based sex work may remove some of the stigma at least symbolically; however sex workers on the street continue to experience stigma and also continue to resist it. The stigma attached to street-based sex work is based on deeply ingrained norms about female sexual behaviour, and moral discourses surrounding sex workers. For instance, the idea that sexually liberal woman are deserving of abuse, that all street-based sex workers are drug addicts, and all drug addicted women are to be pitied and exist below the rest of society.

Further, the PRA is limited in its capacity to address violence towards sex workers. There is still a reluctance to report violence amongst sex workers. This relates in part to the stigma attached to sex work and sex workers earlier experiences reporting sexual violence. Since prostitution does not exist in a social vacuum, the continued reluctance to report violence also relates to earlier experiences in life with the police and reflects codes and patterns of behaviour amongst some social groups. Specifically this relates to the commitment not to 'nark' on others. Overcoming these barriers is therefore far from simple. In part this requires significant relationship building between the police and sex workers to gain trust. This alone is not enough and broader ideas about victimization need to be challenged so that all victims of violence feel equally entitled to justice.

This chapter has argued that the PRA represented an important first step in promoting the human rights of sex workers globally. The experience in New Zealand shows that decriminalization can empower sex workers to challenge exploitation and violence in their work. The law signals that sex workers rights are important though cannot ensure these rights are always respected. To strengthen the law there needs to be greater awareness in society of the realities of sex work and erosion of the patriarchal norms that construct the behaviours of female street-based sex workers as deviant. Only then might the human rights of these sex workers be fully realized.

Acknowledgements

I would like to thank Associate Professor Jan Jordan, Dr Elaine Mossman, and Catherine Healy for their helpful comments and suggestions on earlier drafts of this chapter.

References

Abel, G. and Fitzgerald, L. (2010a). 'Decriminalisation and stigma', in G. Abel et al. (eds) *Taking the Crime out of Sex Work: New Zealand Sex Workers' Fight for Decriminalisation*. Bristol: Policy Press.

Abel, G. and Fitzgerald, L. (2010b). 'A public health perspective of the PRA', in G. Abel et al. (eds) *Taking the Crime out of Sex Work: New Zealand Sex Workers' Fight for Decriminalisation*. Bristol: Policy Press.

Abel, G., Fitzgerald, L. and Brunton, C. (2007). *The Impact of the Prostitution Reform Act on the Health and Safety Practices of Sex Workers*. Christchurch: Department of Public Health and General Practice, University of Otago.

Abel, G., Fitzgerald, L. and Brunton, C. (2009). 'The Impact of Decriminalisation on the Number of Sex Workers in New Zealand', *Journal of Social Policy*, 38, 515–31.

Abel, G., Healy, C., Bennachie, C. and Reed, A. (2010). 'The Prostitution Reform Act', in G. Abel et al. (eds) *Taking the Crime out of Sex Work: New Zealand Sex Workers' Fight for Decriminalisation*. Bristol: Policy Press.

Barnett, T., Healy, C., Reed, A. and Bennachie, C. (2010). 'Lobbying for decriminalisation', in G. Abel et al. (eds) *Taking the Crime out of Sex Work: New Zealand Sex Workers' Fight for Decriminalisation*. Bristol: Policy Press.

Boynton, P. and Cusick, L. (2006). 'Sex workers to pay the price', *British Medical Journal*, 332, 190–1.

Buckley, T. (2009). Locals sweep sex workers off the streets, *Sunday News*, 19 April.

Efthimiou-Mordaunt, A. (2002). 'Sex-working drug users: out of the shadows at last', *Feminist Review*, 72, 82–94.

Eldred-Grigg, S. (1984). *Pleasures of the Flesh: Sex and Drugs in Colonial New Zealand, 1840–1915*. Wellington: Reed.

Eldred-Grigg, S. (2008). *Diggers, Hatters and Whores: The Story of the New Zealand Gold Rushes*. Auckland: Random House.

Espiner, C. (2005). Number of prostitutes rises 40%, *The Press*, 19 April, 1.

Farley, M. (2004). '"Bad for the Body, Bad for the Heart": Prostitution Harms Women Even if Legalised or Decriminalised', *Violence Against Women*, 10, 1087–125.

Farley, M. (2008). 'What really happened in New Zealand after prostitution was decriminalised in 2003?' [online: Prostitution Research and Education], available at: http://www.prostitutionresearch.com/Report%20on%20NZ%2010-29-2008. pdf [accessed 15 February 2009].

Fitzgerald, L. (2010). 'The media and the PRA', in G. Abel et al. (eds) *Taking the Crime out of Sex Work: New Zealand Sex Workers' Fight for Decriminalisation.* Bristol: Policy Press.

Garrett, D. (2006). Sex law does more harm than good, *New Zealand Herald*, 17 April.

Guy, D.J. (1991). *Sex and Danger in Buenos Aires: Prostitution, Family and Nation in Argentina.* Lincoln: University of Nebraska Press.

Hallgrimsdotir, K.H., Phillips, R. and Benoit, C. (2006). 'Fallen Women and Rescued Girls: Social Stigma and Media Narratives of the Sex Industry in Victoria, B.C., from 1980 to 2005', *The Canadian Review of Sociology and Anthropology*, 43, 265.

Healy, C., Bennachie, C. and Reed, A. (2010). 'History of the New Zealand Prostitutes' Collective', in G. Abel et al. (eds) *Taking the Crime out of Sex Work: New Zealand Sex Workers' Fight for Decriminalisation.* Bristol: Policy Press.

Hubbard, P. (1998). 'Community Action and the Displacement of Street Prostitution: Evidence from British Cities'. *Geoforum*, 29, 269–86.

Jordan, J. (1991). *Working Girls: Women in the New Zealand Sex Industry Talk to Jan Jordan.* Auckland: Penguin.

Jordan, J. (2010). 'Of whalers, diggers and "soiled doves": a history of the sex industry in New Zealand', in G. Abel et al. (eds) *Taking the Crime out of Sex Work: New Zealand Sex Workers' Fight for Decriminalisation.* Bristol: Policy Press.

Kinnell, H. (2006). 'Murder made easy: the final solution to prostitution?' in R. Campbell and M. O'Neil (eds) *Sex Work Now.* Cullompton: Willan, 141–68.

Kinnell, H. (2008). *Violence and Sex Work in Britain.* Cullompton: Willan.

Koskela, H. and Tani, S. (2005). 'Sold out!' Women's practices of resistance against prostitution related sexual harassment. Women's Studies International Forum, 28, 418–29

Lowman, J. (2000). 'Violence and the Outlaw Status of (Street) Prostitution in Canada', *Violence Against Women*, 6, 987–1011.

Manukau City Council (2009). 'Manukau resolves to make street prostitution illegal' [online: Manukau City Council], available at: http://www.manukau.govt.nz/EN/ News/NewsArticles/Pages/Manukauresolvestomakestreetprostitutionillegal. aspx [accessed 15 April 2009].

McKeganey, N. and Barnard, M. (1996). *Sex Work on the Streets: Prostitutes and their Clients.* Bristol: Open University Press.

Ministry of Justice (2009). *Review of Street-based Prostitution in Manukau City.* Wellington: Ministry of Justice.

Mossman, E. (2008). *International Approaches to Decriminalising or Legalising Prostitution.* Wellington: Ministry of Justice.

Mossman, E. and Mayhew, P. (2008). *Key Informant Interviews Review of the Prostitution Reform Act 2003*. Wellington: Ministry of Justice.

Mullins, C.W. (2008). 'Negotiating the streets: women, power, and resistance in street-life social networks', in T.L. Anderson (ed.) *Neither Villain nor Victim: Empowerment and Agency among Women Substance Abusers*. New Brunswick: Rutgers University Press, 65–83.

New Zealand Herald (2005). Man fined for endangering prostitute, *New Zealand Herald*, 13 July.

O'Neill, M., Campbell, R., Hubbard, P., Pitcher, J. and Scoular, J. (2008). 'Living with the Other: Street sex work, contingent communities and degrees of tolerance', *Crime Media Culture*, 4, 73–93.

Östergren, P. (2004). 'Sex workers critique of Swedish prostitution policy' [online], available at: http://www.petraostergren.com/pages.aspx?r_id=40716 [accessed 14 September 2008].

Pascoe, N., Fitzgerald, L., Abel, G. and Brunton, C. (2007). A critical media analysis of print media reporting on the implementation of the Prostitution Reform Act, 2003–2006, Christchurch. Christchurch: University of Otago.

Prostitution Law Review Committee (2008). *Report of the Prostitution Law Review Committee on the Operation of the Prostitution Reform Act 2003*. Wellington: Ministry of Justice.

Prostitution Reform Act (2003). Wellington: Ministry of Justice.

Raymond, J.G. (2004). 'Prostitution on Demand: Legalizing the Buyers as Sexual Consumers', *Violence Against Women*, 10, 1156–86.

Renzetti, C.M. (2008). 'Foreword', in T.L. Anderson (ed.) *Neither Villain nor Victim: Empowerment and Agency among Women Substance Abusers*. New Brunswick: Rutgers University Press, xiii–xv.

Robinson, J. (1983). 'Of diverse persons, men and women and whores': Women and Crime in Nineteenth Century Canterbury. MA Thesis in Sociology. Christchurch: University of Canterbury.

Sanders, T. (2004). 'A continuum of risk? The management of health, physical and emotional risks by female sex workers', *Sociology of Health & Illness*, 26, 557–74.

Sanders, T. (2008). *Paying for Pleasure: Men Who Buy Sex*. Cullumpton: Willan.

Sanders, T. and Campbell, M. (2007). 'Designing out vulnerability, building in respect: violence, safety and sex work policy', *The British Journal of Sociology*, 58, 1–19.

Shannon, K., Kerr, T., Strathdee, S., Shoveller, J., Montaner, J. and Tyndall, M. (2009). 'Prevalence and structural correlates of gender based violence among a prospective cohort of female sex workers', *British Medical Journal*, 339, b2939.

Sullivan, M.L. (2007). *Making Sex Work: A Failed Experiment with Legalised Prostitution*. North Melbourne: Spinifex.

Tapaleao, V. (2009a). Renewed call to outlaw street prostitution, *New Zealand Herald*, 15 April.

Tapaleao, V. (2009b). Sex workers given one month's grace, *New Zealand Herald*, 22 April.

The Dominion Post (2008). Concern over child prostitution, *The Dominion Post*, 25 January.

The Press (2008). More street sex control sought, *The Press*, 21 December, 1.

Wright, M. (2006). *Disposable Women and Other Myths of Global Capitalism*. New York: Routledge.

PART II
Methodology:
Doing Sex Work Research

Chapter 4

Tackling Taboos: Men who Pay for Sex and the Emotional Researcher

Natalie Hammond

Sex work research is now an established area of study exploring the whole spectrum of the industry such as exotic dancing (Egan 2003); male sex work (Whowell 2010); adult entertainment premises (Hubbard et al. 2008) and male clients (Sanders 2008). Yet despite the continuing emergence of sex work research, researching sex is problematic, regardless of the topic under investigation. Sex work in particular has a specific set of characteristics meaning that research into this area can be challenging and complicated. For example, sex work research has been considered to be dangerous and problematic due to the often sensitive and stigmatized nature of the topic under investigation, and gaining access is often fraught with difficulties due to the hidden nature of prostitution (Sanders 2008). Yet as I discovered during my doctoral research, researching the sex industry also has the potential to elicit significant emotional responses, as demonstrated in the extract below:

> Tomorrow is the first day of actual proper field work – interviews – feel like I'm throwing myself in at the deep end with face to face [interviews] first. Am really nervous … in case I … can't ask the questions … and … what happens if he's crazy or a nutter? … I really hope I don't get any crazies … I can't believe that I'm actually at this point now – finally – after all the work and stress! I'm hoping that after tomorrow I'll feel better and happy – not that I'm unhappy – [it's] more fear of the unknown (Research Diary, 9 January 2008.)

Such emotional responses have potential impacts for the research process, the researcher and the research findings. Taking note that emotions are part and parcel of the research process early on may enable a researcher to prepare for and anticipate that such responses may occur, and in doing so may be able to overcome what can sometimes be methodological barriers to research.

The empirical data that this chapter is based on was gained from an ESRC funded qualitative PhD project about men who pay for sex with women in the UK which commenced in September 2006. It demonstrates how sex work research can be emotionally demanding in multiple ways. This chapter will explore this empirical data and suggests that reflexive accounts of researchers' emotional journeys are essential to understand how a researcher's emotional responses can be generated

60 *New Sociologies of Sex Work*

through interactions with both participants and with those with whom the researcher comes into contact with beyond the project. These reflexive accounts can also indicate the ways in which these interactions shape the interpretation of data and contribute towards knowledge production. In doing so, this chapter engages in the often intense emotionality of sex work research, including highlighting how the researchers' identity becomes fused with the project and topic under investigation. The chapter also explores the ways in which emotion shapes the processes through which knowledge is produced and the resultant data collected and analysed.

Researching Sex Work

Researching sex work has been fraught with challenges due to stigma, the perceived dangerousness of participants and the barriers faced in reaching hidden populations. These barriers may be encountered when attempting to gain ethical approval, negotiating access and recruitment of research participants, and being confronted with prevailing stereotypes (Melrose 2002, O'Neill 1996, Sanders 2006b, Shaver 2005). Researching men who pay for sex has further methodological barriers due to stigmatization, desire for anonymity amongst participants and a number of legal ambiguities surrounding the industry (Sanders 2008). These ambiguities are often further exacerbated by the political climate, for instance in the UK tackling the demand for commercial sex became a priority in a Home Office report of the same name (Home Office 2008).

Despite these barriers, a variety of successful projects that explore male clients have been undertaken, drawing on a range of methods for access, recruitment and data collection. These have included using sex worker accounts (O'Connell Davidson 1996, Lever and Dolnick 2000); working through sexual health clinics (Ward et al. 2005); training brothel staff to conduct surveys (Xantidis and McCabe 2000, Plumridge et al. 1997); undertaking on-street interviews (McKeganey and Barnard 1997); using media advertisements (Grenz 2005); large scale surveys utilizing kerb-crawler re-education programmes (Monto 1999); red light area observation of cars (Hoigard and Finstad 1992) police interviews for secondary data (Sharpe 1998); the internet for content analysis of commercial sex websites (Earle and Sharp 2008, Holt and Blevins 2008); and the online community to recruit for interviews (Sanders 2008).

Yet despite such success in collecting data on male clients, methodological difficulties remain which relate to the nature of the topic. Researching sex can be challenging as it is considered to be a private and taboo topic. Furthermore, anything other than monogamous heterosexual relations is considered to deviate from social norms, means that talking about sex may not be a common occurrence for some people (Grenz 2005). Thus, teasing out people's sexual stories requires sensitivity and emotional awareness in order to encourage disclosure during interviews, especially when faced with language barriers, embarrassment, discomfort or strong emotional responses (Robinson et al. 2007, Campbell 2002, Meadows 1997).

Additionally, sex work research opens up the possibility for the disclosure of sensitive or illegal information including exploitation, violence and misogynistic attitudes, consequently listening to such narratives can be emotionally draining for the researcher (Sanders 2005). Sanders (2006a) suggests that significant emotional effort is invested when researching sex work due to the practicalities of conducting fieldwork and the strain of constantly attempting to understand, reflect and analyse one's own position. Melrose's (2001), study of juvenile entrance into sex work provides a thorough account of the emotional aspects of sex work research. She reveals feelings of distress, shock and anger in parallel to participants' feelings of 'guilt, powerlessness and frustration' (2001: 347). Melrose (2001) also discusses the unrealistic expectations she placed upon herself to be a good researcher or manage her feelings. O'Connell Davidson and Layder disclosed feelings of horror and disgust as well as being 'sickened and disturbed' by misogynistic attitudes they encountered during research with men who pay for sex abroad (O'Connell Davidson and Layder 1994: 216.) Sanders (2006: 462) similarly describes feelings of anger and contempt and infrequently 'pure rage' in her research among male clients in the UK. She further discusses the emotional effort as not only having to face sexist attitudes and ignorant practices, but also in response to absorbing and reacting appropriately to participants' difficult emotions (Sanders 2008). In contrast, she also describes listening to other stories in which positive emotions were expressed, particularly concerning, fun and pleasure.

Emotions and Reflexivity

Beyond these important accounts, few emotional narratives exist in methodological literature. This emotional absence is not exclusive to sex work research, as Kleinman and Copp (1993: 17) argue that emotional accounts are missing from research more generally due to a desire to present ourselves as objective and neutral. Furthermore, reflexive work tends only to be published when the 'professional coast is clear … when we are less vulnerable to others' criticisms'. Despite this, over the past decade reflexive practice has risen up research agendas and the social context in which knowledge is produced is beginning to be acknowledged. Feminist methodologies have sought to expose how knowledge is contextually specific and the researcher's biography affects what they find and therefore, what we know (Stanley and Wise 1993). Additionally, there is now an increasing awareness that 'how knowledge is acquired, organized and interpreted is relevant to what the claims are' (Altheide and Johnson 1994: 486, see also Widdowfield 2000 and Holland 2007). These developments, parallel to Plummer's (1995) notion of sexual stories, in that being reflexive opens up space for researchers' to see how emotions are part of the process of constructing knowledge. When describing our emotional journeys, we must also recognize and reflexively analyse our own (and others') emotional responses throughout and towards the work in order to develop our insights (Harris and Huntington 2001, Stanko 1997).

Despite the rise of reflexive practice, some emotions are still considered taboo, such as feelings of inadequacy as a professional, dislike towards participants, sexual attraction in the field and unexpected empathy with deviant populations. Additionally, the impact of such research on one's identity, feelings and behaviour are still relatively underrepresented in reflexive accounts (Kleinman and Copp 1993, Newton 1993, Scully 1990, Wesely 2006). However, there is some recognition that when researching sensitive topics, such as sex work, emotional difficulties may arise for both researcher and participant. Consequently, methods to support researchers such as debriefing are recommended as strategies for limiting the dangers of emotionally charged research (see Campbell 2001, Coles and Mudaly 2009, Dickson-Swift et al. 2009). Yet, these methods tend not to distinguish between experiencing emotion and recognizing emotion. I argue that it is not until we recognize emotion that we are able to see the impacts of these experiences on the researcher, data collection and analytic thinking.

The remainder of this chapter gives voice to the 'emotional' researcher by presenting both the experience and recognition of emotion within the research process through an honest account from a novice sex work researcher. Having first set out the study including discussing my own positionality, the remaining sections use specific examples to explore first, some of the emotions I experienced during the research and second, the significance of recognizing these emotions for knowledge construction.

The Self and the Study

As this chapter both explores my emotions and my emotional reactions to others' emotional responses throughout the research process, it is pertinent to first locate myself within the research (Cylwik 2001). I am a white, well-educated female who was in a long-term, long-distance heterosexual relationship prior to the project starting. At 26, I was relatively young in contrast to the majority of participants who were on average 50 years old. My interest in sex work grew out of reading The Natasha's by Victor Malarek and the progressive realization at the time that there was limited literature surrounding male clients. I have never worked in the sex industry and my only previous contact was a result of my Master's degree during which I undertook qualitative interviews with police about their opinions regarding street based prostitution, as well as two visits to strip clubs as a student. Therefore, I had little first-hand knowledge or experience of sex work.

Much work on male clients focuses exclusively on the commercial sex encounter and seeks to explore themes such as motivations (Xantidis and McCabe 2000); intimacy (Bernstein 2007, Lever and Dolnick 2000); violence (Monto 1999), sexual health and prevalence (McKeganey and Barnard 1994, Ward et al. 2005); emotional involvement (Sanders 2008); and internet facilitation of paid for sex (Holt and Blevins 2009). There is little documented about clients outside of the commercial sex encounter with minimal exploration of their subjective relationship experiences both within and outside of commercial sex (for an exception within commercial sex see Sanders 2008). My PhD explored the relationships of men who pay for sex in both their commercial and non-commercial lives, in order to add to the growing body of knowledge surrounding paying for sex and to locate male clients more broadly in contemporary sexual culture. By considering the relationship experiences and sexual lives of these men, before, during (and at times after) their involvement in commercial sex and exploring their experiences within it, the parallels and dichotomies, as well as the leakages, between the commercial and non-commercial worlds that the men took part in were explored.

I put out a call for participants using an online commercial sex message board and an article in the local paper. I also requested biographies from each participant in order to gauge what they would talk about, their attitudes to the study and as a safety mechanism in order to screen for fantasists' or anybody who expressed any overtly sexual or dangerous tendencies. I received approximately forty responses of interest and no one was rejected on the basis of the biography they submitted. Ultimately, face-to-face, telephone and MSN instant messenger semi-structured interviews which explored commercial sex involvement, relationships, sexuality, intimacy and policy were conducted with thirty-five men.

Experiencing Emotion

In order to explore the emotional experience of researching men who pay for sex called for by Sanders' (2008), the discussion now turns to a detailed account of my emotional journey during research. Throughout the entire research process, I experienced a broad range of emotions, yet it was not until I left the field that I began to recognize them. I focus on four key areas of emotion that I experienced which will be pertinent to both the novice researcher and those conducting sensitive research. These emotions include fear, anxiety and inadequacy, sadness and sympathy and anger.

Fear

Two important events set the context for this project; the murder of five sex workers in Ipswich in 2006 and a Government legal review 'Tackling the Demand' in 2008 (Home Office 2008). Both of these events constructed male clients as potentially violent, dangerous men (Kinnell 2008, Sanders and Campbell 2009). There was little public acknowledgment either of the spectrum of the industry or the diverse nature of male clients. Thus, the research was conducted during a time when paying for sex was the focus of much public negative debate, scrutiny and stigma. Such representations of clients raised a number of concerns amongst my friends and family, as well as within the university. This 'fear' of clients from other people became particularly evident whilst I was arranging a public space in which to conduct interviews.

64 *New Sociologies of Sex Work*

In order to balance my safety, but facilitate the research, a different university department to my own was contacted for office space, in case interviewees did not wish to visit the sociology building. Although I was offered office space, this was mediated by stipulations about how I should behave and practice precautions. Negative constructions of clients were clear, as I was instructed by the department to meet men in the reception area and to escort them out of the building once the interview finished. It was explained to me that staff were 'concerned about men wandering about the building under their own steam'. As these concerns were expressed and as they multiplied, I found myself absorbing the apprehension of others regarding bringing men into the building, as demonstrated in the following extract from my field diary:

> Staff feel very concerned about men trotting round building on their own – visions of monsters on the loose! ... Was in bed last night and got that anxious feeling again! What if today's the day I meet that one 'crazy' nutter ... Hopefully not though ... Been really upset by people shouting or stressing at me regarding safety ... [people are] very worried about my safety ... due to the stereotypes (Research Diary 27 September 2007.)

Others' fears regarding male clients were not limited to the university environment, where people's concerns seemed to revolve around encountering the men. Concerns were raised about exposing too much of my real identity and regarding my physical safety during interviews. People in my personal life asked why I was using my real name, whether it was a good idea to give out my department address and whether I would be accompanied by someone during interviews. The accumulation of such comments led me to question my methods. I wondered whether I was in fact actually putting myself in danger. These fears also simultaneously began to seep into my personal life, where I absorbed them even more deeply. Unsurprisingly, by the time I started interviewing, the emotional reactions of other people to the figure of the male client had a significant impact on me and I also became fearful of them and the dangers that they were claimed to represent. Subsequently, I would dread undertaking interviews. I was apprehensive before every face-to-face interview and fearful of what I was to encounter.

Anxiety

Due to the methodological challenges of researching hard to reach populations, people persistently enquired, with curiosity, although not necessarily critically, about how I would locate the population, how I would successfully recruit and retain participants and why respondents would even consider taking part in such a study. Despite the increase in knowledge surrounding clients, their relative absence in research added further pressure. Each participant became extremely valuable, not only to my project, but to the broader body of knowledge. I felt that I had been given an opportunity; a window into a world that was mysterious and frequently out of reach. Therefore, I felt that if I let one participant slip through the net, I was not only letting myself, but also the project and the wider academic research community down. These issues, coupled with concern about my lack of first hand knowledge and experience of the sex industry itself and of actually undertaking research led me to fear that I was not up to tackling such a challenging project. At times I felt out of my depth, that I did not really know what I was doing and I found it difficult and awkward to direct the interview in the way I wanted it to go. This was particularly the case as some of the questions were complex and either hard for participants to respond to or concerned sensitive issues, such as problematic relationships or sexual inexperience. The dialogue below, which preceded a conversation concerning Matt's strained marriage, reveals my reluctance to probe interviewees:

> **Matt:** I don't know if you got from that what you want, if you want to push a little harder I'll try [pause] as I say it's not a subject I discuss much.
> **NH:** no that's fine, I don't know how we could, sometimes it's hard to put into words.
> **Matt:** yes it is.
> **NH:** just to jump to something very different now though...

As the dialogue demonstrates, I not only reject his offer to expand on what may have been an extremely interesting area of discussion, I also move the conversation on, not just to the next question in the similar area of relationships but to something different. Events such as this would leave me incredibly frustrated with myself and anxious that I had lost the opportunity to obtain significant insights and crucial bits of data.

Overall my anxieties were unfounded. Participants were friendly and mostly very open about their experiences and I did not feel threatened or physically uncomfortable at any point during the interviews. However, fears about the actual interview encounters, regarding my safety or adequacy were not my only type of emotional response. In addition, I also experienced significant emotional reactions towards the stories that participants disclosed during our conversations.

Sadness

At times I experienced sadness upon hearing the stories from interviewees. They told stories of being bullied and laughed at for being a virgin, wanting, but not being able to get a girlfriend and the ways in which commercial sex highlights and reinforces men's inadequacies and loneliness. I have been told tales of devastation over marriages that are devoid of emotion and physical contact. One man said that he wanted his 'soul mate back', cried and went on to ask if he needed therapy. There were further moments of extreme sadness especially with the widowed men. Dave discussed how his wife had died of breast cancer and whilst I was reading the interview transcript, his account of family life during this time and continuing after her death reduced me to tears. Alan discussed the loss of his wife, just as they were about to start on a new stage in their lives together as their children had left home. His description of events and the story of how his wife 'went and died on me' particularly saddened me. Not long after interviewing began my grandfather passed away, so I was in a heightened emotional state whilst dealing with my own personal grief and was therefore possibly more sensitive to these stories of grief and loss. I responded to the men's emotional accounts of their unhappiness and sadness by experiencing my own feelings of sadness and sympathy. These poignant stories challenge stereotypes of clients as dangerous and instead imply a state of human vulnerability.

Anger

Alongside my feelings of sympathy towards the men, I also experienced feelings of anger. It was difficult at times to listen to stories from married men about their involvement in commercial sex whilst they simultaneously claimed that their wives were their 'best friend', that they loved them and that they 'would not want to hurt' them. In addition, the stories of how men felt they were so close to sex workers but still claimed to have a good relationship with their wife, apart from the lack of sex, were at times emotionally testing. What I saw as the deceit and false foundations that their relationships were built on, of a secretive double life, challenged my own opinions on relationships. The men did not explicitly blame their wives for their involvement in commercial sex, but they did use their wife's behaviour to justify their own. Due to my nervousness, despite the fact that I was experiencing these emotions, I felt a degree of numbness whilst in the field and it seemed my emotions were suppressed by anxieties about generating data. However, upon leaving the field, after reflecting on my findings, I began to recognize the intense emotions I had experienced. These are discussed in the following section.

Recognizing Emotion

I must have been aware at some level that I was experiencing these emotions as I was actively recording them, either in my research diary, in notes of reflection after interviews or during transcription. However, I made no attempt to either address them or examine their relevance. Possibly due to my own naivety and also the desire to avoid unpleasant emotions, I simply chose to distance myself from my feelings on the issue. Later, however, I realized that I had significantly misjudged this ability to distance oneself from research.

As has been noted by others (Woodthorpe 2009, Cylwik 2001), it is often only upon leaving the field and having time to reflect that researchers are able to see that emotional responses are connected to the project and it is only at this point that it becomes possible to recognize these emotions. This recognition of my emotions was fundamental to the research process in three significant ways. First, doing research can be emotional and these emotions can influence how we collect our data. Second, doing emotionally demanding research can have a profound effect on the researcher's own identity, which in turn influences interpretation and analysis. Finally, I contend that researchers' emotional responses can form part of our data and offer analytical insight. In the following section I elaborate on each of these points in turn.

Data Collection and Emotions

The anxieties surrounding feeling inadequate as a researcher, which maybe common to other researchers, are rarely discussed, perhaps for fear of exposing oneself to critique. These are especially pertinent for novice researchers who have little experience of research, the wider academic community and often the topic they investigate. Kleinman and Copp (1993: 4) claim that at times, even as experienced researchers, we may not know what we are doing and are thus open to persistent feelings of insecurity and vulnerability. Woodthorpe's (2007, 2009) account of a novice researcher's experience of researching death describes many parallel anxieties that I felt about my own research. She describes feelings of inadequacy, being unprofessional and not meeting the academic standards of a 'neutralized' researcher (2007: 4). I wish to expand on my own feelings of inadequacy, which, from talking with fellow qualitative doctoral students seem to be common and also to demonstrate how these influenced the research process. I take heed of Humphrey's warning that reflexive accounts can result in 'the charge of self-indulgence and narcissism' (2005: 853). Yet, as he demonstrates, rich methodological insights can be gleaned from these accounts which, he claims outweigh this risk.

Similar to Woodthorpe (2007), despite having undertaken qualitative research training at both Masters and Doctoral level, nothing was able to prepare me for the reality of being in the field. There were moments of sheer elation, such as when a potential participant agreed to take part and I could add him to 'the list' or shared humour with participants as I listened and related to their stories. However, I found transcription horrific. As well as being incredibly laborious, I had to listen to my own mumbling, pauses, stuttering and stammering to find the words as well as listening to myself make – what I thought was – mistake after mistake with how I conducted the interviews, such as speaking too fast or filling silences with questions. This was a source of my own private embarrassment and yet I still did not connect my conduct during interviews with the emotions I had been experiencing. However, when the transcripts were completed and the voices turned to text and read in conjunction with my research diary and reflective interview notes, I finally started to see the connections between them and to recognize my own anxiety. This link became apparent as despite having over forty-four hours of face-to-face or telephone typed transcripts, seven internet chat transcripts and many other email second interviews, I was still extremely anxious that I did not have 'good' enough data. I felt that I was unable to see anything within it. My recognition of these feelings of anxiety sparked a realization that they were in fact not new, but that I had been experiencing them throughout the whole recruitment and data collection process. I then began to recognize that my preoccupation with meeting academic standards, obtaining enough of these 'hard to reach' participants and not letting the wider sex work research academic community down, had impacted upon the way interviews were conducted, in that my anxieties and nervousness had muted participants. I realized that I had rushed interviews simply as I wanted them over as quickly as possible, that I had not probed some questions and thus obtained superficial answers. In an attempt not to miss out on what I perceived to be key questions and get the right data, I began to appreciate, upon re-reading transcripts, that I had not let participants speak, and that pauses were met with me launching into the next question. Had I not set expectations of myself so high, I may have been a little less nervous during some of the interviews and I may have felt able to let participants fill some of the silences instead of feeling that I had to.

Hubbard et al. (2001) similarly describe how the researcher's emotions influence the data collected. They reveal how, after one particularly emotional interview, the researcher conducted subsequent interviews differently. In an attempt to manage her emotions she deliberately failed to establish rapport with participants so they would not open up too much about their experiences; she managed her emotions by stifling the opportunity for participants to disclose emotionally-fraught events and when given hints to push participants, as I was by Matt, she failed to probe further. They infer from this that the data collected is therefore different to what could have been produced if rapport had been established, but they stress that this does not make the data any less valid, it just produced different data than would otherwise have emerged. The reflection I engaged in after I had left the field provided me with the distance I needed to recognize that my emotional experience of anxiety towards wasting participants and getting good data had such a profound impact on the data collection process as described. This allowed me to appreciate that similar to Hubbard et al., had I been less nervous, different data could have emerged, thus providing important methodological reflections and insight.

Identity and Influence

Due to the dominant discourse around clients I prepared myself for misogynistic attitudes and stories of abuse. However, one thing that I did not consider was the potential emotional impact of the research on my own identity and relationship. As Sanders describes, her work with female sex workers involved 'having to do some personal soul searching also made me confront my stereotypes and prejudices about sexuality and lifestyles. A consideration which is not something that is generally written into research design' (2006b: 463). In addition to not being incorporated into the research design, there is relatively little documentation of this soul searching and the powerful effect of undertaking sensitive research upon the researcher's own identity (for an exception see Moran-Ellis 1996).

Upon leaving the field and sometime later, perhaps, it is hard to be specific now, I began to realize that I had been analysing myself and my own life. Whilst I do tend towards self-introspection, I recognized that I had been thinking specifically about relationships, marriage and sex a lot, perhaps more than was normal for me. It was then that, instead of experiencing the emotions of sadness or anger towards participants, I began to recognize that they were having a significant effect on both me and my identity. I began to see the possibility that the relationship I was in at the time may not last forever. This realization scared me and consequently I began to feel that it was the most precious thing in my life and developed a perhaps somewhat unhealthy obsession with the idea that if it ended that would be the end of the world! I became preoccupied with the idea that I would inevitably become the boring sexless women that my participants spoke about. Relationships became central to my world, as was the sadness experienced over men's loss of their relationships, which contributed to my fear that I would not experience the positive aspects of relationships that some participants had mentioned such as, marriage and raising a family. I remain unsure as to the full effects of this reassessment of my own sexual subjectivity and I think this is a matter for further reflection, perhaps with more distance from the actual project itself. However, although the connection between my increased awareness of relationships and sex in my own personal life was a shock, it also had the effect of demonstrating the normality of men's ideas about their lives and relationships, providing me with a basis on which to understand their responses. Rather than inhabiting a separate darker category of 'otherness', these were lives I could identify with. As well as recognizing that I could relate to interviewees and that the research raised questions about my own identity, life and feelings, I began to recognize that some of the emotions I had experienced were due to the fact that my identity became fused with the project and participants (Israel 2002). My emotions had resonance with those that my participants experienced in being a male client. This parallel between their experiences and my own allowed me to link my own emotions as an important analytic tool.

Emotions as Data: Fused Identity

I was surrounded by supportive people throughout the project, although there was a lack of understanding or knowledge surrounding my work and frequently, stereotypical assumptions of commercial sex were held by those around me, especially in my personal life. Comments such as 'Natalie's doing a PhD in "prostitution"' followed by laughing were common during the initial stages, as well as some people wanting to know why, whilst at the same time not really recognizing that anyone would want to work in this area. Furthermore, a number of people questioned why somebody would want to talk with 'the perverts' reflecting their perceptions of men who pay for sex. Similar to Braun (1999), I consequently found myself, on some occasions, being exceptionally vague about my PhD. I sometimes claimed that it just focused on 'gender'. In cases in which people were unaware that I was doing a PhD, I simply stated that I was at university studying sociology and did not correct their assumption that I was an undergraduate, as a strategy to forestall questions about the content of my research. My own fears about my safety suggest that despite my attempts to assume a non-judgemental attitude and my increased knowledge about my participants, I too was still drawing on dominant stereotypes by sensing that I could in some way be in danger, thus reinforcing the spoiled identities of the men.

In some ways the fears I felt during the research were, in part, a result of the fact that I internalized the fears and the personal reactions of people around me. Therefore I 'experienced' the effects of the dominant stereotype. My 'fused identity' allowed me to 'feel' the stigma and danger that men take on when they start paying for sex. The men's own emotional articulation of these difficulties, together with my own experience of having to manage my identity as a sex work researcher, allowed me to empathize and understand how this troubled them. My powerful experience of feeling this stigma, in conjunction with participants' disclosure of difficulties associated with being a male client, such as the conflict with other identities that the men had in their work and personal lives, allowed me to see the significance and complexities of inhabiting a male client identity. The centrality of my own conflicts with regards my identity in my personal and professional life, either in terms of how I reassessed or managed it, led to identity becoming a key conceptual tool in my thesis. Thus recognizing and engaging with our emotions as researchers can be key for understanding the 'pre-scientific' way in which we interpret our data and arrive at our theoretical frameworks.

Exploring the Third Space: Emotions as Data

Although I experienced significant emotional responses throughout the project, just reporting on my emotional experiences could be liable to critique as being too self indulgent or 'intellectually sloppy' (Letherby 2000). However, as I have shown, reflecting on our emotions gives us a different level of understanding of our research (Harris and Huntington 2001). I have documented how I experienced a number of emotions throughout the research process as a result of interactions with both people around me and with research participants. As such, I have laid out how my emotional experiences, once recognized, offered insight into the lived experience of being a male client and the ways in which this enriched the project.

Whilst the emotions I experienced took place within the context of being a novice sex work researcher, I have little doubt however that I am not alone in my experience. As such, I am convinced that the feelings of anxiety about being good enough and securing enough participants to produce a valid study, parallel the feelings of other novice (and perhaps experienced) researchers. My concern about my safety can further be transferred to other research topics, and even perhaps ones where participants are not thought of as dangerous; entering the unknown has the potential to generate fear, whatever the context. Finally, researchers are all human beings and I defy anybody who undertakes research with other people, whether relating to personal and intimate lives or to something that could be conceived as emotionally 'safe', to be able to remain completely neutral throughout the research process and experience no emotion. It is here that the process of recognizing our emotions becomes central to allow us to see that emotions are not a hindrance, however painful. Instead the awareness and utilization of our emotions can increase the quality of our research as 'the researcher becomes the research instrument' (Gilbert 2001: 11). As this chapter has shown, researching the sex industry can be emotional and for the novice researcher this can be heightened due to the lack of experience. Therefore, in parallel to addressing taboos related to the topic of sex work research, this chapter begins a project of addressing a similar reluctance to document emotional journeys. My open account of my experiences of sex work research is offered as a resource for other novice researchers, regardless of their research topic, and also as one that demonstrates how the 'emotional researcher' contributes to the construction of knowledge and should thus no longer remain silent.

References

Altheide, D. and Johnson, J. (1994). 'Criteria for assessing interpretive validity in qualitative research', in N. Denzin and Y. Lincoln (eds) *Handbook of Qualitative Research*. London: Sage, 485–99.

Bernstein, E. (2007). *Temporarily Yours: Intimacy, Authenticity and the Commerce of Sex*. London: The University of Chicago Press.

Braun, V. (1999). 'Breaking a taboo? Talking (and laughing) about the vagina', *Feminism and Psychology*, 9(3): 367–72.

Campbell, R. (1998). 'Invisible men: making visible male clients of female prostitutes in Merseyside', in J. Elias, V. Bullough, V. Elias, and G. Brewer (eds) *Prostitution: On Whores, Hustlers and Johns*. New York: Prometheus Books, 155–71.

Campbell, R. (2002). *Emotionally Involved: The Impact of Researching Rape*. New York: Routledge.

Coles, J. and Mudaly, N. (2009). 'Staying safe: strategies for qualitative child abuse researchers', *Child Abuse Review*, 19(1): 56–69.

Cupples, J. (2002). 'The field as a landscape of desire: sex and sexuality in geographical fieldwork', *Area*, 34(4): 382–90.

Cylwik, H. (2001). 'Notes from the field: emotions of place in the production and interpretation of text', *International Journal of Social Research Methodology*, 4(3): 243–50.

Dickson-Swift, V., James, E., Kippen, S. and Liamputtong, P. (2009). 'Risk to researchers in qualitative research on sensitive topics: issues and strategies', *Qualitative Health Research*, 18(1): 133–44.

Earle, S. and Sharp, K. (2008). 'Intimacy, pleasure and the men who pay for sex', in G. Letherby, K. Williams, P. Birch and M. Cain (eds) *Sex as Crime?* Cullompton: Willan, 63–79.

Egan, D. (2003). 'I'll be your fantasy girl, if you'll be my money man: mapping desire, fantasy and power in two exotic dance clubs', *Journal for the Psychoanalysis of Culture and Society*, 8(1): 109–20.

Gilbert, K. (2001). Introduction: why are we interested in emotions? in K. Barry (ed.) *The Emotional Nature of Qualitative Research*. London: CRC, 3–15.

Grenz, S. (2005). 'Intersection of sex and power in research on prostitution: a female researcher interviewing male heterosexual clients', *Signs*, 30(4): 2091–113.

Harris, J. and Huntington, H. (2001). 'Emotion as analytic tools: qualitative research, feelings, and psychotherapeutic insight', in K. Barry (ed.) *The Emotional Nature of Qualitative Research*. London: CRC, 129–45.

Hoigard, C. and Finstad, L. (1992). *Backstreet: Prostitution, Money, and Love*. Cambridge: Polity Press.

Holland, J. (2007). 'Emotions and research', *International Journal of Social Research Methodology*, 10(3): 195–209.

Holt, T. and Blevins, K. (2009). 'Examining sex work from the client's perspective: assessing johns using online data', *Deviant Behavior*, 28(40): 333–54.

Home Office. (2008). *Tackling the Demand for Prostitution: A Review* [online], available at: http://www.homeoffice.gov.uk/documents/tackling-demand [accessed 12 December 2008].

Hubbard, G., Backett-Milburn, K. and Kemmer, D. (2001). 'Working with emotion: issues for the researcher in fieldwork and teamwork', *International Journal of Social Research Methodology*, 4(2): 119–37.

Hubbard, P., Matthews, R., Scoular, J. and Agustin, L. (2008). 'Away from prying eyes? The urban geographies of "adult entertainment"', *Progress in Human Geography*, 32(3): 363–81.

Humphreys, M. (2005). 'Getting personal: reflexivity and autoethnographic vignettes', *Qualitative Inquiry*, 11(6): 840–60.

Israel, T. (2002). 'Studying sexuality: strategies for surviving stigma', *Feminism and Psychology*, 12(2): 256–60.

Kinnell, H. (2008). *Violence and Sex Work in Britain*. Cullompton: Willan.

Kleinman, S. and Copp, M. (1993). *Emotions and Fieldwork* (Qualitative Research Methods Series: Vol. 28). London: Sage.

Letherby, G. (2000). 'Dangerous liaisons: auto/biography in research and research writing', in S. Linkogle and G. Lee Treweek (eds) *Danger in the Field: Ethics and Risk in Social Research*. London: Routledge, 91–113.

Lever, J. and Dolnick, D. (2000). 'Clients and call girls: seeking sex and intimacy', in R. Weitzer (ed.) *Sex for Sale*. London: Routledge, 85–100.

Malarek, V. (2004). *The Natashas: The New Global Sex Trade*. London: Vision.

McKeganey, N. and Barnard, M. (1994). *Sex Work on the Streets: Prostitutes and their Clients*. Philadelphia: Open University Press.

Meadows, M. (1997). 'Exploring the invisible: listening to mid-life women about heterosexual sex', *Women's Studies International Forum*, 20(1): 145–52.

Melrose, M. (2002). 'Labour pains: Some considerations on the difficulties of researching juvenile prostitution', *International Journal of Social Research Methodology*, 5(4): 333–51.

Monto, M. (1999). 'Female prostitution, customers, and violence', *Violence Against Women*, 10(2): 160–88.

Moran-Ellis, J. (1996). 'Close to home: the experience of researching child sexual abuse', in M. Hester, L. Kelly and J. Radford (eds) *Women, Violence and Male Power*. London: Open University Press, 176–87.

Newton, E. (1993). 'My best informant's dress: the erotic equation in fieldwork', *Cultural Anthropology*, 8(1): 3–23.

O'Connell Davidson, J. (1996). 'Prostitution and the contours of control', in J. Weeks and J. Holland (eds) *Sexual Cultures: Communities, Values and Intimacy*. New York: St Martin's Press, 180–98.

O'Connell Davidson, J. and Layder, D. (1994). *Methods, Sex and Madness*. London: Routledge.

O'Neill, M. (1996). 'Researching prostitution and violence: towards a feminist praxis', in M. Hester, L. Kelly and J. Radford (eds) *Women, Violence and Male Power*. London: Open University Press, 130–47.

Plummer, K. (1995). *Telling Sexual Stories: Power, Change and Social Worlds*. London: Routledge.

Plumridge, E., Chetwynd, J., Reed, A. and Gifford, S. (1997). 'Discourses on emotionality in commercial sex: the missing client voice', *Feminism and Psychology*, 7(2): 165–81.

Robinson, V., Hockey, J. and Maher, A. (2007). 'Representing "sex" in the research process', *International Journal of Social Research Methodology*, 10(3): 181–94.

Routledge, P. (1996). 'The third space as critical engagement', *Antipode*, 28(4): 399–419.

Sanders, T. (2006a). 'Researching sex work: dynamics, difficulties and decisions', in D. Hobbs and R. Wright (eds) *The SAGE Handbook of Fieldwork*. London: Sage, 201–42.

Sanders, T. (2006b). 'Sexing up the subject: methodological nuances in researching the female sex industry', *Sexualities*, 9(4): 449–68.

Sanders, T. (2008). *Paying for Pleasure: Men who Buy Sex*. Cullompton: Willan.

Sanders, T. and Campbell, R. (2009). 'Why hate men who pay for sex? Investigating the shift to tackling demand and the calls to criminalise paying for sex', in V. Munro (ed.) *Demanding Sex? Critical Reflections on the Supply/Demand Dynamic in Prostitution*. Aldershot: Ashgate, 179–93.

Scully, D. (1990). *Understanding Sexual Violence: A Study of Convicted Rapists*. New York: Routledge.

Sharpe, K. (1998). *Red Light, Blue Light: Prostitutes, Punters and the Police*. Aldershot: Ashgate.

Shaver, F. (2005). 'Sex work research: methodological and ethical challenges', *Journal of Interpersonal Violence*, 20(3): 296–319.

Stanko, E. (1997). '"I second that emotion": reflections on feminism, emotionality, and research on sexual violence', in M. Schwartz (ed.) *Researching Violence against Women: Methodological and Personal Perspectives*. London: Sage, 74–85.

Stanley, L. and Wise, S. (1993). *Breaking Out Again: Feminist Ontology and Epistemology*. London: Routledge.

Ward, H., Mercer, C., Wellings, K., Fenton, K., Erens, B., Copas, A. and Johnson, J. (2005). 'Who pays for sex? An analysis of the increasing prevalence of female commercial sex contacts among men in Britain', *Sexually Transmitted Infections*, 81, 467–71.

Wesely, J. (2006). 'Negotiating myself the impact of studying female exotic dancers on a feminist researcher', *Qualitative Inquiry*, 12(1): 146–62.

Whowell, M. (2010). 'Male sex work: exploring regulation in England and Wales', *Journal of Law and Society*, 37(1), 125–44.

Widdowfield, R. (1999). 'The place of emotion in academic research', *Area*, 32(2): 199–208.

Woodthorpe, K. (2007). 'My life after death: connecting the field, the findings and the feelings', *Anthropology Matters*, 9(1): 1–11.

Woodthorpe, K. (2009). 'Reflecting on death: the emotionality of the research encounter', *Mortality*, 14(1): 70–86.

Xantidis, L. and McCabe, M. (2000). 'Personality characteristics of male clients of female commercial sex workers in Australia', *Archives of Sexual Behavior*, 29(2): 165–76.

Chapter 5

Walking the Beat:
Doing Outreach with Male Sex Workers

Mary Whowell

Introduction

> I climbed into the back of the outreach van and breathed in the smell of stale milk, the remnants of a spillage from the days when it used to serve as a tea-and-condom-bus for the homeless. Ed lit a cigarette and I opened the window to try and let in some air. We started the engine and set off from the office, on outreach, to the Industry Street area. A well-known cruising ground where some of our project participants 'did rent'.[1] We turned the corner past a male sauna onto Industry Street itself and a hooded figure came round the corner on a low riding bike. 'Is that Darren?' asked Mo. 'Yeah', Ed replied, 'out renting for his mum's booze again, come on, lets see what he's up to'. (Fieldwork Diary 2006)

This quotation is taken from a fieldwork diary that I kept whilst undertaking PhD research on the practice (where and when sex is sold); performance (how sex is sold) and regulation (how sex work is regulated by different groups) of street based male sex work in Manchester, UK. Data collection for the research comprised of 28 interviews with 31 key stakeholders;[2] and 600 hours of participant observation completed whilst volunteering with two male sex work outreach projects in the city. Outreach can broadly be described as mobile outreach provision, delivered either in a vehicle or on foot to communities that are unable to access mainstream service provision. Described above therefore, is a moment 'on outreach', which would typically involve loading up the outreach van (or sometimes my car) with condoms, tea, coffee, hot chocolate and signposting information, and heading into the city with two professional outreach workers to the areas where the men worked. Once there, we would seek to engage with the men to deliver a basic level of service provision. As well as dispensing advice and harm minimization materials, we would help them access emergency accommodation, and book

---

1   'Doing rent' is slang for selling sex. A cruising ground is an area where men meet for sex.

2   Interviewees included sex work project participants, outreach workers, the police, members and employees of the City Council, bar and club managers and public health workers amongst others. See Whowell (2009) for specific details on methodology.

appointments, so they could come to the office and access a more advanced level of assistance. This might include organizing more permanent accommodation, offering help around finance, emergency food supply, and working on issues surrounding mental, sexual and physical health. 'Doing outreach' was the central way in which outreach teams were able to access men selling sex; it was also the central way I learnt about street based male sex work in Manchester, and the spaces or 'beats' used for sex work. It constituted a valuable source of data for my thesis. However, doing outreach was not a simple process, and did not involve distributing materials indifferently. Learning to 'do outreach' was central to my experience as a researcher, and became the means through which I used participant observation to collect data. By volunteering with outreach services, I learnt about the local commercial sex scene, the practice of outreach teams, and the important role they played in the wider red light landscape. Maintaining a dual role as participant observer/outreach worker gave me a double responsibility of collecting data whilst also maintaining a duty of care towards outreach project participants. I at once embodied an 'insider/outsider status' that had to be negotiated, but which also allowed for a unique insight into how outreach was practiced on the ground.[3]

This chapter is largely empirical, and draws from my experience as a volunteer outreach worker, as well as interviews with professional outreach workers to explore the process of doing outreach. The analysis presented here is not instructive of how researchers should approach their projects, nor is it an analysis of participant observation as a research methodology (see Cloke et al. 2004, Cook 2005, Cook and Crang 2007, Hoggart et al. 2002, Silverman 2006). Instead, it contributes to the wider literatures on prostitution by illuminating the complexity of outreach as a way of offering social care to sex workers on the street; an issue researchers may find fruitful to consider as part of their wider analysis. The complexity of the outreach experience could also be usefully considered by PhD students, especially in terms of risk assessment, ethics and health and safety when planning fieldwork. As previously mentioned outreach does not just consist of 'giving stuff out', it constitutes developing relationships, garnering a specialist knowledge of the spaces in which sex workers operate and in essence, learning how to work safely in the red light landscape.

To explore these issues, the first section contextualizes the practice of outreach with sex work projects more generally, describing its recent history and their general function. Moving forward I describe the spaces in Manchester in which I practiced outreach between January 2006 and July 2008. I will suggest that in order to 'do outreach', outreach workers (and researchers) must do three things: (i) they must have a knowledge and regular presence within the space; (ii) they must be engaged in the social networks active in that space; and (iii) they must be able to react to the volatility of the street environment and be able to manage risk in order to work effectively.

---

3   There were significant ethical issues that had to be untangled as part of this negotiation. These are explored in full in Whowell (2009).

Walking the Beat: Outreach in Manchester

> Outreach work comes in all shapes and sizes, but it is almost a definition of outreach that workers meet clients where they are at, existentially but also geographically. (Hall and Smith 2009: 3)

Although the definition of 'outreach' will vary from project to project (both in praxis and concept), the basic premise remains the same; outreach teams offer mobile service provision to communities who feel they are socially and/ or physically unable to access what could broadly be described as mainstream health and wellbeing services. Teams access a variety of populations including the homeless, drug users, at risk youth and sex workers. They are often third-sector, not-for profit organizations, and are central to the landscape of social care provision existing in towns and cities in the UK and internationally (Alexander 1999, Coyle et al. 1998, Crimmens et al. 2004, Hall and Smith 2009, Montgomery 1999, Pitcher 2006, Rowe 1999, Wolffers 1999). In the 1980s when the first outreach teams accessing street based sex workers were established, services focused on safer sex and HIV prevention. Now however, a more varied provision is available nationally and internationally, incorporating a multitude of services from healthcare and accommodation to language lessons for migrant sex workers, to the publication of guides on 'selling sex' for those working in different parts of the industry; for example as escorts, in pornography, as fetish workers and brothel workers (Alexander 1999, Gaffney 2002, Pitcher 2006, UKNSWP 2008, www. xtalkproject.net/). Since the inception of outreach projects and especially over the last decade, sex work researchers have used engagement with social care providers to access research participants working in different areas of the sex industry. Much of the literature describing this explores the methodological concerns of researchers seeking to engage sex workers in research, yet few papers have asked and answered questions about how outreach teams themselves negotiate access and develop the necessary relationships to deliver outreach provision to heterogeneous sex working communities (Boynton 2002, Coy 2006, Hubbard 1999, Sanders 2005, Shaver 2005).

There were two male sex work outreach projects operating in Manchester when I completed fieldwork between January 2006 and July 2008. The first being MSWOP (the Male Sex Work Outreach Project), a project within Lifeshare, an organization providing services to the homeless in Manchester, and the second being The Blue Room, a creative arts based project. MSWOP provided access to essential services including emergency accommodation, condoms, food parcels, medical appointments, and assistance with finance. The Blue Room utilized the arts (broadly defined) to explore important issues facing the men selling sex on the streets and hosted exhibitions and performances of the work the men completed with the project. They also operated a referral service to other social care agencies.

78   *New Sociologies of Sex Work*

Approximately 40 men over the age of 18 accessed these services during the period I was volunteering with them.[4]

Geographically, there were two key spaces in Manchester where men publically sold sex: the internationally-known Gay Village[5] located in the south-east of Manchester City centre, and a lesser-known, public sex environment (PSE), the Industry Street area. MSWOP accessed both spaces, whereas the Blue Room worked primarily in the Village. Both spaces were locally known to have rich sexual histories and constituted 'red light landscapes' given their association with public and paid sex (Glinert 2008, Taylor et al. 1996). Outreach with MSWOP was conducted two evenings a week, and involved driving between the areas in a vehicle and walking around them on foot. MSWOP sought to gather knowledge about the local scene. The team engaged with non-sex working 'regulars', distributed condoms, booked appointments, talked, drank coffee and hot chocolate, and spent time conversing with the men. The Blue Room had a space in a tent and then in a shop in the Village one evening a week, and ran sessions from this location. The men would come in, play games, work on projects, eat together, talk, laugh, drink tea and coffee, eat biscuits, and access help and advice. Outreach teams of two people would also go out from Blue Room sessions to let other men working know about the provision available.

Doing outreach involved being on the move, usually outside, walking around the spaces where men sold sex. The city streets became a space through which the team and I gathered knowledge about when, where and how men sold sex, and what their service needs were (Hall 2009). Volunteering allowed me to observe how outreach workers operated across the red light landscape. Through this, I sought to 'unearth' and tried to understand the 'taken for granted' actions of outreach workers (Herbert 2000: 551). Perhaps one of the most significant elements of 'doing outreach' was the amount of walking around the city the team did, which was necessary to access project participants 'on the ground.' Outreach was physical and felt 'like the weather – close or cold, or bracing or wet' (Hall and Smith 2009: 5). When on outreach you brush up and against the urban fabric: wet paving stones, grotty pavements and corners, nooks, crannies and crevices. You feel the streets and the cobble-stones through your boots, you avoid disregarded sex litter, used condoms, empty packets of lube, and the occasional syringe. You purposefully step over putrid puddles. You shelter under umbrellas, in doorways

---

4   Men under the age of 18 also accessed the projects. However they were not written into the research as the ethical framework stipulated by the university, and agreed by the outreach projects stated that only those over the age of 18 could be involved.

5   Hereafter known as 'the Village'. The Village is identified as a space of sex work in this chapter as it is identified as such in Manchester City Council (2007). However the 'Industry Street' area is made anonymous as that space is not referred to as a beat area in publicly available documentation.

Walking the Beat

and in the musty bars in the Village where men sold sex.[6] You walk over sticky carpets, use rancid and often un-lockable toilets, and avoid the glances of inquisitive locals. You watch your drink, other people's drinks and your surroundings. You learn to sense when spaces are safe, when to stay and when to leave, and *I* learnt how to do all this by going 'on outreach'. You learn through doing. Outreach does not leave spaces 'un-marked', it is a multi-sensorial experience, 'it is *hard* on the feet and sometimes on the knees' (Hall and Smith 2009: 5, emphasis as original[7]). Outreach workers rely on their senses, and their knowledge of the city to provide a service on the beat; knowledge required to operate skillfully. Likewise, participant observation requires that researchers (like professional outreach workers) must engage their senses in research to learn about the social and cultural processes and actions active in those spaces (Herbert 2000, Hall and Smith 2009). These processes are discussed in subsequent sections, and it is on this note we move to the first theme to be explored: the notion that outreach workers must have a knowledge of the beat and a regular presence in spaces of sex work in order to practice successfully.

Becoming a Regular and Learning about Spaces of Sex Work

During fieldwork, outreach workers consistently entered the same spaces in which men sold sex twice a week. Outreach was conducted mostly in the early evening for two to three hours between 18:00 and 21:00, with other visits out of these hours taking place between 09:00 and 17:00. These extra visits were made when outreach workers were looking for particular project participants who were not in the areas where they normally sold sex during regular outreach sessions. The regularity with which the teams and I as a researcher entered the spaces, allowed us to gain a greater depth of understanding about the areas in which the men worked. Thus like Hall (2009: 578, emphasis as original), in his work on urban outreach in Cardiff, the regular walks around the areas where men sold sex were in fact 'given over to gleaning further knowledge of a known but shifting *landscape*'. The more the team went on outreach, the more I learnt about geographies of the beat, namely, the particular streets, corners, steps, doorways and pubs from which the different men worked.

When the men were not in the areas where they were commonly known to sell sex, outreach workers saw this as an indication that something was different or potentially taking place in the area, such as: 'the police [being] about or drug dealers…looking for [their] money. You can usually pick up [what is going on]' (Outreach Worker 2, 2008). Through regularly entering the Village, outreach teams and I as a researcher learnt to read these markers and subtle nuances. It

---

6   Note that men did not sell sex in all of the bars in the Village, only a select few. See Whowell (2009) on bars and sex work in the Village.

7   See Hall and Smith (2009) for an excellent multi-sensorial description of outreach.

80 New Sociologies of Sex Work

was deemed important by outreach workers to take in the 'geography, and the locations…what's around you' (Outreach Worker 7, 2007). To stay safe teams had to work around other activities on going in the space. For example, people drinking and partying in bars in the Village, others using the paths running through the Industry Street area for sex or for access to the city centre, people under the influence of drink or drugs. We had to note if there were any 'dodgy' characters[8] around, and be careful not to disturb the men if they were with clients, we had to observe carefully and work with the situation as it was presented. These are all issues researchers working with outreach teams should consider in order to keep themselves and their research participants safe. Yet, it was only through regularly entering the areas in which the men worked, that outreach workers were able to read and react to these signs and signals on the street.

Outreach workers recognized and used triggers in the streetscape to develop a nuanced understanding of place, and a depth of understanding about how the streets were used by the men selling sex, clients, police and the general public. As well as using sight to interpret signs and triggers in the cityscape, they also relied on how they *felt* when walking the beat:

> Yeah [you] definitely feel that the atmosphere at different times, there's different feelings, when you don't feel safe really, and sometimes you feel you can cut the atmosphere with a knife, and you don't know why but you know from the minute of entering the Village something's amiss. It's really strange whether it's because it's not the normal faces, they're not stood where they should be, that's usually because there's police in the area, you'd be like oh, where is everybody? (Outreach Worker 2, 2008)

The repetitive routes the outreach team walked at regular times of the day and night, allowed the team and I to garner a nuanced understanding of the streetscape; and how it was marked by the men working there (see also Brown 2008, Wunderlich 2008). Rendell (2000) has reflected on the power of rhythmic footsteps in place, suggesting that walking in the city as an embodied act is, in itself, transformative, and the means through which spatial meanings writ large in the city are broken and remade. Walking the beat allowed myself and the team to 'sensorially and reflectively interact with the urban environment', we developed a relationship and understanding of the street spaces, and the sexual practices taking place within them (Wunderlich 2008: 125). Outreach workers walk to learn about the spaces in

---

8 In this context 'dodgy characters' could be described as clients the men had reported to be violent or aggressive, and others usually involved in the underground economies (for example drugs, the sale of stolen goods) and general street scene of the Village and Industry Street area. Not everyone involved in these activities was considered 'dodgy' by the outreach team, however there were certainly some individuals who were described in this way.

which they work and to engage with those seeking to access service provision. By using outreach as a way to collect research data researchers are able to do this too.

Regularly entering the areas in which the men worked was also central to developing relationships of trust. The consistency of outreach workers also aided this, as only one paid member of permanent staff left MSWOP and The Blue Room team remained the same throughout the fieldwork. This was important as there was no consistent police presence in the Village and the Industry Street areas until the summer of 2008 when neighbourhood policing teams were established. Outreach teams have however provided service provision on the beat since May 2000 when Lifeshare (the charity housing MSWOP) began offering outreach for male sex workers. MSWOP took over the outreach provision in 2003. The regularity and consistency with which teams entered the beat areas allowed outreach workers to offer a level of 'informal regulation' and protection in spaces of sex work:

> We did feel because the lads knew we'd be out at a particular time or day, it was a safety thing for them... it was our spot for those times, and we would look round just to make sure that the lads[9] that were out were safe, and [to see] if there was anything dodgy, or that we perceived as dodgy, going on down there. It wasn't just sitting in the van, we would walk around and have a look round [Industry Street], the same in the Village, that's all part of what we're doing, so for that particular time we did make it our space, we did regulate that space really (Outreach Worker 7, 2007).

More than the material practice of distributing condoms, offering hot drinks and dispensing advice, the regular presence of the team offered the men working the street a regular time and place through which they could access support:

> If the lads are nervous, or they've been with a bad punter or whatever they'll come straight over to us and [say] ooh such-a-body's there, I've had a bad experience. So we'll say right, well come on, walk with us, they're not going to bother with you while you're with us and we'll just usually walk them to the other side of the Village, sit down and just have a chat and sometimes the person they're afraid of will crock up [turn up] and do-one [leave] themselves because they've seen us (Outreach Worker 2, 2008).

It was clear from fieldwork that the outreach workers played a key role on the lives of the men. The team offered an informal regulatory presence, and some degree of protection or relief in the Village from the stresses associated with street sex work, such as long periods spent alone on the street, isolated working environments, constantly having to negotiate with clients, having to always be

---

9 The term 'lads' here refers to men to who sell sex, it is a generic term used by service providers to describe the project participants. All those who took part in the PhD research were aged 18 or over.

82   *New Sociologies of Sex Work*

aware of the environmental surroundings to stay safe and negotiating the 'street scene' more generally. What was also stressed in interviews with the sex work project participants was that outreach workers provided a 'friendly face' and a level of respite, in what was a turbulent and volatile street space:

> *you know the face*, like Ed, everyone knows Ed and they'll go and speak to Ed if they see him, say 'hi how you doing?, Have another drink,[10] and then go again because you feel better that you've had a chat and got everything off your chest about what's going on. (Sex Work Project Participant 4, 2008, emphasis added)

Knowing the faces of outreach workers (and their volunteers), contributes to the relationship building process, which can only be attempted if the outreach provision is consistent, regular and well informed.

The Importance of Social Networks

Relationships between outreach teams and sex workers were also developed through engagement in social networks in the Village and Industry Street area. Not only did engaging with sex workers and their peer group (some of whom sold sex, whilst others did not) lead to more participants learning about the services of MSWOP and The Blue Room, but engaging in street networks allowed important information to be gleaned and passed on between outreach workers and the men working the street. Outreach workers could pass information about 'dodgy punters', when MSWOP or Blue Room sessions were on and when they would be in the office and available for appointments. Whereas the men would pass on snippets of information about what might be happening on the street that night, who was working where, which clients were out and looking for business, if the police had been in the area, and what the word on the street was. In addition, there were other 'locals' who have used the Industry Street area and the Village for a variety of purposes for many years. Some of these people frequented the pubs and clubs, some worked there, others were part of the street scene, and could be seen wandering around at different times of the day, whilst others were members of the (heterogeneous) homeless community. Perhaps because of the regularity with which the outreach teams were in the Village and Industry Street area, these individuals would often approach us to talk, to pass time and to pass on tidbits of information:

> There are people I have come across, people who may not be involved...with the lads, or sex work or drugs or alcohol they were just there just for whatever reason, maybe they had a past where at one time they did work [sell sex] but you do occasionally come across people who come around there who were just there,

---

10   The term 'drink' here refers to a non-alcoholic drink as provided by the outreach projects.

Walking the Beat

part of the scenery and they would speak to you because they got to know you and you would speak to them quite often really (Outreach Worker 7, 2008).

Outreach was not only shaped by the presence of outreach workers and sex workers, but also by third parties who were not directly linked to the sexual exchange. Listening out to learn about what might be happening on any given night was therefore important. As Hall and Smith (2009: 5) reflect: '[h]earing is conventionally one of the more sympathetic senses: it is receptive and open, and [is a] qualit[y] that outreach work requires – a good ear (a thick skin is also important). Add to that an ear to the ground' (Hall and Smith 2009: 5). As well as being useful to outreach workers, listening to what was being said on the street was a key way in which I learnt about street-based male sex work.

Outreach workers would, when appropriate, use this network to send discreet messages out to the men accessing the outreach projects: '[w]e can share and pass information as well within that web, if there's maybe a dodgy punter or somebody doing a lot of street robberies then you can put the word out to be watchful through your little network.' (Outreach Worker 2, 2008). This works in a similar way to the messages about 'dodgy punters' passed out by outreach projects for female sex workers (Sanders 2004, UKNSWP 2007), and is consistent with examples from the wider literature about the value of 'street gossip'. Policek's (2009) research on street sex working in Edinburgh suggests that sex workers will exchange knowledge and information about drug deals with police so they can continue to work on the street and avoid being moved on (see also McKeganey and Barnard 1996). This is not to say that these types of relationships are unproblematic, but they demonstrate the complex ways in which street sex workers negotiate the right to work in public space (see also Hubbard and Sanders 2003).

Outreach workers were nevertheless, trained to be aware of who they were talking to, and the implications this might have both ethically, and on the project and its' participants. Outreach workers never passed on information or talked about project participants to others, and conversations were often general. For instance, a licensed premise we regularly visited employed a female member of staff who had worked there for over 25 years. Due to the continual presence of outreach teams over time, we gained the trust of this particular staff member, so she would sometimes pass on pieces of information, but the team had to be careful so not to implicate her or others further:

> She would say 'some of your lads are over there', and that was it and that was fine for me, that's all I ever wanted to hear to be honest with you… I never went up to her and said 'have you seen any of our lot today' or anything, because… she's not trained for it…she might be aware of the individuals and what's going on but she might not know about the histories, boundaries and those sorts of things. (Outreach Worker 7, 2008)

84 *New Sociologies of Sex Work*

Networks and the webs of people involved in different ways with the street scene, did exist and were to some extent useful to, and used by the outreach workers. Learning and engaging with different actors in the red light landscape was also a fascinating way to learn about how the commercial street scene operates, and provided rich research data. Networks also demonstrate the complexity of the street scene, which is commonly portrayed to only comprise sex workers and their clients, whilst further evidence from my research showed that other individuals were also linked to the sale of sex. Notably some security staff, managers of particular bars in the Village, and some regular drinkers were involved in the buying and selling of sex. Researchers would do well to consider the complexity of the sexual exchange and move beyond research which focuses solely on sex workers and their clients (Agustin 2006). Using outreach as a tool to learn about the extended networks of people involved in the commercial sex scene is one way to do this.

Managing Risk

The ability to manage difficult and potentially risky situations was central to the role outreach workers played on the street. Although scenarios when outreach workers or participants were actually in danger were rare, skillful negotiating skills and the ability of outreach workers (and researchers) to remain calm were necessary in order to practice outreach. Two experiences drawn upon here illustrate how outreach workers manage risk encountered on the street. The first example refers to managing aggression or threatening language when on outreach. The second example refers to an incident which demonstrates the material impact of how having a regular presence on the beat and being involved with street networks can contribute to the safety of outreach workers.

In the spring of 2008, I wrote about an incident in the Industry Street area in my research diary. The team was attempting to engage with two men, both new to selling sex on the street. Although the team had met the men a couple of times, we were finding it difficult to sustain contact and wanted to use the time we had with them to talk and find out if there was anything MSWOP could offer. They were not alone, but were accompanied by an older man who I described in my fieldwork diary was 'big with a skin head'.[11] He seemed very interested in who we were. When we were giving out condoms, he snarled 'I don't need them, I do it bareback'.[12] At this point one of the professional outreach workers stepped in to calm the situation down. Up to that point he had maybe been a little detached, but not aggressive:

> We have a laugh and call our condoms wellies... I'll say sometimes 'you've got
> to watch it because you need double wellies, waders, devils and snorkels before

---

11 The term 'skin head' refers to a person whose hair is closely shaven or cropped.
12 Bareback in this context refers to sex without a condom.

Walking the Beat

you go down there!'... I've had occasions where people may have got a little bit aggressive with me and said no, 'I do it bareback'. So [you have to] not be scared and say that's a really foolish thing to do and try go into a little bit of sexual health and try and push condoms, well not forcing them on but I have had a quite a few occasions where I've been told to F off... I think sometimes you just deal with it, when it's happening, it's your job. (Outreach Worker 2, 2007)

Laughter and humour, and essentially letting people talk to you before leaving the scene was a key skill used by outreach workers to placate potentially volatile situations. After distributing condoms to the two men, and leaving our contact details we left the Industry Street area to continue outreach in the Village. The potential to bump into, or have to engage with unknown third parties is relatively high whilst on outreach. Spaces of sex work are not only populated by sex workers and their clients. Also common are male or female partners, peers, others seeking to gain economically from the exchange of sex, protectors, and sometimes personal enemies of sex workers. Although threatening interactions were in my experience rare, researchers working with outreach teams must learn how to act when engaging with potentially risky street environments. I followed risk assessments drawn from the projects and approved by the university, but in reality it very much depended on the situation in hand. Thankfully, there were few occasions were I actually felt 'at risk' of harm, and on those few occasions, the decision to placate and then exit worked.

Also key to avoiding risk was being able to 'sense' trouble. If the team entered the areas where the men worked, and sensed that something was amiss, outreach workers could usually, based on their existing knowledge, decipher what might be happening on the street based on who was stood where, if police were in the area, what the weather was like (more men work indoors when it rains), or if known gangs or threatening individuals were in the area. On some occasions outreach workers were able to find out what was going on from one of the project participants or regulars to the area: 'Within 50 yards of walking into our normal entry into the Village we'll probably know the reasons why [something feels strange] because we'll bump into one of our networks...' (Outreach Worker 2, 2008). Being well networked in the areas in which the men worked was key to staying safe. Also important to being accepted by the men on the beat as social care providers (and I as a researcher) was the reputation of the outreach teams, forged through many years of consistent and regular outreach work, engagement in networks on the street, and crucially having a proven track record of assisting the participants. One of the most fascinating outcomes of this was that the reputation of the team was proven (on one occasion at least) to offer some level of safety against the petty criminal element present in the Village:

I did have an interesting encounter a couple of weeks ago. I was walking through the Village, there were two thuggy street robbers sat there pretending to be rent boys, and they obviously weren't, but as I was walking past, one of my

86 *New Sociologies of Sex Work*

colleagues overheard him saying 'oh he's alright him, leave him alone', and she thinks he was referring to me, as in saying, don't go there, do you know what I mean? (Interview with Outreach Worker 1, 2007)

It is possible that the visibility of the outreach team entering the Village and engaging with the men provided two-way protection. The outreach workers were viewed positively by the men, and others involved in the petty criminal element of the Village did not hassle or target the outreach workers, perhaps because they knew about the service we provided, or they may even have known some of the men who accessed the project.

Thus by working with street networks, individuals, sex workers and their peers and reacting to triggers and the volatility of the street environment, outreach workers were able to deliver service provision on the street with few questions asked and little hassle. They were also protected from harm, precisely because of the sustained engagement they had with the men working the beat, and knowledge gleaned through practice on how to work safely in street environments.

Conclusion

Although there has been much research (especially over the last decade) wherein researchers have used outreach agencies as gatekeepers to access sex workers, there has been little consideration of how outreach itself is practised and performed on the ground. This chapter has revealed that outreach constitutes more than the material practice of giving out condoms and dispensing advice to men who sell sex. It is complex, embodied and entwined within wider social networks, street practices and social performances. Doing outreach requires a depth of understanding of commercial sexual practice and the development of relationships, not just with project participants but with a variety of actors across the red light landscape. Outreach teams and researchers must be able to react and engage with volatile street environments and learn how to manage risk, they must use their senses to keep themselves and project participants safe. Therefore knowing how to 'do outreach' is an important concern for researchers seeking to gather data by joining an outreach team.

The empirical data presented in this chapter highlights three important facets of outreach work worthy of consideration by researchers: (i) that it is necessary for outreach teams to enter spaces of sex work regularly and consistently; (ii) that outreach teams engage in street networks to glean and share information and finally (iii) that outreach workers must know how to manage risk and confrontation on the street. Aside from these substantive issues, other concerns highlighted included: taking notice of what was happening on the street (who was stood where, if police were in the area and such), knowing how to placate a potentially volatile situation, knowing when to leave and when to stay, being aware of potential dangers and knowing when it is appropriate to approach sex work project participants. These issues are important to consider prior to fieldwork, especially when seeking to meet the increasingly stringent ethical, risk assessment and health and safety requirements of universities. Finally, it would be interesting for projects incorporating outreach as methodology to publish more on how outreach is practised, as opposed to focusing on the collection of data. Future work could also consider the emotional and sensorial experiences of outreach in greater depth.

Acknowledgements

I would like to thank Sarah Kingston, Kate Hardy and Ian R. Cook for comments on earlier drafts of this chapter. I would also like to thank DFAIT and the Government of Canada for providing the post-doctoral funding which allowed me to work on this publication.

References

Agustin, L. (2006). 'The cultural study of commercial sex', *Sexualities*, 8(5): 618–31.

Alexander, P. (1999). 'Health care for sex workers should go beyond STD care', *Research for Sex Work*, 2, 14–16.

Boynton, P.M. (2002). 'Life on the streets: the experiences of community researchers in a study of prostitution', *Journal of Community and Applied Social Psychology*, 12(1): 1–12.

Brown, G. (2008). 'Ceramics, clothing and other bodies: affective geographies of homoerotic cruising encounters', *Social and Cultural Geography*, 9(8): 915–32.

Cloke, P., Cook, I., Crang, P., Goodwin, M., Painter, J. and Philo, C. (2004). *Practising Human Geography*. London: Sage.

Cook, I. (2005). 'Positionality/situated knowledge', in D. Atkinson et al. (eds) *Cultural Geography: A Critical Dictionary of Key Ideas*. London: I.B. Tauris, 14–24.

Cook, I. and Crang, M. (2007). *Doing Ethnographies*. London: Sage.

Coy, M. (2006). 'This morning I'm a researcher, this afternoon I'm an outreach worker: Ethical dilemmas in practitioner research', *International Journal of Social Research Methodology*, 9(5): 419–31.

Coyle, S., Needle, R.H. and Normand, J. (1998). 'Outreach-based HIV prevention for injecting drug users: a review of published outcome data', *Public Health Reports*, 113(1): 19–30.

Crimmens, D., Factor, F., Jeffs, T., Pitts, J., Pugh, C., Spence, J. and Turner, P. (2004). *The Role of Street-Based Youth Work in Linking Socially Excluded Young People Into Education, Training and Work*. York: Joseph Rowntree Foundation.

Gaffney, J. (2002). 'Guidelines for development of outreach work with men who sell sex', in K. Schiffer (ed.) *Manual: Tips, Tricks and Models of Good Practice for Service Providers Considering, Planning or Implementing Services for Male Sex Workers*. Amsterdam: European Network Male Prostitution.

Glinert, E. (2008). *The Manchester Compendium*. London: Allen Lane.

Hall, T. (2009). 'Footwork: moving and knowing in local space(s)', *Qualitative Research*, 9(5): 571–85

Hall, T. and Smith, R. (2009). *Urban Outreach as Sensory Walking*. Paper at the annual conference of the Royal Geographical Society (RGS), University of Manchester,UK, 26–28 August.

Herbert, S. (2000). 'For ethnography', *Progress in Human Geography*, 24(4): 550–68

Hoggart, K., Lees, L. and Davies, A. (2002). *Researching Human Geography*. London: Arnold.

Hubbard, P. (1999). 'Research, action and "critical" geographies', *Area*, 31(3): 195–8.

Hubbard, P. and Sanders, T. (2003). 'Making space for sex work: female street prostitution and the production of urban space', *International Journal of Urban and Regional Research*, 27(1): 75–89.

Manchester City Council (2007). *Manchester Prostitution Strategy* [online], available at: http://www.manchester.gov.uk/downloads/Appendix_1_ Manchester_Strategy_2007.pdf [accessed 26 January 2009].

McKeganey, N. and Barnard, M. (1996). *Sex Work on the Streets: Prostitutes and their Clients*. Buckingham: Open University Press.

Montgomery, R. (1999). 'There aren't even any written materials in the clinic to read', *Research for Sex Work*, 2, 3–5.

Pitcher, J. (2006). 'Support services for women working in the sex industry', in R. Campbell and M. O'Neill (eds) *Sex Work Now*. Devon: Willan, 235–62.

Policek, N. (2009). *Policing the Truth: Sex Workers as Police Informants*. Paper presented at Annual Socio-Legal Studies Association conference, De Montfort University, Leicester, 8 April.

Rendell, R. (2000). 'Pursuits', in S. Pile and N.Thrift (eds) *City A–Z*. London: Routledge, 196–8.

Rowe, M. (1999). *Crossing the Border: Encounters Between Homeless People and Outreach Workers*. London: University of California Press.

Sanders, T. (2004). 'The risks of street prostitution: punters, police and protestors', *Urban Studies*, 41(9): 1703–17.

Sanders, T. (2005). *Sex Work: A Risky Business*. Devon: Willan.

Shaver, F.M. (2005). 'Sex work research: methodological and ethical challenges', *Journal of Interpersonal Violence*, 20(3): 296–319.

Silverman, D. (2006). *Interpreting Qualitative Data*, 3rd Edition. London: Sage.

Taylor, I., Evans, K. and Fraser, P. (1996). *A Tale of Two Cities: A Study in Manchester and Sheffield*. London: Routledge.

United Kingdom Network of Sex Work Projects (UKNSWP) (2007). *Ugly Mugs and Dodgy Punters* [online], available at: http://www.uknswp.org/resources/GPG1.pdf [accessed: 24 March 2010].

United Kingdom Network of Sex Work Projects (UKNSWP) (2008). *Sorted Men: A Guide to Selling Sex* [online], available at http://www.uknswp.org/resources/RSW3.pdf [accessed: 5 May 2010].

Whowell, M. (2009). Inappropriate sexualities? The practice, performance and regulation of male sex work in Manchester. Unpublished PhD Thesis, Loughborough University.

Wolffers, I. (1999). 'Appropriate health services for sex workers', *Research for Sex Work*, 2, 1–3.

Wunderlich, F.M. (2008). 'Walking and rhythmicity: sensing urban space', *Journal of Urban Design*, 13(1): 125–39.

Chapter 6

New Technologies, New Territories: Using the Internet to Connect with Sex Workers and Sex Industry Organizers

Suzanne Jenkins

Introduction: The Transformation of Sex Work

Given the plethora of literature on sex work that now exists, it could be argued that the subject of commercial sex has now been so well researched that it no longer necessitates further academic inquiry. Since the turn of the century alone, many valuable empirical studies have already been published in the UK (see for example O'Neill 2001, Sanders 2005 and 2008, Brooks-Gordon 2006, Day 2007). However, the nature of sex work and the working methods used by those who sell sexual services are constantly evolving. New technologies such as the Internet provide for a greater variety of sexual services such as online pornography and webcam performances as well as offering alternative ways of advertising and negotiating the sale of direct sexual encounters (see Sharpe and Earle 2003).

To remain relevant and useful sex work research needs to adapt to these developments. However, as yet there is little evidence of modification in terms of research strategy. For example, historically, due to the hidden nature of the sex industry, researchers have commonly accessed participants through contact with sexual health outreach services or with the use of snowball sampling techniques, (Sharpe 1998, Phoenix 1999, O'Neill 2001, Day 2007). Partly as a result of limited access, and partly because it is seen as the most problematic form of prostitution, research into sex work has usually focused on female prostitutes working from the street. The case in the UK is that far fewer women are working this way, and even in major cities street sex work is thought to be less than thirty per cent (Scambler 2007).

Indoor sectors of the sex industry in contrast are said to be 'booming' (Sanders 2006: 91). This includes women and men working in sex flats, saunas, and massage parlours and as escorts, many of whom have turned to the Internet as their primary means of marketing and communication (Hughes 1999, Bimbi and Parsons 2005). Although sex work is now far less visible on public streets, it is very readily identifiable by almost anyone who searches the Internet. One implication of this shift is that while off-street sex workers have historically been hard to identify, let alone access for research purposes, the Internet now offers sex work researchers new prospects for access.

Although there has been reluctance to accept the use of Internet technology in academic research, the growth in new communication technology has presented social researchers with a number of new opportunities and since the 1990s, Internet-based research methods have been used increasingly in academic studies (McGlothlin 2003). However, although several studies have used Internet technology to access and communicate with male escorts for the purpose of sexual health research (for example Davis et al. 2000, Minichiello et al. 2008), as yet, few have used the opportunity that the Internet offers to investigate other aspects of the industry or to access and communicate with female sex workers (for an exception see Sanders 2005).

Drawing upon my own empirical research with escort sex workers, in this chapter I illustrate how the Internet is useful in three ways: first, by providing access to previously hidden populations; second, by facilitating efficient and dynamic means of administering surveys; and third, by providing an effective yet sensitive means of communication for interview purposes. Additionally, I use the example of sex work industry managers to highlight how Internet technology can offer an opportunity to extend the scope of sex work research into new territories by providing a platform for the voices of people working in areas of the industry about which little is known. In doing so I explain how the use of Internet-mediated communication can overcome some of the barriers imposed by more conventional research approaches, and argue that if used appropriately, they can provide a valuable contribution to sex work research methodologies and extend knowledge about sex work into hitherto unexplored territories.

Computer-mediated Surveys: Transcending the Quantitative/Qualitative Divide

Research methods that utilize new technologies such as the Internet are usually referred to as computer-mediated-communication (hereafter CMC) methods. An example of their use as a data collection method can be seen in the way that CMC methods have been used to replace traditional methods of administering self-completion survey instruments. Rather than administering surveys by post, electronic mail (hereafter email) offers almost instantaneous transmission and distribution of a questionnaire via the Internet and also returns the collected data in a format ready for analysis. Unsurprisingly, as De Vaus (2002: 123) observes, 'since the mid-1990s the Internet has become an increasingly viable and popular means of administering questionnaires'.

Social surveys are usually considered to be a quantitative data collection method, and regardless of their mode of administration, survey methods, and quantitative research methods more generally, have been subject to certain criticism by some social researchers. For example, in the early 1980s, several feminist social researchers proposed that the principles and practices associated with quantitative research were incompatible with feminist research on women, partly because they were seen to objectify social life and partly because they were bound up with male values of control; that is, control of the research participant and control of the research context (Oakley 1981, Bryman 2001). Also, social surveys were seen as a one-way process in which the interviewer presumed the right to ask the questions that *they* deemed relevant without offering anything in return. This top-down approach prompted feminists to argue that it was indefensible to 'use' other women in this way (Bryman 2001). It was argued further that if one of the primary aims of feminist research is to uncover the unheard voice of women and to reflect women's subjective experience, it needed to be reflexive, respondent-focused and interactive (Illingworth 2001, Hesse-Biber 2007). For many feminists, this meant research had to be qualitative in orientation. Although feminists are not the only researchers that have expressed antipathy towards quantitative research methods, it is within feminist research that this critique has been particularly noticeable (Bryman 2001).

Technological developments have lead to new opportunities for social science to apply survey methods in order to learn about social life. Technology has not only revolutionized the way in which surveys are administered, it has also impacted on the mediated interface between the researcher and the respondent. Although still largely a non-interactive process, in comparison to traditionally-distributed surveys, Internet-mediated surveys can be designed to be more respondent-friendly, offer participants more control over the process and can more easily encourage people to express their personal narratives through open questions. Indeed, according to Bryman (2004), it is questionable whether web-based survey instruments should be regarded as structured interviews or self-completion questionnaires, although he maintains that in a sense they are both. Therefore, although a number of researchers have suggested that open-ended questions are best used when respondents can answer verbally (for example Gunn 2002, De Vaus 2002), this may be less relevant in the case of computer-mediated surveys. For example, there is evidence that respondents tend to give longer answers to open-ended questions in electronic surveys than in printed surveys (Schonlau et al. 2002). Schaefer and Dillman (1998), who examined this issue more closely in a comprehensive review of previous Internet studies, conclude that email versions elicit much longer responses to open-ended questions than paper versions (forty rather than ten words) whilst others have reported that respondents have been known to write what is effectively a 'mini-essay' (Comley 1996).

Of course, the number of words written in response to an open-ended question is not the only important factor when evaluating a research method; the value of any data lies in its relationship to the research aims. As such, a number of researchers have reported that not only do respondents write lengthier comments when communicating electronically, they also demonstrate a higher rate of self-disclosure than in traditional surveys and there is evidence that answers tend to be more honest and insightful in other ways (see for example Mehta and Sivadas

1995, Comley 1996). Self-disclosure, defined as 'the act of revealing personal data to others' (Archer 1980: 183, Joinson 2001), usually involves the divulging of intimate, socially controversial or otherwise sensitive facts, feelings or opinions. Research has shown that in responding to open-ended questions, email respondents wrote more clarifying and illuminating comments than traditional mail respondents (Mehta and Sivadas 1995). Therefore, while the higher number of words typed may, in part at least, be simply due to the speed of typing over handwriting, the likelihood is that there is more to it than just speed. Certainly it would seem then that CMC methods may be well suited to open-ended questions and it is the quality of the responses in terms of fullness and verbosity that is most clearly demonstrated in the literature. Given the way that online surveys appear to encourage more productive and rewarding responses similar to those elicited using interactive approaches, the binary and static distinction between quantitative and qualitative data may no longer be a useful distinction in this context.

In light of this, and given the aim in my research design to elicit at least some descriptive data from the survey, I decided to include a high proportion of open-ended questions in my survey. Moreover, of the 40 questions on the questionnaire, almost all questions provided space for unlimited text to be added should respondents wish to qualify their answers. In response to feminist criticism of the way that surveys assume the right to ask only questions deemed relevant by the researcher, as well as providing extra space for additional information, any questions that respondents preferred not to answer could be skipped without explanation.

The survey was sent to a database of email addresses taken from escort sex workers' websites and this resulted in over five hundred responses, many of which provided lengthy, elaborate answers. While a small number of participants did little more than tick boxes, many wrote several pages of text. Analysis of the word count produced by the survey suggests that they each typically provided between 600–1,200 words, with the most verbose typing over 4,000 words of text. Open questions in the survey therefore produced a wealth of data. Furthermore, as well as being positive in terms of the quantity of words used, in many cases, responses were extremely insightful and revealing. For example, some women used the survey space to contextualize their sex work by writing about their personal relationships, childhood, or career history, while others described their feelings about the lived experience of doing sex work and elaborated on topics such as their emotional and sexual health.

Overall, the survey – a method normally assumed to be quantitative – produced a huge volume of qualitative data through the use of open questions, much of which were useful and enlightening. In this way, the distinction between qualitative and quantitative research methods became blurred, in line with Bryman's (2001) prediction. Of course asking people to divulge personal information via an online survey will not, however, always be the most suitable strategy. The characteristics of a particular research sample may necessitate the use of more traditional methods of communication such as face-to-face interviewing. However, the appropriateness

New Technologies, New Territories 95

of a survey in this research was that the individuals in my sample used the Internet as a marketing and communications tool in their work. Therefore, they were likely to be familiar with computer-mediated communication and already spent considerable amounts of time on the Internet. Many of their websites indicated that email was their preferred means of communication, suggesting that they were likely to be comfortable with communicating online. With this in mind, using the survey as a tool for recruiting interview participants, I included the option of online communication methods also as an interview method. Interviewees could select this as their preferred mode of interaction. Many respondents did select online methods for interview purposes, including many women. However, before discussing the advantages and disadvantages of those interviews, in the following section I consider what other researchers have observed about CMC interview methods and in particular, discuss how computer-mediated interview methods fit with feminist research practice.

Online Interviewing: What Constitutes a Woman-friendly Environment?

The prospect of conducting qualitative research using online personal interviews is an exciting opportunity that new technologies such as computers and in particular, the Internet, have made possible. These can be conducted in either synchronous mode, such as instant messaging or asynchronous mode, such as email. Although academic researchers are beginning to capitalize on the benefits that online interviewing offers, there are still some reservations about whether CMC methods are as effective as more traditional face-to-face methods in social research. For example, in the early days of CMC research methods, one of the pressing concerns about communicating 'remotely' was the impact this might have on response quality. As Joinson (2005: 22) explains, 'early theories of Internet behaviour (and more specifically CMC) tended to focus on what was lost during Internet-based interaction'. For example, one merit of face-to-face interviews is that by communicating directly, the interaction includes not just words, but also body language and gestures; conversely, without that direct interaction, we lose out on what words alone cannot convey, such as humour, sarcasm or other emotions which people may feel or intend by their responses.

Yet establishing a rapport and creating an environment that facilitates frank discussion is not always achievable even by the most skilled researcher. Moreover, it is not clear that establishing a personal rapport or connection with your participant is always the best way to extract information. Not only do many Internet-based studies provide results comparable to non-Internet ones in terms of volume of data (Hewson et al. 2003), but more significantly, there is evidence that there are certain important advantages to providing a shield from the direct exposure of face-to-face methods. For example, it could be argued that with no direct personal interaction between interviewer and interviewee, there is less incentive to adopt or maintain a 'public' image or facade. As Gies (2008: 317–18) points out, 'the appeal of the Internet is not invariably that it allows us to be someone else but also that it allows us to be ourselves'. Therefore, rather than being a barrier to frank disclosure, visual anonymity may help to lessen inhibition and coyness.

Moreover, whilst a lack of direct physical interaction could result in difficulty establishing a rapport or social connection with some participants, as Joinson (2005) argues, this will not always be the case and instead, the presence of a researcher may hinder candid response for some participants (see also Selwyn and Robsons, 1998). Online research can offer respondents greater freedom to communicate their feelings about sensitive subjects (Illingworth 2001). Indeed, Illingworth found that a number of her participants emphasized that they would have been reluctant to participate in her study on involuntary infertility if research been conducted in a more conventional face-to-face setting.

Researching Sex Workers Online

The enabling factors associated with visual anonymity were something that several of my interview participants mentioned. That is, that if they had had to meet with me in person they would not have agreed to be interviewed. For some participants, this was, in part at least, about their convenience, but four women explained that they were more comfortable discussing their sex work online and they could express themselves better this way without risk. That risk was not necessarily about the legality of their work, and it could be argued that providing written statements could pose a higher risk of the information being used against them. Instead, it was sometimes simply that not everyone finds face-to-face interaction a comfortable setting in which to share their private thoughts. For some it can be too embarrassing, intimidating, or potentially emotional. The face-to-face interviews that I conducted bore this out, with many poignant moments of reflection and emotion infiltrating the flow of discussion. In addition, the motivation not to engage direct physical interaction was sometimes about avoiding what interviewees perceived as offensive or patronizing attitudes in response to disclosure about their work. One female participant suggested:

> You can say what you like online and get away with it … you know, without getting "the look" or the "there there now love" like they do when they feel sorry for you or think you're off your head and that … but you don't know me from Adam so it's like "whatever".

As well as offering a 'safe' environment in which to disclose personal experiences and emotions, Illingworth contends further that the electronic environment is an effective tool which presents a more neutral and egalitarian space in which to communicate. Not only were such notions alluded to by many of the female participants in my own research, but several male participants also explained their preference for online interview communication in terms of their heightened level of confidence with communicating without visual contact. Illingworth (2001) suggests that an online environment anonymity allows feelings and experiences to be discussed which would be withheld in other interactive contexts, and this was confirmed by interviewees who turned down my offer to come to meet them in person in favour of using instant messaging, saying that they knew they would find it easier to express themselves online or that they felt they could be more truthful online.

That my physical presence represented a barrier to open discussion became evident in other ways. For example, two female participants who I interviewed face-to-face, both with whom I felt I had had a frank exchange, later contacted me to say that there was something I should know that they had not felt able to disclose. One emailed me and admitted to suffering from a psychological disorder that she had denied when face-to-face. The other telephoned me to disclose a very negative experience from her childhood that she had not disclosed in the two hours we had spent together, much of which had focussed on her family background. Both explained their non-disclosure in terms of it being hard to talk about such sensitive experiences in person. What is not clear, of course, is whether, had we not met first, these disclosures would have occurred at all. These example do reinforce the notion that face-to-face interviews are not necessarily the easiest way for all people to feel comfortable about disclosing their personal experiences.

Although in recent years there has been a softening of the attitudes of feminists towards quantitative research (see Sprague 2005), the use of CMC methods is an aspect of social research that feminists have as yet to take full advantage of. Given its significance as a feminist issue, feminist researchers have been responsible for much of the existing literature on sex work and this has provided a valuable insight into the subject of commercial sex. However, as feminist social researchers we do need to try to elicit the views of a wide range of sex workers, not just those who are most comfortable communicating in a face-to-face setting. By including the option of online interviews in research design feminists may offer an opportunity to further empower some women by providing a choice of context within which they may feel more ready to contribute.

Winning Trust Online

Regardless of the legal status of prostitution, commercial sexual services 'occur in a fragile and hostile legal climate' (Sanders and Campbell 2008: 53). Sex workers are accustomed to being guarded, defensive and secretive about their work. Sex work researchers will need to overcome barriers in terms of access that are raised both by the stigma attached to sex work and the complex legal status of prostitution. Indeed, several recipients of my invitation to take part in my sex work survey declined stating that they were not prepared to take part because they felt that there was no guarantee how the data would be used or who would have access

98 *New Sociologies of Sex Work*

to it. As Sanders (2005) argues, it is harder for researchers to establish their bona fide status online, than in offline situations.

I found that issues of trust tended to be of less concern to male participants, perhaps because they have not typically been subject to the same degree of legal intervention or social stigmatization as female sex workers (Weeks 1991, Marlowe 1997). This may also be why, proportionately, more women than men chose face-to-face interviews rather than online. Nevertheless, many participants, male and female, expressed concerns about confidentiality and privacy. Being offered a choice of interview style allowed participants to base their decision on their own experiences and priorities and this was often reflected in their explanations both for choosing face-to-face interviews as well as to be interviewed online. For example, a female escort explained why online interviewing would be unsatisfactory to her:

> I prefer in-face ... I like to see a person's face, and I like to know who I'm talking to ... to tell where a person is really coming from ... I want to see what this person really thinks, how this person looks at this and what this person is really like and you can't do that on MSN or whatever.

These feelings were not uncommon, and several other participants explained their preference for meeting in person in similar ways. Two women said that the fact that I had *offered* to meet them in person was sufficient reassurance that I was genuine and they were therefore happy to be interviewed online. For others, the opportunity to be interviewed without having to meet in person provided them with a necessary sense of anonymity to discuss their work freely. Being offered choice about how to communicate for research purposes may therefore have more significance in the context of sex work than in other areas of research. Given the illicit and deviant nature of sex work, offering a choice about the level of anonymity may be particularly valuable. McKenna et al. (2002) argue that not only is the social cost of self-disclosure reduced through anonymity but that there is also a reduction in a person's power to use the disclosed information against the person who has divulged this information. This may be especially pertinent to sex workers fearful about having their sex work identity exposed.

Not only is there less risk of information being used against them, but research has shown that, in the absence of visual anonymity, people are more likely to disclose information about themselves that would not normally be socially acceptable because don't have to explain themselves or face disapproval (Bargh, McKenna and Fitzsimons 2002, Di Marco and Di Marco 2003). Sex workers, at risk of both social disapproval and being challenged about the legality of their work, may feel that such risks are effectively reduced by mediating via a computer interface. Regardless of whether in reality the risks are any different, this was the perception of at least some of the men and women that I interviewed.

Altogether, 65 per cent of the respondents (n=147) who agreed to be interviewed, chose an online interview and 35 per cent (n=79) per cent asked to be interviewed in person. Although telephone interviews had not been offered as an option, some participants asked if the interview could be conducted this way and so 11 per cent (n=12) of the interviews were conducted by telephone. Proportionally, slightly more women selected face-to-face interviews. As Table 6.1 shows, of the 108 sex workers I finally interviewed, less than half of respondents, regardless of gender, chose to meet with me in person for their interview.

Table 6.1   Number of interviews by methods and gender

	Female	Male	Transwomen	Total
Face-to-Face	36	10	5	51 (47%)
Telephone	6	4	2	12 (11%)
Online	28	15	2	45 (42%)
Total	70 (65%)	29 (13%)	9 (8.33%)	108 (100%)

Comparing the Data

In comparing these two interview methods, the face-to-face interviews produced almost twice as much data in terms of words of text. Regardless of interview method, interviews with male participants produced, on the whole, fewer words than those with female participants and transwomen. However, as suggested earlier, higher verbosity alone does not necessarily equate to a successful interview. For example, some verbal exchanges, no matter how convivial and quantitatively productive, may offer little value in terms of addressing the research questions. Also, although online connections present a distinct set of distractions such as receiving messages from other contacts, I found that most people minimized possible distractions during our online interviews which were always prearranged for a suitable time. Conversely, in face-to-face situations there was a greater tendency to react to distractions in the environment or to go off at a tangent onto other topics of little research value.

Direct comparison between the number of words produced using the two methods is also difficult because in online interviews, not only were distractions less common, but people also tend to respond to instant messaging and emails using as few words as necessary. There was also a tendency to use acronyms and emoticons, which convey meaning without words. This does mean that the data can be open to interpretation; for example, symbols such as a smiley face may not reflect the participant's true feeling. Nevertheless, such inconsistencies can also occur in face-to-face situations between the spoken word and the felt emotion and can be minimized to some extent by varying question types and themes to provide response validation.

In terms of data quality, both face-to-face and online interviews provided very rich, descriptive data. While online interviews did so in fewer words, it was not clear that they necessarily brought about a greater level of disclosure from participants. There were very similar levels of disclosure and what appeared to be honesty and openness in sharing private and sometimes sensitive information; that some were done using fewer words did not necessarily render them less valuable. I argue therefore that while verbosity is usually desirable, criteria for successful data collection is more complex and is not about the quantity of words. Instead, the pertinence and significance of the words used, and consequently, the degree to which they illuminate the inquiry, is a more useful indication of successful data collection.

Reflecting upon the data produced in these interviews, it was also evident that in comparison to synchronous methods, email communication led to greater wordiness. This is probably because the respondent could choose *when* as well as *whether* to respond, allowing more time for contemplation and reflection. Likewise, whereas in instant messaging or in face-to-face situations both participants and researchers have to think 'on the spot', with email the researcher has the advantage of taking time to think about a response prior to posing the next question to a participant. However, as I became more experienced at online interviewing I found that the pace of synchronous interviews could be controlled and that messaging need only be as 'instant' as the communicators choose. For example, slowing down the pace of my questions led to a corresponding slowing down of the respondent's pace. This resulted in an increase in the fullness of their answers. Therefore although the first few online interviews were fairly short, later interviews typically took around the same time as face-to-face ones and sometimes considerably longer. In this way, as Kivits (2005) argues, for both the interviewer and the interviewee, online methods can be a reflective process, not only in practical terms but also due to the time for reflection before expressing questions and/or answers (Kivits 20050: 49). Although the idea of using computers as an interface will not appeal to everyone, for those who were practiced at communicating in this fashion – as many of my participants were – this was a comfortable and convenient form of communication as well as a productive and ethical one.

Unexpected Consequences: Accessing Sex Work Organizers

Non-visual forms of communication are particularly valuable when discussing details of a personal and sensitive nature, especially when this is also in the context of a deviant or illicit activity. I would argue that it makes sense to offer CMC methods when participants are being asked about behaviours that are criminalized. This has been used to good effect in other contexts. For example, Coomber's (1997) research with drug dealers used CMC methods to reach and communicate with participants who were 'notoriously difficult to reach', due to their criminality. Coomber recruited his respondents through advertising on newsgroups and he sent emails to potential participants. Given the difficulties of accessing drug dealing populations, Coomber's success in managing to glean some interesting indicative information on this sensitive subject was only made possible by his use of CMC.

Given the illegality that surrounds third party organizers involved in the sex industries, the use of CMC may be of particular value. Despite the attention that has been paid to the individual workers and their clients, at present, the management of prostitution remains an understudied area of sex work research. This is probably due, in part, to problems of access, given its criminalized status. It may also be that stereotypical images of what or who constitutes either a 'pimp' or a 'madam' deem such individuals to be unworthy of academic discussion within what is presumed to be an inherently exploitative industry, those who make profit from individual sex workers are considered to be the 'lowest of the low'. Excluding these actors reduces our knowledge of the social organization of the sex industries. As Sanders (2008: 55) argues, such assumptions of inherent exploitation 'detracts from the reality that the majority of the indoor markets are not exploitative but are in fact practising good management'.

Due to the advantages of online research, while sex work organizers were not a deliberate part of my research sampling strategy, I was able to include the views of six individuals who managed or owned brothels or escort agencies as they replied to the survey. The data this produced was very enlightening and cohered with many of the views about industry organizers that were provided by sex worker participants themselves. Third parties varied in their approach to management and there is much to be learnt from analysing their working practices and their interaction with sex workers. Without these individuals being caught in the net, these insights would not have been possible.

Conclusions

The Internet offers sex work researchers the opportunity to identify, access, and communicate sensitively with a wider range of sex workers and sex industry organizers than has been possible using conventional research methods. Overcoming the usual quantitative/qualitative divide, sex workers can now be effectively surveyed using well-designed questionnaires to collect large datasets of both a qualitative and quantitative nature. Although using Internet technology would inevitably still exclude some sex workers, this is likely whatever strategy and method is used. Furthermore, despite feminist preference for face-to-face interview techniques, I have argued that face-to-face settings are not necessarily always the most sensitive, or most productive, way to communicate with people, especially when the subject matter is of a personal or controversial nature. The data produced through online interviewing can be rich and enlightening, and can offer a unique insight into thoughts and experiences that can be difficult for some people to articulate in person. While using computers to administer surveys or conduct interviews may not appear to fit as neatly with traditional feminist research practice, they need not be any less in line with feminist requirements for facilitating the voices of women; rather, in some instances they might offer the perfect setting in which to draw out hitherto unheard voices. Therefore, CMC methods can, if used appropriately, provide a sensitive contribution to an overall research strategy.

In addition, sex work researchers should attempt to communicate with sex work organizers and other third parties with whom sex workers have working relationships. Internet technology may be of particular use in this context. Both quantitative and qualitative data on the management and organization of sex work could be generated and used to challenge assumptions about the sex industry. Regardless of whether researchers strive to engage with sex workers, their clients, or sex industry organizers, many participants will inevitably continue to express a preference for direct face-to-face contact with their interviewers, and this method of communication will probably continue to be among the most valuable ways to gain an understanding about the complex nature of commercial sex. However, whilst the use of online interview methods will not always be appropriate, my contention is not that they should replace face-to-face interviews but that they should be offered as an alternative means of interview communication, and moreover that they should not necessarily be rated as inadequate or inferior. What is evident is that the sex industry does not remain static and just as one cannot hope to fully understand changes in any other industry without including the motivations, agendas and aims of those who manage and facilitate the business, nor can we hope to understand sex work without the inclusion of the many men and women who make their living organizing or facilitating sex work for others. To do this, new technologies are simply another tool, albeit a particularly useful one, to include in the social researcher's repertoire. If sex work research is to remain current, and therefore relevant, it must use the full range of methodological resources available and moreover, it must support an inclusive approach to those who work in this ever-changing industry.

References

Archer, J.L. (1980). 'Self-disclosure', in D. Wegner and R. Vallacher (eds) *The Self in Social Psychology*. London: Oxford University Press, 183–204.

Bargh, J.A., McKenna, K. and Fitzsimons, G. (2002). 'Can you see the real me? activation and expression of the "true self" on the Internet', *Journal of Social Issues*, 58(1): 33–48.

Bimbi, D.S. and Parsons, J.T. (2005). 'Barebacking among Internet-based Male Sex Workers', *Journal of Gay & Lesbian Psychotherapy*, 9(3/4).

Brooks-Gordon, B. (2006). *The Price of Sex*. Devon: Willan.

Bryman, A. (2001). *Social Research Methods*, 2nd Edition. Oxford: Oxford University Press.

Bryman, A. (2004). *Social Research Methods*, 2nd Edition. Oxford: Oxford University Press.

Comley, P. (1996). *The use of the Internet as a data collection method*. Paper at *Research Methodologies for 'The New Marketing'* Symposium, ESOMAR/ EMAC Publication Services, 204, 335–46. Available at: http://virtualsurveys. com/papers/email.htm [accessed 2 November 2009].

Coomber, R. (1997). 'Dangerous drug adulteration: an international survey of drug dealers using the Internet and the World Wide Web (WWW)', *International Journal of Drug Policy*, 8(2): 18–28.

Davis, M., Bolding, G. Hart, G., Sherr, L. and Elford, J. (2004). 'Reflecting on the experience of interviewing online: perspectives from the Internet and HIV study in London', *AIDS CARE*, 16(8): 944–52.

Davis, S., Bimbi, D.S. and Parsons, J.T. (2000). 'Barebacking among Internet-based male sex workers', *Journal of Gay and Lesbian Psychotherapy*, 9(3/4): 85–105.

Day, S. (2007). *On the Game: Women and Sex Work*. London: Pluto Press.

De Vaus, D. (2002). *Surveys in Social Research*, 5th Edition. London, Routledge.

Di Marco, A. and Di Marco, H. (2003). 'Investigating cybersociety: a consideration of the ethical and practical issues surrounding online research in chat rooms', in Y. Jewkes (ed.) *Dot.cons: Crime, Deviance and Identity on the Internet*. Devon: Willan, 148–64.

Gies, L. (2008). 'How material are cyberbodies? Broadband Internet and embodied subjectivity', *Crime, Media, Culture*, 4(3): 311–30.

Gunn, H. (2002). 'Web-based surveys: changing the survey process', *First Monday*, 7(12). Available online at http://firstmonday.org/issues/issue7_12/ gunn/ [accessed 2 November 2009].

Hesse-Biber, S.N. (2007). 'Putting it together: Feminist research praxis', in S.N. Hesse-Biber and P.L. Leavy (eds) *Feminist Research Practice*. Thousand Oaks, CA: Sage, 329–52.

Hewson, C., Yule, P., Laurent, D. and Vogel, C. (2003). *Internet Research Methods: A Practical Guide for the Social and Behavioural Sciences*. London: Sage.

Hughes, D. (1999). 'New technologies and the sex industry: pimps and predators on the Internet globalizing sexual exploitation of women and children', available at: http://www.uri.edu/artsci/wms/hughes/ppsi.htm [accessed 2 November 2009].

Illingworth, N. (2001). 'The Internet matters: exploring the use of the Internet as a research tool', *Sociological Review Online*, 6(2). Available at: http://www. socresonline.org.uk/6/2/illingworth.html [accessed 2 November 2009].

Joinson, A. (2001). 'Self-disclosure in computer-mediated communication: the role of self-awareness and visual anonymity', *European Journal of Social Psychology*, 31(2): 177–92.

Joinson, A. (2005). 'Internet behaviour and the design of virtual methods', in C. Hine (ed.) *Virtual Methods: Issues in Social Research on the Internet*. Oxford: Berg Publishers, 21–34.

Kivits, J. (2005). 'Online interviewing and the research relationship', in C. Hine (ed.) *Virtual Methods: Issues in Social Research on the Internet*. Oxford: Berg Publishers, 35–49.

Marlowe, J. (1997). 'It's different for boys', in J. Nagle (ed.) *Whores and Other Feminists*. London: Routledge, 141–4.

McGlothlin, J. (2003). 'The infusion of Internet-based Surveys and Postal Surveys: Guidelines for counselors', *Journal of Technology in Counseling*, 3(1).

McKenna, K.Y.A., Green, A.S. and Gleason, M.E.J. (2002). 'Relationship formation on the Internet: what's the big attraction?', *Journal of Social Issues*, 58(1): 9–31.

Mehta, R. and Sivadas, E. (1995). 'Comparing response rates and response content in mail versus electronic mail surveys', *Journal of the Market Research Society*, 37(4): 429–39.

Minichiello, V., Harvey, P.G. and Marino, R. (2008). 'The sexual intentions of male sex workers: an international study of escorts who advertise on the web', in G. Letherby, K. Williams, P. Birch and M. Cain (eds) *Sex as Crime*. Devon: Willan, 156–71.

Oakley, A. (1981). 'Interviewing women: A contradiction in terms', in Roberts, H. (ed.) *Doing Feminist Research*. London: Routledge and Kegan Paul.

O'Neill, M. (2001). *Prostitution and Feminism: Towards a Politics of Feeling*. Cambridge: Polity Press.

Phoenix, J. (1999). *Making Sense of Prostitution*. Basingstoke: Palgrave Publishers Ltd.

Sanders, T. (2005). *Sex Work: A Risky Business*. Devon: Willan.

Sanders, T. (2006). 'Behind the personal ads: the indoor sex markets in Britain', in R. Campbell and M. O'Neill (eds) *Sex Work Now*. Devon: Willan, 92–115.

Sanders, T. (2008). *Paying for Pleasure: Men who Buy Sex*. Devon: Willan.

Sanders, T. and Campbell, R. (2008). 'What's criminal about female indoor sex work?', in G. Letherby, K. Williams, P. Birch and M. Cain (eds) *Sex as Crime*. Devon: Willan, 47–62.

Scambler, G. (2007). 'Sex work stigma: opportunist migrants in London', *Sociology*, 4(6): 1079–96.

Schaefer, D.R. and Dillman, D.A. (1998). 'Development of a standard E-Mail Methodology: results of an experiment', *Public Opinion Quarterly*, 62, 378–97.

Schonlau, M., Fricker, R.D. and Elliott, M.N. (2002). *Conducting Research Surveys via E-mail and the Web*. Santa Monica, CA: Rand.

Selwyn, N. and Robson, K. (1998). 'Using email as a research tool', *Social Research Update* (21) (published quarterly by the Department of Sociology, University of Surrey, Guildford GU2 7XH, England). Available at: http://sru.soc.surrey.ac.uk/SRU21.html [accessed 2 November 2009].

Sharp, K. and Earle, S. (2003). 'Cyberpunters and cyberwhores: prostitution on the Internet', in Y. Jewkes (ed.) *Dot. cons: Crime, Deviance and Identity on the Internet*. Devon: Willan, 36–52.

Sharpe, K. (1998). *Red Light, Blue Light: Prostitutes, Punters and the Police.* Aldershot: Ashgate Publishing.

Sprague, J. (2005). *Feminist Methodologies for Critical Researchers: Bridging Differences*. Walnut Creek, CA: Altamira.

Weeks, J. (1991). *Against Nature: Essays on History, Sexuality and Identity.* London: Rivers Oram Press.

PART III
Mobility, Sex Work and Consumption

Chapter 7

Situating the Female Gaze: Understanding (Sex) Tourism Practices in Thailand

Erin Sanders

The gendered dynamics of tourism processes, traditionally overlooked in tourism studies, have more recently started to be included as a category of analysis by social theorists (Butler 1994, Aitchison 2001). While tourism has often been seen as a masculine endeavour, there has been some analysis done on the way that women use social spaces as part of their tourist experience (Elsrud 2001). The sex industry in Thailand has often been understood as a masculine space, constructed to satisfy the whims and desires of western male tourists. Most authors, both academic and journalistic, that deal with sex tourism in Thailand point to the hordes of male tourists who visit the country every year in search of sexual (and sometimes romantic) relationships with Thai sex workers (Enloe 1989, Truong 1990, Manderson 1992, Seabrook 1997, Bishop and Robinson 1998). However, there has been relatively little discussion about western women's interactions with these sexualized spaces, despite the fact that numbers of western women tourists have (on average) been increasing over the past few decades (TAT 2007). Indeed, western women have often been overlooked in their tourist capacity in Thailand and often rendered invisible in academic analyses. This chapter will challenge the assumption that sexualized spaces and venues in Thailand are reserved or marked out solely for male tourists.

Drawing upon empirical data collected in Thailand over several months during 2007 and 2008, this ethnographic study explored women's interactions with various sexual markets in Thailand. Observational, survey, and interview data suggest that women tourists access a variety of sexualized spaces as part of their holiday 'experience', and see the sex industry as a 'normal' part of Thai culture. Women's interactions with these spaces, opens up debates about the nature of 'sex tourism' and the role of race and gender in tourism structures and practices. This chapter will highlight the overlap between tourist and sex tourist markets through the lens of women's tourism 'experiences' of sexualized venues.

Gendered Sex Tourists

This section begins by asking who exactly is the imagined 'sex tourist'? Sanchez Taylor (2001: 749) argues that 'the stereotypical image of the "sex tourist" is that of the Western man who travels to Thailand or the Philippines in order to pay for sex with Go Go bar/brothel prostitutes'. This stereotypical man, the male sex tourist, is seen in much of the literature on sex tourism practices. Academic and journalistic accounts of sex tourism (particularly in Thailand) tend to focus on the western men who travel to sun-drenched foreign locales to engage in sexual relations with Other women. While there has been some debate in academic literature about issues such as intentionality and the nature of the sexual relationship involved in male sex tourism (Opperman 1999, Ryan and Kinder 1996), generally sex tourism is seen as an extension of prostitution, in which men are configured as 'users' of prostitutes.

There was been some acknowledgement that western women also engage in sexual relationships with foreign men as part of their holiday experience. However, discussions around women who engage in similar sexual activities have been much more contentious and hotly debated within the social sciences. This controversy is due to a number of factors: firstly there is a gendered/feminist argument about the extent to which women are victims or agents and if they are capable of exploitation (Barry 1996, Jeffreys 1997, Nagle 1997, Segal and MacIntosh 1992). Secondly, because sex tourism is often defined in a narrow way – as directly related to prostitute-use – this has made it much more difficult to talk about female sex tourism related to the sex industry, because women are not generally associated with using prostitutes, nor are they connected to commercial sexual exchanges more generally.

In contrast to male sex tourists who are often understood to be exploiting local women, the actions of female sex tourists have sometimes presented in a more benevolent but also a more contradictory way. They are sometimes seen as rather innocent as 'romance tourists' (Pruitt and LaFont 1995), or even cast as hapless dupes being exploited by local men (Jeffreys 2003). Sanchez Taylor (2001, 2006) suggests that female 'romance tourists' are understood as women 'who buy meals and gifts for her local sexual partner [and are] enjoying a "romance", not using a prostitute'. Tourist women are often seen as 'passive innocents, "used" by local men who are actively seeking money, a ticket off the island and maybe love, as well as sexual experience' (2001: 750). Sanchez Taylor persuasively argues sex tourism is not simply about 'male patriarchal privilege and female powerlessness' (2001: 749). Indeed, she suggests that:

> female tourists' sexual-economic relationships with local men are predicated upon the same global economic and social inequalities that underpin the phenomenon of male sex tourism. The fact that parallels between male and female sex tourism are overlooked reflects and reproduces weaknesses in existing theoretical and commonsense understandings of gendered power, sexual exploitation, prostitution, and sex tourism (2006: 43).

This analysis of sex tourism takes gender relations into account, but also provides a critical reflection about other types of power including those based on race and

Situating the Female Gaze

class, that are often obscured by focusing so exclusively on gendered power. Indeed, these categories of power are sometimes absent from discussions around sex tourism. A more nuanced picture begins to emerge around the set of issues that underlies women's sexual engagement with local men if we begin to understand women tourists 'as being motivated by racist sexual stereotypes and using sex tourism to bolster their privileged race and class status' (Jeffreys 2003: 25). By employing this understanding it is possible to analyse female sex tourism without focusing *exclusively* on gender injustices, and instead other crucial structural inequalities, such as race and class, can also be included.

Women's role and position within the sex tourism is a contested area. Indeed there is a broader question about what exactly constitutes sex tourist behavior, and what defines 'sex tourism'. The common assumption about sex tourism is that western men travel to foreign countries to engage in sexual relations with, usually younger, poorer, deprived, local women. However, definitions of sex tourism as associated with prostitute use, and understandings of sex tourists as men looking to exploit Other women are too simplistic to account for the nuances and complex realities of sexual tourism. Indeed, defining sex tourism as the consummation of 'commercial sexual relations' oversimplifies the phenomenon and excludes a wide range of other examples in which tourism and commercial sex may converge (Opperman 1999: 252).

Rather than starting from the position that sex tourism can be simply categorized as western men travelling for sex, therefore, it might therefore be more useful to look at the power relations that govern interactions between tourists and foreign Others. Moreover, it is useful to develop an analysis that does not rely so exclusively on essentialist assumptions about the nature of women's and men's sexual relationships. We might more usefully define sex tourism as 'a broad term to describe the activities of individuals who, whether or not they set out with this intention, use their economic power to attain powers of sexual command over local women, men and/or children while travelling for leisure purposes' (O'Connell Davidson 1998: 75). This type of definition would allow for a much wider scope for defining sex tourism and sex-tourist activities. It can refer to a wider range of people (both male and female), geographical locations, and sexual practices, geographical locations (O'Connell Davidson 1998: 75). This definition acknowledges the power difference between 'first world' tourists and 'third world' sex workers, without subscribing to an essentialist gender ideology.

Discourses on sex tourism, both male and female, often focus on the physical nature of the sexual interactions between a 'couple', that is a sex tourist and a local sex worker. However, the role of visual interactions within sexual spaces/places have also begun to be acknowledged (Opperman 1999, Hall and Martin 2001, Johnston 2001, Wonders and Michalowski 2001, Johnston 2002). The importance of the tourist process itself has also been highlighted: 'sex tourism masks the complex processes by which individuals choose to seek sexual gratification, first within prostitution, and *secondly as part of the tourist experience*' (Kruhse MountBurton in Opperman 1999: 252). The role of the visual in tourism and sex tourism is key in shaping touristic engagements with both sexual spaces and places and with eroticized/exoticized Others. Indeed, many red light districts around the world constitute major attractions for tourists who do not pay for sexual services, but rather visit those places for voyeuristic purposes (Opperman 1999: 252).

Some authors have begun to explore the role of western women in sexualized tourist destinations. Opperman (1999: 254) notes that western women engage in voyeuristic behaviors in a Thai context, suggesting they visit go-go bars 'in a voyeuristic role observing male sex tourist behavior'. Manderson (1995: 314) also highlights the particular problem of tourist voyeurism in the Thai sex industry, noting that 'whether or not the commoditization shifts from voyeurism to active sex, sex remains the commodity, and the bar a commercial venue for the sale of sex'. This emphasis on *voyeurism* as part of sex tourism and the tourist experience more generally is important as it moves away from a narrow classification of sex tourism as related to prostitute use and allows for a broader discussion about sex tourism as the commodification of Other/exotic/erotic people and bodies. Importantly, the boundaries between 'normal' tourism and 'sexual' tourism become more blurred as visual and touristic processes are considered (Bishop and Robinson 1998).

The sex tourist market in Thailand is uniquely positioned, due to the history and social contexts that have helped develop Thailand as a tourist destination, which have also worked to develop it as a *sex* tourist destination (Truong 1999, Bishop and Robinson 1998, Boonchalaski and Guest 1998). Thailand's red light areas host a wide range of sexual entertainments which include male, female, and transsexual sex workers, employed at a wide variety of venues, shows, bars, nightclubs, cabarets, massage parlours and so on. While some of these sexual spaces and places are set up to employ sex workers and sell direct sexual services to clients who want to engage in sexual relations. However, many of them offer more than simply cash-for-sex exchanges and are not built not upon selling sex, but rather on enticing in customers to buy drinks (Wilson 2004). While prostitution is certainly at the centre of much of the tourist-oriented sex market, the Thai sex industry is remarkably varied in the types of entertainment that is on offer to a wide variety of men, women, and even children.[1] Common forms of sexual entertainment include go-go bars where scantily-clad male and female sex workers often dance on stage while tourists are invited to watch their movement, perhaps inviting them for a drink or taking them off the premises. Transsexual cabaret shows feature male-to-female transsexuals, wearing sequined gowns and elaborate costumes, lip-synching to western songs for a seated audience. Cabaret singers sometimes sell sex to customers, although this seems to happen more frequently at smaller cabarets than the large-scale venues. In ping-pong shows female sex workers perform a variety of 'tricks' on stage, usually pulling strange

---

1   Children of western tourists were often seen in highly sexualized areas, including sexualized pedestrian streets and transsexual Cabaret shows. Even guidebooks like the Lonely Planet (2007) suggest that these shows are suitable as family entertainment.

or unwieldy objects out of their vaginas. Many ping pong show workers also sell sex to audience members.

These shows and venues are designed specifically to draw the tourist gaze. Writing about a notorious sexual area in Bangkok, Wilson (2004: 79) notes that the architectural and spatial orientation is configured to elicit the customers gaze, stating that 'this infrastructure of seating and lighting maximizes the customers view of an array of women and directs the gaze away from customers as a whole... Bars sell spectacle and fantasy, affection and flattery, and access to an array of available young women'. Importantly, she also points out that the sale of drinks is the primary source of income for many sexualized venues, but adds that this profit relies on the spectacle of women in order to attract custom.

Manderson's (1992) work highlights the sexual/voyeuristic motivations in tourists' desires to see ping pong shows in Thailand, situating these shows as an integral part of the broader sex industry. Manderson herself visited a ping pong shows to observe the interactions of male customers with Thai female sex workers and suggests that the Thai female dancers are objects of lust for these voyeuristic male clients. She notes that 'Thai women perform for and act out the presumed fantasies of foreign men' (1992: 454) and further claims that these are designed by and for men. Manderson acknowledges that women tourists are also present at the show (as is she herself) but still insists that the shows are designed exclusively for male tourists. While this claim is still possible, the fact that women are visiting ping pong shows, and that their presence there is acknowledged, but not analysed, calls for further reflection the role of women in (sexual) tourism settings. This chapter will try to unravel some of the reasons why western women might be accessing the sexualized spaces of go-go bars, red light areas, and ping pong shows in Thailand. By expanding the definition of sex tourism out from direct sexual contact to visual consumption, it might be possible to examine some of the issues related to the role of western women in (sexual) tourism, and specifically to understand the importance of gender, but also race and class in these dynamics.

The Female Gaze?

Wolff (1985) has argued that the male gaze means that women in public spaces are objects of (men's) attention which they cannot escape. As such, women are generally thought to be unable to look at or watch others, nor can they actively gaze. While psychoanalytic and cultural theory debates have focused on the gendered nature of sexuality and perversion and the possibility of a female gaze (Kaplan 1991, Welldon 1992), these arguments have tended to ignore race and nationhood. Yet in Patpong, Thai women certainly are the objects of a white/western gaze enacted by both men and women. It is difficult to suggest that they are simply under the scrutiny of the male gaze, as women also visit these areas to 'take a peek' or to 'have a look' at the Thai Other. White western women's racial, social and national power gives them the ability to walk around these areas without being objects of fascination or desire themselves and this relative power allows them to take a position of control.

While psychiatric understandings of voyeurism and scopophilia have largely positioned men as active watchers and women as objects of the gaze (Stoller 1986, Kaplan 1991, Pajaczkowska 2000), the tourist literature acknowledges that travellers (both male and female) are watchers as well. Chi (1997) suggests that tourism is the scopophilia of modern consciousness, with the 'eye' or 'seeing' taking precedence over other forms of touristic understanding and this gaze is both socially organized and systematized (Urry 2002). Indeed, part of being a modern day tourist means that one often gazes upon a variety of scenes, people, and places that are 'out of the ordinary' (Urry 2002). The gaze focuses on local features that are marked off as unusual, or different to 'everyday' encounters and revolve around the collection of signs and symbols: 'the tourist is interested in everything as a sign of itself... All over the world the unsung armies of semioticians, the tourists, are fanning out in search of the signs of Frenchness, typical Italian behavior, exemplary Oriental scenes, typical American thruways, traditional English pubs' (Culler cited in Urry 2002: 3). Tourists search for the authentic or the real as part of their travels and they consume these authentic scenes through the tourist gaze (MacCannell 1976).

While tourists are on their quest for signs of authenticity, what they choose to look at is marked for them by a variety of sources, including film, television, music, and in particular, guidebooks (Jacobs 2001). Tourist guides and professionals impact on the direction of the gaze and particular objects that are highlighted by the tourist industry as suitable for tourists to gaze upon (Urry 2002). Changing values associated with class, gender, and distinction of taste can have an impact on what is marked out (by the tourist industry) as culturally relevant and which objects are fit for visual consumption. What counts as a suitable object of the (tourist) gaze can be almost anything, but their essential feature is that whatever this object is, it must be different to the 'normal' objects from home; it must be out of the ordinary. Sanchez Taylor (2000) argues that consuming difference is a critical component of the tourist experience, and that exotic Others are positioned as markers of cultural authenticity.

For many women in Thailand, the sex industry was a 'must see' – something that all tourists (regardless of gender) should see during their visit. For Gemma,[2] who had not been to a ping pong show but was considering whether to visit one, she wanted to go to watch the watchers, but she also implicitly suggested that the sex industry is part of how some tourists see Thailand, and that this something (other) tourists do when they visit:

> For me it would be just to have seen it. What I always do is to watch other people watching things like that too because you get an open view of another view on the whole country and why people are going there.

---

2   The names of all participants have been changed to protect their identity.

Situating the Female Gaze

Seeing red light areas or going to a bar or a show was considered a must-see for many women, something that all tourists (regardless of gender) should do whilst in Thailand. In an interview with two women in Pattaya, this positioning became clear:

> **Eliza:** It's like, everybody have to see the shows…
> **Interviewer:** I haven't been to a show yet.
> **Diane:** You haven't?! But you have to! You have to go before you leave Thailand!

When I told Eliza and Diane that I hadn't been to a show in Thailand, they were astounded. Partly it seemed because I was researching the sex industry and 'shows' to them summed up what the sex industry was about, but also because they saw this as a quintessential experience to have whilst in Thailand. Eliza had been to Thailand several times over the past few years and admitted that the sex industry was something she 'saw' on every visit. In fact, she admitted that she frequently took other colleagues to see the shows in Bangkok.

> For Loreta, the sex industry was also something she felt she needed to see as part of her trip to Thailand, and something she acknowledged was not necessarily 'pleasant' to watch, but something that *should be seen* nonetheless.
>
> I mean people were saying it's like nothing you've ever seen before, it will blow your mind, you know, not necessarily in a good way, but it's something that you kind of need to do – it needs to be seen to be believed sort of thing and to be honest with the other local attractions in Bangkok, the temples and such, they were nice, but no one ever said 'it blew my mind, I've never seen anything like it'. So it was a bit of a tourist attraction situation.

It is clear, then, that sex industry functions as a tourist attraction, alongside the famous temples and Thai architecture sits the infamous ping pong show, something that all tourists, regardless of gender, should go and see. In fact, seeing a ping pong show seemed to surpass other Thai tourist sites. Ancient temples pale in comparison to the thrill of a ping pong show, which will 'blow your mind'. One tourist in Phuket, when asked what made her decide to see a sexualized show, replied:

> **Alison:** Um, I think it's just one of those touristy things that you do – you go to the elephant show – which I'd go see the elephant show again but I wouldn't see the lip-syncing cabaret again, but then again I do love the stage costumes and all that goes along with it.

Seeing the sex industry is thus seen as simply part of the normal Thailand tourist experience, just as going to see an elephant perform tricks in a tourist show might

116 New Sociologies of Sex Work

be. In this sense, the sex industry comes to be the marker of authentic Thai culture. Going to see a ping pong show was understood by most participants as something essentially 'Thai'. While the women I spoke to all talked about different reasons for wanting to go to engage with the sex industry, the sex industry as a cultural experience, as an authentic Thai experience, was a defining feature of their narratives.

It is important to remember that it is not simply the sex industry as a structure that they are going to look at; they are also going to look at Thai sex workers and other subjects. They are going to look at actual people working at go-go bars, the western men there to buy sex, the lady boys lining the streets and the bodies of Thai women. As such, while the vast majority of female participants did not buy sex or engage in explicit sexual activity with Thai men or women, many did go to *watch* Thai women working in the sex industry. It is this visual consumption that is a key part of the process for them: looking, watching and seeing were all verbs that women used when they talked about their interactions with the sex industry. A French tourist in Pattaya says simply, When asked why she liked to visit Walking Street, on French tourist in Parraya simply said 'I really like to have a look'.

For this woman, one of the reasons she goes to Walking Street is to *look*. The pleasure that is afforded in the act of looking is the key action that many women highlight. I interviewed Amanda on the beach in Pattaya, she told me she likes to go to Walking Street so she can 'sit and people watch'. I asked her if she had ever been to any of the 'shows' on offer. Amanda replied that while she doesn't often go into the clubs or the girl bars now but she used to go with her ex-partner: She said, 'we never participated, if you know what I mean… we just came to watch'. For Amanda, looking does not extend to participating, instead these are separate activities with different meanings attached to them.

Looking, however, is not passive, nor is it innocuous. Many psychoanalytic theorists note the sadism and violence associated with the gaze (Socarides 1974, Stoller 1986, Moore and Fine 2000). Within tourism studies, Urry (2002) notes that power is also wrapped up in the act of looking. He suggests that the act of looking is a fundamental part of the tourist experience which places tourists in a relatively powerful position over the 'exotic' Others that they gaze upon. As Maoz (2006: 222) puts it, 'the gaze, which has the potential to discipline and normalize the locals' behaviour, is said to lie within the power of the Western, well to do, heterosexual, capitalist, white male'. Within tourist studies, there is recognition that there is power attached to the act of looking, and as Maoz suggests, this power is dedicated not only to white tourists, but white *male* tourists. There is a power relationship inherent in tourist relations with economically, socially, and politically underprivileged Others that tourists look at as part of consuming an authentic tourist experience. In Thailand female tourists are accessing sexual spaces and engaging with these spaces in a visual way: women come not only to *look*; they specifically come to look at the Thai Other.

Pruitt and Lafont (1995) suggest that for women engaging in sexual relationships with local men, these female 'romance tourists' are freed from the normal constraints of their western, gendered existence, whilst local men can benefit by creating new ways of engaging in intimate relationships. It is certainly possible to argue that western female tourists in Thailand are likewise freed from certain gendered constraints, Jenks (1995: 150) writes about the condition of the male gaze as having been 'formative of the cultural products and traditions of modernity. While excluding the feminine it has systematically disempowered the feminine, and one symbolic representation of this is a gendered imbalance of ocular practice. Women do not look, they are looked at'. In Thailand western women are in a sense freed from the traditional constrictions that they would normally be governed. They are no longer the objects of the gaze, rather Thai women become the object in this particular space. Yet there is little reciprocity going on here. Western women go to these places to look at Thai women, few had conversations or meaningful interactions with sex workers, Thai women were simply cast as objects of the tourist gaze.

Women Watching, Women Watchers

While research on sex tourism in Thailand has largely focused on the prostitution-related aspects of the sex industry, exploring the ways that tourists engage with sexual shows highlights the multiple ways that power functions in tourist (and sex tourist) relations in Thailand. In this context, it is clear that both male and female become gazers. Going to see a ping pong show for many women was a way of satisfying a curiosity about the sex industry and 'having a look' was a critical part of their discourse. The politics of watching and gazing in sexualized settings positions sex workers as objects of the female tourist gaze and western women as active (visual) consumers of the sex industry. The discursive lines that are drawn between western women tourists and female sex workers are based on these visual interactions. Western women are watching Other bodies, and the visibility of Thai women contrasted with the invisibility of western women in the same sexualized space requires an investigation into the way that bodies socially read. Casper and Moore (2009: 1) argue that bodies are made visible in the modern world. They argue that we are trained to 'visually process and meticulously read bodies – our own and others – for social cues about love, beauty, status, and identity (2009: 1). In this regard, the way sex workers bodies are read by western women creates a boundary between 'normal' white, western bodies and 'deviant' sexual, grotesque Other bodies. As such, this visual commodification of sex workers bodies reinforces binary dualisms of self/other, tourist/guest, normal/deviant; western women read and interpret Thai women working in the sex industry as touristic objects, markers of authenticity, and exotic/erotic Others. Female tourists' voyeuristic engagement triggers a process that renders Thai women as objects, as abject, and as exotic/ erotic Others.

It is useful here to remember that part of the aim of tourism is not just to sexually arouse or excite (Enloe 1989, Cohen 2001). However, rendering exoticized local people *as Other* is essential to tourism. Casting tropical spaces as idyllic and using racist tropes to describe the local people (as either sexual, happy, subservient, indolent, or all of the above) naturalizes difference. In this sense, the bodies of local women in Thailand are exoticized, eroticized, racialized, and importantly, commodified. Local people (and women in particular) can then be cast as Other, and certain destinations such as Thailand and the local people there are understood in a way that is 'consistent with an ideology that postulates as natural the opposition between a primitive dark-skinned "other" and a civilized white-skinned "self"' (Cohen 2001: 62).

Bhattacharyya (2002) makes a persuasive argument about power and this element of the 'exotic'. Drawing on a definition that suggests that 'exotic' links to the foreign, the bizarre, the strange – she examines the ways in which 'new cultures of exoticism can illuminate... power struggles' and ties this specifically into ideas around racialized difference. This focus on race is important as she considers the way that the gaze is an essential aspect of exercizing power over the racialized, sexualized Other. Indeed, racialized/sexualized Others are placed in a vulnerable position by the materially, racially, politically and socially privileged. The Other becomes the object of the (tourist) gaze and this gaze, this powerful, exoticizing gaze, is made possible by the power of the viewers/watchers/tourists. In order to maintain this gaze, the object of the gaze must be suitable. They must be sufficiently different and exotic in order to be visually consumed. Western tourists do not go to Thailand to look at western sex workers – they come to look at the exoticized, sexualized, racialized Thai women – who are not only markers of Thailand, but also function as a sign or symbol of dangerousness/Otherness. As 'the exotic relies upon an explicit and comprehensible power disparity' (Bhattacharyya 2002: 106), in this instance Thai women become understood as 'lesser', not only by western men, but by western women as well.

Conclusion

The visual consumption of exotic/erotic Others as part of one's holiday 'experience' has implications for the way we might understand sex tourism more generally. If we refer to O'Connell Davidson's broad definition of sex tourism, then our understanding of visual sex tourism behaviour could well be considered as part of a continuum of sex tourism. There are of course differing levels of exploitation, and a distinction should be made between tourists who engage in overt sexual relationships with multiple local women, to those tourists who randomly wander through a red light area during their visit. However, recognizing that women are contributing to the maintenance of the sex industry in Thailand by going to watch/look and by constructing this experience as exciting/normal/must-see propagates the sex industry, and works to objectify and commodify Thai sex workers further.

Recognizing that women can, in some senses, 'do' sex tourism too is important, and that this visual consumption of the sex industry is part of what funds and motivates the sex industry suggests that simply looking at gendered categories of analysis does not go far enough in evaluating the true nature of situation in Thailand. A more detailed analysis of race and class in western women's motivations to see and engage with sex shows and sexualized spaces would allow for movement beyond the dyad of men as sexual/aggressive and women as asexual/passive, towards a more nuanced analysis of which power relations underlie commercial sexual encounters. There is a need for further research in the areas of female and visual/voyeuristic sex tourism and the impacts these reinterpretations may have on (re)defining and furthering understandings around 'sex tourist' behaviours.

References

Aitchison, C. (2001). 'Theorizing Other discourses of tourism, gender and culture: Can the subaltern speak (in tourism)?', *Tourist Studies*, 1(2): 133–47.

Barry, K. (1996). *The Prostitution of Sexuality*. New York: New York University Press.

Bhattacharyya, G. (2002). *Sexuality and Society: An Introduction*. London: Routledge.

Bishop, R. and Robinson, L.S. (1998). *Night Market: Sexual Cultures and the Thai Economic Miracle*. London: Routledge.

Butler, K. (1994). 'Independence for Western Women through Tourism', *Annals of Tourism Research*, 21, 487–9.

Casper, M. and Moore, L. (2009). *Missing Bodies: The Politics of Visibility*. London: New York University Press.

Chi, R. (1997). 'Toward a New Tourism: Albert Wendt and Becoming Attractions', *Cultural Critique*, 37, 61–105.

Cohen, C. (2001). 'Island is a woman: women as producers and products in British Virgin Island tourism', in Y. Apostolopoulos, S. Sonmez and D. Timothy (eds) *Women as Producers and Consumers of Tourism in Developing Regions*. London: Praeger.

Elsrud, T. (2001). 'Risk creation in traveling: Backpacker adventure narration', *Annals of Tourism Research*, 28(3): 597–617.

Enloe, C. (1989). *Bananas, Beaches and Bases*. London: University of California Press.

hooks, b. (1992). *Black Looks: Race and Representation*. Cambridge, MA: South End Press.

hooks, b. (2003). 'The Oppositional Gaze: Black female spectators', in A. Jones (ed.) *The Feminism and Visual Culture Reader*. London: Routledge.

Jacobs, C. (2001). 'Folk for Whom? Tourist Guidebooks, Local Color, and the Spiritual Churches of New Orleans', *The Journal of American Folklore*, 114(453): 309–30.

Jeffreys, S. (1997). *The Idea of Prostitution*. Melbourne: Spinifex Press.

Jeffreys, S. (2003). 'Sex Tourism: do women do it too?', *Leisure Studies*, 22, 223–38.

Jenks, C. (1995). 'Watching Your Step: The history and practice of the *flaneur*', in C. Jenks (ed.) *Visual Culture*. London: Routledge.

Johnston, L. (2001). '(Other) Bodies and Tourism Studies', *Annals of Tourism Research*, 28(1): 180–201.

Johnston, L. (2002). 'Borderline Bodies', in L. Bondi et al. (eds) *Subjectivities, Knowledges, and Feminist Geographies: The Subjects and Ethics of Social Research*. New York: Rowman and Littlefield.

Kaplan, L. (1991). *Female Perversions*. London: Penguin.

MacCannell, D. (1976). *The Tourist: A New Theory of the Leisure Class*. London: MacMillan.

Manderson, L. (1992). 'Public Sex Performances in Patpong and Explorations of the Edges of Imagination', *The Journal of Sex Research*, 29(4): 451–75.

Manderson, L. (1995). 'The Pursuit of Pleasure and the Sale of Sex', in P. Abramson and S. Pinkerton (eds) *Sexual Nature, Sexual Culture*. Chicago: University of Chicago Press.

Maoz, D. (2005). 'The Mutual Gaze', in *Annals of Tourism Research*, 33(1): 221–39.

Moore, B. and Fine, B. (eds) (1990). *Psychoanalytic Terms and Concepts*. London: The American Psychoanalytic Association and Yale University Press.

Nagle, J. (1997). *Whores and Other Feminists*. London: Routledge.

O'Connell Davidson, J. (1998). *Prostitution, Power and Freedom*. Ann Arbor: University of Michigan Press.

Opperman, M. (1999). 'Sex Tourism', *Annals of Tourism Research*, 26(2): 251–66.

Pajaczkowska, C. (2000). *Ideas in Psychoanalysis: Perversion*. Cambridge: Icon Books.

Pruitt and LaFont. (1995). 'For love and money – Romance Tourism in Jamaica', *Annals of Tourism Research*, 22(2): 422–40.

Ryan, C. and Martin, A. (2001). 'Tourists and strippers: Liminal theater', *Annals of Tourism Research*, 28(1): 140–63.

Ryan, R. and Kinder, R. (1996). 'Sex, tourism, and sex tourism: fulfilling similar needs?', *Tourism Management*, 17(7): 507–18.

Sanchez Taylor, J. (2001). 'Dollars are a girl's best friend? Female tourists' sexual behavior in the Caribbean', *Sociology*, 35(3): 749–64.

Sanchez Taylor, J. (2001). 'Tourism and "embodied" commodities: sex tourism in the Caribbean', in S. Clift and S. Page (eds) *Tourism and Sex: Culture, Commerce and Coercion*. London: Pinter.

Sanchez Taylor, J. (2006). 'Female sex tourism: a contradiction in terms?', *Feminist Review*, 83, 42–59.

Schellhorn, M. and Perkins, H. (2004). 'The Stuff of which Dreams are Made: Representations of the South Sea in German-language Tourist Brochures', *Current Issues in Tourism*, 7(2): 95–133.

Seabrook, J. (1997). *Travels in the Skin Trade*. London: Pluto Press.

Segal, L. and McIntosh, M. (eds) (1993). *Sex Exposed: Sexuality and the Pornography Debate*. Piscataway: Rutgers University Press.

Socarides, C. (1974). 'The Demonified Mother: A Study of Voyeurism and Sexual Sadism', *International Review of Psychoanalysis*, 1, 187–95.

Stoller, R. (1986). *Perversion: The Erotic Form of Hatred*, 2nd Edition. London: Karnac.

Tourist Authority of Thailand (TAT). http://www2.tat.or.th/stat/web/static_tts.php [accessed January 2008].

Truong, T. (1990). *Sex, Money and Morality: Prostitution and Tourism in Southeast Asia*. London: Zed Books.

Urry, J. (2002). *The Tourist Gaze*, 2nd Edition. London: Sage.

Welldon, E. (1992). *Mother, Madonna, Whore: The Idealization and Denegration of Motherhood*. London: Karnac.

Wilson, A. (2004). *The Intimate Economies of Bangkok: Tomboys, Tycoons, and Avon Ladies in the Global City*. London: University of California Press.

Wolff, J. (1985). 'The Invisible Flaneuse: Women and the Literature of Modernity', *Theory, Culture & Society*, 2(3): 37–46.

Wonders, N. and Michalowski, R. (2001). 'Bodies, borders, and sex tourism in a globalized world: a tale of two cities – Amsterdam and Cuba', *Social Problems*, 48(4): 545–71.

Chapter 8

The Place of the Gringo Gulch: Space, Gender, and Nation in Sex Tourism

Megan Rivers-Moore

Introduction

Despite being located only a few dozen blocks from one another, the various neighbourhoods where sex is sold in San José, Costa Rica are represented as entirely distinct. The area now known as Gringo Gulch was previously associated with the city's elite, a bourgeois neighbourhood where efforts were made to keep working class people, and especially sex workers, out (Marín Hernández 2007). Throughout the 1990s and 2000s, however, the area has become increasingly associated with sex tourism. Residents lament that the last desirable place to live in the centre of San José is being turned into a centre of prostitution like other neighbourhoods in the capital (Fonseca 2008).

In this chapter, I explore the ways in which selling sex is constituted in city space, arguing that discursive and material practices produce different types of sex work in different spaces. To do so, I explore how Gringo Gulch has been made into a space that is defined as foreign, in contrast to the historical red light district. In particular, I consider the deployment of gendered national identity in constituting the spaces of sex work in the city of San José. In doing so, I argue that transnational sex tourism is not about the transcendence of national boundaries, but rather that it continues to depend on long-held notions of national identity and national power. These are both highly gendered and experienced differently by different subjects.

I begin with a discussion of the different contexts, in which sex is sold in San José, and then go on to consider the role of the state in constituting Gringo Gulch as a foreign, and therefore non-national, space. Next, I discuss the experiences of sex tourists in Gringo Gulch in order to demonstrate the crucial role that their national identities play in their experiences in Costa Rica. Finally, I assess how sex workers' understandings of national identity also contribute to the production of differential spaces within San José's sex industry.

Selling Sex in San José

There are three main sectors in which sex work takes place in San José. Street and brothel based sex work are concentrated in the city's red light district. The area has a high concentration of commercial land use and very few residences, as well as numerous abandoned lots. Many of the businesses are tiny hotels used as temporary or permanent lodging for those working in the area, including sex workers. Street level sex work is dominated by older women, often in their forties, fifties, and sixties, or by younger, but drug addicted women. Street sex work is poorly paid, irregular, and women face harassment from municipal police and business owners. Younger women in the district tend to be found in brothels, where sex work is better paid and more regular, though health and safety conditions are often dubious at best. Clients in the red light district are primarily working class Costa Rican men and some Central American migrants. In contrast to the concentration of street and brothel work, sex work in massage parlours is less centralized, and businesses can be found in various parts of the city. Women are treated like employees with regular hours and sometimes even uniforms and some include bars, where women can make extra money by getting a cut when clients buy them drinks. Although massage parlours similarly attract working class Costa Ricans, a significant number of these clients are also drawn from the middle classes.

In contrast, sex tourism is concentrated in the central and north-eastern neighbourhoods of the capital. The area is known as 'Gringo Gulch', primarily by gringos themselves and workers at the bars and hotels that cater to sex tourists. Interestingly, most other Costa Ricans do not refer to the neighbourhood this way. While there are neo-colonial overtones of using a foreign designation, I use it here to indicate the extent of tourism's influence and impact on this part of the city. Although it is only a short walk away from the red light district, Gringo Gulch is worlds apart in terms of its landscape and the daily functioning of the sex industry. While San José is not a city known for its architecture, many remaining historical buildings are found in Gringo Gulch, including several houses once occupied by elite families that have been refurbished as small hotels. The architecture, several sizeable parks and patrols by the newly formed tourism police officers on bicycles that protect tourists and control crime levels make Gringo Gulch one of the prettier and more pleasant areas of San José, in marked contrast to the abandoned lots and rundown infrastructure of the red light district. The overwhelming presence of male tourists that gives Gringo Gulch its name is immediately obvious when walking around the area.

The most iconic sex tourism business in Gringo Gulch is The Prince, a hotel with over one hundred rooms, a casino, several bars, and a restaurant (all open 24 hours). The sex industry in Gringo Gulch takes place largely in hotels and bars not ostensibly set up for this purpose. The Prince Hotel's iconic status makes what goes on inside particularly hard to miss, but many of the other locales where contacts are made between sex tourists and sex workers resemble any other businesses catering to tourists the world over. The owners and managers of hotels and bars in Gringo Gulch were anxious to clarify that they were not running brothels, did not employ sex workers, and had no control over the exchanges of sex and money that took place in their establishments. Indeed, the bars and hotels of Gringo Gulch are extremely careful to ensure that their activities are strictly legal. Tourists and sex workers negotiate directly with no intermediary. The going rate is around US$100, though tourists do their best to bargain for a lower price while sex workers try to maximize their earnings as much as possible. Nonetheless, that is not to say that the businesses do not profit from the sex industry, as their popularity depends on their reputation as places where sex tourists and sex workers can connect. In addition, virtually all of the hotels in Gringo Gulch charge what sex tourists refer to as a 'chica fee', requiring guests to pay an extra charge to bring a woman up to their room.

Gringo Gulch as Foreign

Crossing borders to work and consume in the sex industry is not new, and scholars have explored migration for sex work in diverse settings and moments (Guy 1991, Hicks 1994, Kempadoo 1998, Levine 1994; Bishop and Robinson 1998, Littlewood 2001, Pratt 1992). In this chapter I draw attention to the presence of foreigners, not to suggest that this is an entirely new phenomenon in the sex industry in Costa Rica, but to argue that what has changed is how the sex trade is structured in relation to foreignness. Historical studies show that ten per cent of prostitutes registered in San José between 1869 and 1949 were non-nationals (Marín Hernández 2007). However, there is no evidence that this was cause for concern for the authorities and in fact, English, Italian, French and US prostitutes were particularly sought after by San José's elite (Marín Hernández 2006, see also Guy 1991, McCreery 1986). In contrast, contemporary discourses about the sex tourism industry are very much focused on foreignness and particularly on the presence of migrant sex workers. These foreign sex workers are, according to these discourses, primarily from Colombia, the Dominican Republic, and Nicaragua and importantly, they are concentrated in one very specific Costa Rican place, Gringo Gulch. State practices associated with these discourses include immigration control and expulsion. Whereas historically, foreign sex workers were sought after by locals, now they are to be expelled, both physically from the state and metaphorically from the nation.

The discursive construction of sex workers as foreign was a common theme. Comments which claimed that 'piles of women are coming', and 'most of the muchachas...no, not most, ALL the muchachas are foreigners' were frequently voiced by state and private sector employees, as well as in the national media and in casual conversations. The sex tourism industry was associated with the arrival of migrant sex workers: 'I think that just immigration...has necessarily increased prostitution. If there wasn't so much offer [there wouldn't be so much demand].

There are many people who are willing to accompany a gringo on his vacation' (former director of Costa Rica's department for HIV/AIDS). Sex tourism was associated with specific nationalities, particularly Dominican, Colombian, and Nicaraguan women. These women's bodies were discursively located in The Prince Hotel, the heart of Gringo Gulch. A former senior employee of the Costa Rican Tourism Institute explained that 'many people come here for [sex]. The proof is in The Prince Hotel that is always full of tourists and there are always at least one hundred muchachas there offering themselves. Seventy-five, eighty per cent of the women are foreigners'.

The booming sex tourism trade and the foreign women who are said to staff it are blamed for tarnishing Costa Rica's image. The receptionist at one of Gringo Gulch's biggest hotels estimated that 'eighty per cent [of sex workers] are from the Dominican Republic and Colombia'. She added that it was 'such a shame that Costa Rica has a reputation as a sex tourism destination, when mostly it's foreigners who are involved'. The head of security at the same hotel added that 'this is a peaceful place, muy tranquilo. But then all these foreign women started to come here. All the foreign prostitutes came'. Opinion articles in the country's most important daily newspaper also represent Gringo Gulch as a 'sexual United Nations' and a 'globalized sexual bazaar' (Rodríguez 2006), thus contributing to producing an image of the neighbourhood as a space defined by the presence of foreign women.

It is impossible to quantify the extent of the sex tourism industry in general, and it is even more implausible that the numbers of foreign sex workers could actually be counted. Costa Rican law does not register sex workers, who therefore work independently and informally in Gringo Gulch. Moreover, there is no immigration category for migrant sex workers. Instead, women enter the country as tourists and overstay their visas, have domestic worker permits, or pay lawyers to marry them to unknown Costa Rican men in order to secure residency status. However, my aim here is not to make a definitive conclusion about the numbers of migrants, but rather to describe the discursive representations of the sex tourism trade as dominated by foreigners as one element in the changing spatial organization of San José's sex industry. The notion that the sex industry is made up of foreign women does a certain kind of ideological work in Costa Rica, allowing the state to profit from the sex industry while making sure to maintain the industry's distance from the nation. These discourses about who belongs and who does not are not simply textual, but are also deeply political and made material in significant ways.

Constructions of the spaces of San José's sex tourism industry as 'foreign' serve to constitute, and are constituted by, state practices that literally seek to evict foreign sex workers from the country and reinforce the spatial reorganization of Gringo Gulch as outside the nation. Raids by immigration police are carried out frequently in Gringo Gulch and are highly publicized in national newspapers and on television. According to police officers at the General Directorate for Immigration, raids have been taking place twice per month for several years and one of The Prince's owners confirmed that the hotel is the target of immigration

The Place of the Gringo Gulch   127

raids around twenty times per year. Sex workers discussed the raids constantly, afraid of having their pictures in the newspaper or on television.

During a raid, immigration police arrive suddenly at The Prince, seal the exits, and proceed to check the immigration status of everyone inside the public areas of the hotel, including the bars and casinos. In theory, all foreigners without proper documents are arrested, placed on buses and driven to an immigration detention centre where their cases are investigated, resulting either in deportation or release. The chief of the immigration police was adamant that the raids are about controlling organized crime rather than harassing sex workers. Yet the image that dominates in news coverage is of dozens of women, usually covering their heads with coats and sweaters, being placed on buses by police officers. One officer even stated that 'the raids are to catch foreign prostitutes who are here illegally. We only focus on the women, no one else is even asked to show identification'.

The raids represent state anxieties about immigration and are an example of the ways in which 'governments often stage high-profile spectacles to make themselves visible ... The "weakness" of everyday stateness is often countered by attempts to make state power highly visible. In this endeavor, issues of security, crime, and punishment occupy a privileged arena for performance of sovereign power' (Hansen and Stepputat 2005: 29). The spectacle of raids in Gringo Gulch suggests that issues of sexuality and morality are also central to the performance of state control. Though dozens of women are detained during each raid and filmed and photographed by the media as they are loaded onto buses, immigration data does not include information on where detainees were caught, making it impossible to determine how many deported women are actually from Gringo Gulch. Many sex workers interviewed had heard stories of women that had been detained by police officers who demanded money and/or sex in exchange for their release. Media coverage of the raids also emphasizes the foreignness of the women found in Gringo Gulch, reporting for example that 'seventy-eight Colombian, Dominican, and even Costa Rican women were surprised by immigration and municipal officials' (Serrano 2007; emphasis added). Though immigration police said they also carry out raids in nightclubs in other areas of the city, the media coverage is virtually exclusively focused on Gringo Gulch.

Whether or not significant numbers of sex workers are actually deported, state practices, and the media coverage of those practices, effectively represent Gringo Gulch as a foreign space where most sex workers are non-nationals. This is an example of how 'geographies of sex work' are produced through the spatially selective enforcement of national legislation (Hubbard et al. 2008). By focusing immigration control practices on Gringo Gulch, the neighbourhood is produced as a space where certain national laws are enacted in particular ways, which fall disproportionately on the backs of sex workers. Non-reproductive sexuality, including prostitution, has long been positioned as outside discourses of national identity, citizenship and belonging (Mosse 1985, Parker et al. 1992). Thus sex workers are represented as 'foreign' and excluded from the nation, yet still subject to the state's power. As states are centrally implicated in gender relations and ideas about nations and national identity, the policing of particular kinds of sex is not just about appropriate sexuality but about what kinds of sexuality imperil the nation and what kinds promote citizenship. This is what Nagel (2003) calls 'the moral economy of nationalism', which is

> gendered, sexualized, and racialized. National moral economies provide specific places for women and men in the nation, identify desirable and undesirable members by creating gender, sexual, and ethnic boundaries and hierarchies within nations, establish criteria for judging good and bad performances of nationalist masculinity and femininity, and define threats to national moral and sexual integrity. (Nagel 2003: 146)

State discourses about sex workers as foreign and the state's immigration raids help to define Gringo Gulch as a place beyond the nation, as this protects the nation's morality while the Costa Rican state still benefits from the money being spent by sex tourists. State discourses and migration controls therefore play a central role in determining precisely which foreign bodies are welcome and which are intolerable.

Untouchable Gringos

By marking Gringo Gulch as foreign, dangerous, and immoral, the rest of the city (and the nation) can remain, in contrast, defined by morality, safety, family values, and national belonging. What is important to note, however, is that the foreign bodies that occupy Gringo Gulch are not just those of sex workers, but also of sex tourists. Yet television and newspaper coverage of immigration raids at The Prince Hotel never picture tourists. Though several tourists interviewed admitted to being undocumented (having overstayed their tourist entrance visas), none seemed particularly concerned and indeed many sex workers explained that immigration police do not even ask to see tourists' passports during raids. After requesting anonymity, an immigration police officer confirmed that tourists are not required to produce documents because 'if we detain a gringo, their embassy is on the phone immediately and they are a huge pain.'

The immigration raids are thus aimed specifically at sex workers and it is the bodies of these women, not those of sex tourists that are used to mark the space of Gringo Gulch as foreign. It seems that only some kinds of foreign bodies are intolerable in Costa Rica, not all. Both gender and nation therefore play a critically important role in defining who belongs and who is excluded. The state's definition of gringos as untouchable also points to the 'portability of national identity' (Sassen 1998) and demonstrates the importance of geopolitics in the context of sex tourism. Not all passports provide the same kind of mobility or represent the same level of threat. Fears about foreign bodies are never about gringos, but always about women whose passports carry less significance in Costa Rica and whose embassies do not protest (or whose protests go unheard).

The problem of describing sex tourism encounters as 'an interaction between two sets of liminal people' is made explicit through this differential power of passports (Ryan and Hall 2001: 4). As Kempadoo (2004) has argued in the Caribbean, liminality is at best a questionable concept in spaces where tourists are dominant and given preferential treatment. Theorizing sex tourism as liminal assumes that sex tourists and sex workers move around the world in the same way, erasing the materialities of their encounters as well as the effects of geopolitics on who can move where, for how long, and at what cost. Transnational sex tourism is not about the disappearance of national boundaries, but rather continues to depend on gendered and national power relations that are experienced differently by subjects. Gringo Gulch may be produced as a foreign space, but it is a space that remains defined by, and very much in tension with, both the nation and the geopolitics of international relations.

The Costa Rican state's treatment of sex tourists demonstrates just how important gender and nation remain in the context of increased transnational tourism, given the sway of US passports and key role of tourism in Costa Rica's economy. How the state deals with foreign bodies is highly differentiated, and spaces that have become defined as outside the nation are still the targets of state intervention. However, signalling the power of US passports in Costa Rican sex tourism is not to suggest that sex tourists are elite cosmopolitans. While geopolitics plays an important role in how gringos are made to belong in Gringo Gulch, it is still crucial to ask how they themselves engage with being foreign in Costa Rica.

Sex tourists experienced themselves as untouchable in Costa Rica in various ways: none had ever had a problem with the police, and only a tiny minority had been robbed in the streets. Furthermore, few had even bothered to seek out information about the legalities of sex work in the country. Equally none expressed concern about whether or not what they do in Costa Rica is illegal. When specifically asked what they knew about the law, most responded that they had no idea. A few offered imprecise and often incorrect information, including 'I think it's 16' (the legal age to participate in prostitution), 'prostitution is not legal but tolerated', 'it's legal', 'they make the girls carry those cards', and finally 'I don't believe it's illegal, uh, I think it's somewhat regulated. I believe the girls carry a card. I don't know what that card represents, whether it's just ID or a physical check or something like that, I'm not sure'. When asked where they got their information from, most responded vaguely that they had heard it 'somewhere'. This lack of information and concern demonstrates that tourists are able to be in Costa Rica without having to worry about immigration controls or the legality of their actions or presence. Indeed, for sex tourists, both nation and gender combine to make them untouchable.

Latin America has historically been represented as the 'porno tropics' (McClintock 1995), a space of exotic difference sought after by sex tourists. The process of 'Othering' in sex tourism has been discussed in relation to the differences between 'exotic' sex workers and their white clients, because 'commerce depends

130   *New Sociologies of Sex Work*

on the construction of a desirable other – often one that titillates as well as appeals – capable of attracting outsiders' (Bishop and Robinson 1998: 61). Sex tourists' engagements with racialized notions of exotic, sexual 'Others' has been amply documented in the Caribbean and South East Asia (Brennan 2004, Sánchez Taylor 2000, Bishop and Robinson 1998). In Gringo Gulch, sex tourists' descriptions of sex workers emphasized how the women they encountered had particular sexualized features. Illustrative comments from men included, 'Down here, sexuality is different', 'you can just do whatever you want, they love sex, and 'Costa Rican women, they all wear really tight clothes, they know their sexuality, they enjoy sex. There's some truth to the hot Latina blood'. As the latter quote makes clear, these are not merely comments about sexuality, but crucially about a particular racialized sexuality. Sex tourists draw on culturally commonplace ideas about hypersexuality and exoticism that racialize their encounters with sex workers through their association between a different 'Latin' race and a specific sexuality. Racialized 'Otherness' remains central to sex workers' desirability in ways that assume an applicability to all Latin American women, rather than specific national groups. Such a generalized attraction to a racialized 'Latin Americanness' contrasts significantly with state, media, and hotel concerns to emphasize the specific national groups of migrant sex workers.

Sex Workers, National Identity and Space

The spatial constitution and contexts of the sex industry in different parts of San José are discursively and materially produced as separate. Yet sex workers in Gringo Gulch also worked hard to maintain this distinction. The Gringo Gulch area is a 'nice' part of town, unlike the red light district, and sex workers sought to define the red light district as far removed from their experiences in the tourism trade. Sex workers frequently emphasized how comfortable the beds were in the hotels in Gringo Gulch, how nice it was to have air conditioning, how classy most of their clients were. Many of the women interviewed claimed to have no knowledge of the red light district, but would then go on to describe it in great detail. The physical condition of the women who work in the red light district was often brought up; they were referred to as flabby, vulgar and aggressive, in all ways unlike the glamorous women of Gringo Gulch. For Vanessa, 'the level is different. The majority of women who work there are different, they have a different category of education, the places they live, they come from more marginal areas. Something marks them, there's a difference. They don't mind going with another type of man, a man who isn't so clean.' Mariana was even more specific:

> For me, it's terrible, it must be a daily hell. They work in bars that Costa Ricans go to. They'll go with anyone who shows up…Imagine what it's like to be with eight, ten men a day. I think that they live real prostitution. They touch bottom. We all do the same thing, but there is a difference in that they relate to another

The Place of the Gringo Gulch 131

type of person...other social classes, other Costa Ricans. I think there's a big difference.

Sex workers in Gringo Gulch considered prostitution in the red light district as 'real' prostitution, in contrast to what they do. They described in minute detail, and often with visceral horror, the damaged bodies, filthy working conditions, and disgusting clients that they imagined women were forced to contend with, just a few blocks away. Sex workers in the red light district might be described with pity, but just as often they were constructed as vile drug addicts, willing to exchange sex for a pittance. Most important for women in the tourism industry, however, is the fact that their clients are foreign tourists. While the bodies that preoccupy the state are those of foreign sex workers, for women in Gringo Gulch, the bodies they were trying to avoid belonged to Costa Rican men. Beyond explanations about a woman's age, glamour, education, or neighbourhood, having sex with gringos rather than Costa Ricans was the crucial boundary marker for sex tourism workers.

While most women said they have had few or no Costa Rican clients, all agreed that the most important difference between them and the women of the red light district was the nationality of their clients. The reason that this mattered was put the same way again and again: 'el tico es cochino para pagar' (literally the Costa Rican man is a pig when it comes to paying). The preference for gringo clients was thus generally explained in terms of income, as sex with Costa Rican clients meant less money. The ability to charge one hundred dollars to gringos rather than the ten dollars or less charged to Costa Ricans in the red light district was a point of pride and distinction amongst women in Gringo Gulch. Johana explained that

> if there is a Costa Rican and a gringo, you always choose the gringo because he has more money. It's very hard to find a Costa Rican who can pay $100. But [if you find one] then a Costa Rican lasts an hour or maybe more, because he wants to get his money's worth. A gringo takes fifteen or twenty minutes. We prefer the gringo because he's easy money. With a Costa Rican, it's a pisada larga (long fuck).

There are, however, disadvantages to working with gringos. Virginia summed up the main complaint succinctly: 'Costa Ricans are pigs when it comes to paying, they don't pay well. Gringos pay well but are pigs, they smell bad.' The bad smell of gringos was a frequent complaint amongst sex workers, something to be put up with for the sake of earning more money. Cindy went to some length to explain:

> With all due respect, I've never liked gringos. First, they smell bad. They're stupid. They don't know how to dance. I don't like them...My friends say 'what a handsome gringo'. But, my God, I don't see it, I can't see the attraction at all.

132   *New Sociologies of Sex Work*

Beyond the smell, which she described as 'repugnant', Ana added that 'they look at you as if you're obligated to do what they want, whatever they say. They look at you like you're below them, like you're on a lower level'. These complaints about gringos, however, were balanced by the insistence from a few women that they prefer gringo clients for reasons beyond money. Anika explained that

> Americans [sic] are…the majority are very nice people. They have another culture, they have more money, they are more considerate, less machista, you know? There are Canadians, Americans [sic], Chicanos, Mexicans, Europeans, though not many. And there is a marked difference between these men…and it's nice, of course. You have to have the capacity to understand, you know? To deal with different kinds of people.

For Anika and a minority of other women interviewed, part of the attraction of foreign clients goes beyond the question of remuneration and includes a sense of pride in knowing how to successfully interact with men from different countries, a kind of transnational cultural capital that eludes the women of the red light district. Accepting Costa Rican clients, besides implying less money, also means a less exciting, cosmopolitan work place. While most women in the sex tourism industry learn at least a few basic phrases in English, there may also be something to be said for allowing things to get lost in translation. The few Costa Rica clients Johana has had asked her about her family and background, information that she prefers to keep to herself. The choice of gringos over Costa Ricans may also be strategic. Maintaining a transnational clientele, while potentially exciting and challenging, facilitated the division that sex workers make between their work and the rest of their lives. Frequenting the bars and hotels of Gringo Gulch where Costa Ricans rarely venture reduced the risk of running into a family member or neighbour, crucial for women who are hiding their work from their families and communities.

Besides the spatial othering that sex workers in Gringo Gulch performed in order to distinguish themselves from the red light district and the Costa Rican bodies found there, women also described the transnationality of their working lives in terms of their co-workers. In all of the sites where sex tourists and sex workers made contact, the latter always far outnumbered the former, meaning that the most regular, day-to-day encounters were often between the women themselves. Sex work in the tourism industry involved a great deal of sitting around and waiting, time that women filled by talking to one another. While the embodied encounters that sex workers sought out with tourists are most emblematic of sex tourism, women also participated in significant encounters with each other that often involved tensions around questions of national identity.

Some Costa Rican sex workers complained about the presence of foreign women in the sex trade, focusing unsurprisingly on Nicaraguans, Dominicans, and Colombians. Ana argued that 'their way of working is different…for example, they do a lot of things for more money. They do more things. Let's say, anal sex.

The Place of the Gringo Gulch   133

And oral sex without a condom. It's damaging to us [Costa Ricans] because then the clients start seeking them out instead of us'. Nicaraguan women were most often blamed for accepting less money for sex and agreeing to unsafe sex, and the common Costa Rican construction of Nicaraguans as poor, uneducated, troublemakers was frequently voiced (see for example Sandoval García 2004, 2007).

Costa Rican sex workers pointed to Colombian women as being particularly sought after by tourists, complaining that they took away business and had an unfair advantage since so many had had plastic surgery. Colombian women were also frequently referred to as 'mafiosas' and were said to steal from clients, thus falling back on a common if recent stereotype in Costa Rica that links Colombians with organized crime (Cordero 2008). Mariana distinguished between Nicaraguan women, who migrate to Costa Rica in search of dignified work but end up in the sex trade because they are so desperate to send money home to their impoverished families, and Colombian women, who migrate specifically to work in the sex trade and know what they are getting into. However, 'siempre tenemos esa rivalidad entre naciones' (we always have this rivalry between nations), Mariana concluded cheerfully.

By complaining about unsafe sexual practices and dishonourable conduct with clients, Costa Rican sex workers carved out a specific discursive space for themselves in the sex industry. They represented themselves as better educated and more articulate than their poor Nicaraguan co-workers, but more honest and down to earth than their surgically altered Colombian counterparts. However, migrant sex workers were also quick to complain about their treatment in Costa Rica, with Marita, originally from Nicaragua, noting that she had been told by some Costa Ricans to go back to where she comes from. Foreign sex workers were well aware of their association with the sex tourism industry, and many, like Manuela, emphasized 'they say that it's mostly Colombians, but that's not true. The majority are Costa Ricans.' Estela added that 'it's very criticized. But we're contributing a lot [to Costa Rica]. They criticize the foreigners…it's as if everyone comes from outside to do damage to Costa Rica…but nobody ever talks about the Costa Rican [sex workers]'. Colombian sex workers tended to construct Costa Rican sex workers, somewhat defensively, as ugly and ordinary. They were seen to have less education and bad manners because they come from marginal areas. Estela described Costa Ricans in general as 'campesinos' (peasants).

All of the sex workers' attempts to define themselves as different, both spatially and nationally, rested on very similar constructions of women 'Other' than themselves. Other women, whether in the red light district or from another country, were dirtier, less attractive, and less intelligent, allowing particular constructions of identification and difference that permitted women to constitute their own small niches within the sex tourism industry.

Gossip is common in the sex tourism businesses of Gringo Gulch and many sex workers had a great deal to say about their colleagues, usually negative. However, it is worth noting that actual open conflict among women was rare.

While sex workers may resort to national stereotypes when discussing one another, in practical terms women shared food, bus fare, and information without regard for nationality. Several of the sex tourists I interviewed had been present in The Prince Hotel during the immigration raids, and told me that the Costa Ricans left behind would gloat about their good fortune at having some of the competition forcibly removed. While a small minority of women agreed that this is the case (for example Virginia admitted to thinking 'what luck! More work for me!'), most described the raids as unjust, citing examples of hard working migrant friends who send all their money home to their children and condemning the bribes and sexual abuse at the hands of the police that women described when they returned to work. In practical terms, Johana insisted that the raids were bad for business in general: 'After the police leave, the gringos leave too, they go home to bed early, so there is no real benefit for anyone.' Despite frequent national 'Othering', most sex workers ultimately agreed with Andrea that 'we all do the same thing...we all work together so in the end we take care of each other. We support each other.'

Conclusion

The ways that the Costa Rican state has differentially regulated the spaces of commercial sex demonstrates the importance of considering the specificities of local and national policies and practices for understanding how and where sex tourism emerges and becomes institutionalized. Discourses and practices in relation to foreignness in Gringo Gulch demonstrate that not all foreigners are 'Others' in the same way. Although interviews and media reports suggest that very few sex workers as actually deported, the state's immigration raids are a spectacle aimed carefully away from gringo tourists and directed instead at foreign sex workers. These women are excluded not so much from the actual physical territory, then, but more from the possibility of participating as full members of the Costa Rican national community. Sex workers are symbolically excluded from the nation, though their contributions to the Costa Rican economy continue and the state continues to profit. This illustrates the ongoing importance of national identity even in a postcolonial, globalized context (Alexander 2005, Calavita and Suárez-Navaz 2003, Yuval-Davis 1997).

This chapter has demonstrated the central place of gender and nation in sex tourism, looking at how state and public discourses and practices have reorganized the spaces of sex work and defined Gringo Gulch as foreign, as well as how the spatiality of gender and national identity are experienced by sex tourists and sex workers. Spaces that are discursively represented and materially produced as foreign and non-national can remain outside the purview of the state's concern, except in terms of the considerable profits being made. By distinguishing between the spaces and bodies of the sex industry, gendered and national power are maintained and strengthened, serving an important function for the nation-state in preserving its putative morality, cleanliness and order.

References

Alexander, M.J. (2005). *Pedagogies of Crossing: Meditations on Feminism, Sexual Politics, Memory and the Sacred.* Durham: Duke University Press.

Bishop, R. and Robinson, L. (1998). *Night Market: Sexual Cultures and the Thai Economic Miracle.* London: Routledge.

Brennan, D. (2004). What's Love Got to do With it? *Transnational Desires and Sex Tourism in the Dominican Republic.* Durham: Duke University Press.

Calavita, K. and Suárez-Navaz, L. (2003). 'Spanish Immigration Law and the Construction of Difference: Citizens and "Illegals" on Europe's Southern Border', in R.W. Perry and B. Maurer (eds) *Globalization Under Construction: Governmentality, Law, and Identity.* Minneapolis: University of Minnesota Press, 99–127.

Cordero, S.M. (2008). 'Menores refugiados perciben xenofobia en nuestro país', *La Nación,* 20 June [online], available at: http://www.nacion.com/ln_ee/2008/junio/20/aldea1585668.html [accessed 20 June 2008].

Fonseca, Q.P. (2008). 'Mansiones de Otoya terminan como centros nocturnos', *La Nación,* 19 May [online], available at: http://www.nacion.com/ln_ee/2008/mayo/19/aldea1526506.html [accessed 20 June 2008].

Guy, D. (1991). *Sex and Danger in Buenos Aires: Prostitution, Family and Nation in Argentina.* Lincoln: University of Nebraska.

Hansen, T.B. and Stepputat, F. (2005). 'Introduction', in T.B. Hansen and F. Stepputat (eds) *Sovereign Bodies: Citizens, Migrants, and States in the Postcolonial World.* Princeton: Princeton University Press, 1–36.

Hicks, G. (1994). *Comfort Women.* New York: Norton.

Hubbard, P., Matthews, R. and Scoular, J. (2008). 'Regulating sex work in the EU: prostitute women and the new spaces of exclusion', *Gender, Place and Culture,* 15(2): 137–52.

Kempadoo, K. (1998). 'The Migrant Tightrope: Experiences from the Caribbean', in K. Kempadoo and J. Doezema (eds) *Global Sex Workers: Rights, Resistance and Redefinition.* New York: Routledge, 124–38.

Kempadoo, K. (2004). *Sexing the Caribbean: Gender, Race, and Sexual Labor.* New York: Routledge.

Levine, P. (1994). 'Venereal disease, prostitution, and the politics of Empire: the case of British India', *Journal of the History of Sexuality,* 4(4), 579–602.

Littlewood, I. (2001). *Sultry Climates: Travel & Sex.* Cambridge, MA: Da Capo.

Marín Hernández, J.J. (2006). *La Tierra del Pecado, entre la quimera y el anhelo: Historia de la Prostitución en Costa Rica, 1750–2005.* San José: Alma Mater y Nueva Cultura.

Marín Hernández, J.J. (2007). *Prostitución, Honor y Cambio Cultural en la Provincia de San José de Costa Rica: 1860–1949.* San José: Universidad de Costa Rica.

McClintock, A. (1995). *Imperial Leather: Race, Gender and Sexuality in the Colonial Contest.* London: Routledge.

McCreery, D. (1986). '"This Life of Misery and Shame": Female Prostitution in Guatemala City, 1880–1920', *Journal of Latin American Studies*, 18(2): 333–53.

Mosse, G.L. (1985). *Nationalism and Sexuality: Respectability and Abnormal Sexuality in Modern Europe*. New York: Howard Fertig.

Nagel, J. (2003). *Race, Ethnicity, and Sexuality: Intimate Intersections, Forbidden Frontiers*. Oxford: Oxford University Press.

Parker, A., Russo, M., Sommer, D. and Yaeger, P. (1992). 'Introduction', in A. Parker, M. Russo, D. Sommer and P.Yaeger (eds) *Nationalisms and Sexualities*. New York: Routledge, 1–18.

Pratt, M.L. (1992). *Imperial Eyes: Travel Writing and Transculturation*. London: Routledge.

Rodríguez, J. (2006). 'En Vela', *La Nación*, 5 April [online], available at: http://www.nacion.com/ln_ee/2006/abril/05/opinion4.html [accessed 19 October 2006].

Ryan, C. and Hall, C.M. (2001). *Sex Tourism: Marginal People and Liminalities*. London: Routledge.

Sánchez Taylor, J. (2000). 'Tourism and "embodied" commodities: sex tourism in the Caribbean', in S. Clift and S. Carter (eds) *Tourism and Sex: Culture, Commerce and Coercion*. London: Pinter, 41–53.

Sandoval García, C. (2004). *Threatening Others: Nicaraguans and the Formation of National Identities in Costa Rica*. Athens: Ohio University Press.

Sandoval García, C. (2007). *El Mito Roto: Inmigración y emigración en Costa Rica*. San José: Universidad de Costa Rica.

Sassen, S. (1998). 'The de facto transnationalizing of immigration policy', in C. Joppke (ed.) *Challenge to the Nation-State: Immigration in Western Europe and the United States*. Oxford: Oxford University Press, 49–85.

Serrano, F. (2007). 'Detienen a más de 78 mujeres por irregularides migratorios', *Telenoticias*, 14 April [online], available at: http://www.teletica.com/archivo/tn7/nac/2007/04/14/18453.htm [accessed 14 April 2007].

Yuval-Davis, N. (1997). *Gender and Nation*. London: Sage.

Chapter 9

Taxi Dancers: Tango Labour and Commercialized Intimacy in Buenos Aires

Maria Törnqvist and Kate Hardy

Introduction

The afternoon dance at the *Confiteria Ideal* has just started. Visitors are being seated at the tables closest to the dance-floor, while old tango songs from the 1940s and 1950s fill the air. This is one of the traditional tango venues in the middle of town, known for its lush velvet curtains and marble pillars that carry the roof and the weight of sentimentality that tango carries with it. Regular customers wait to be taken to 'their' table. Young local and Argentine dancers in their sixties and seventies arrive fully dressed in suits and long dresses. Amongst them are a small group of first time tourists from West-Coast America. Others just got into town and stare expectantly, with big eyes, at the peculiar details, exchanges and relations in the hall.

When the second *tanda* – a dance-set of three or four songs – starts to play a couple get up on the floor. They belong to a group of newly arrived tourists, sitting in the back of the room. She is dressed in a tight red dress, with a split that exposes more and more of her legs as they move around the hall. He is casual, wearing a pair of jeans and a t-shirt. An older Argentine couple swaps gazes across the room, inviting each others' company through the sublime *cabeceo*. She accepts his invitation, adjusts her shoe-buckle, stands up and approaches the dance floor. Their dancing style is intimate. A tight embrace and small intense movements express the intensity and sadness of the music. As they pass the tables at the back of the hall the newly arrived tourists are transfixed by the woman's grace: 'imagine having her legs and dignity at seventy!', a blonde woman whispers to a friend.

Hours later, the marble hall ambience has reached a crescendo. Most people in the room have been up dancing, including foreign beginner dancers with their newly bought first pair of dance shoes, trying out their purchases on the floor. The dancer in the red dress has ordered her third glass of wine and is talking a little too loudly. As the scene winds down, a man in his early fifties walks in the door. He greets the staff with a familiar kiss and proudly takes a seat next to the dance-floor. Jorge attracts attention with his typical *milonguero* style; a neat pony-tail, black trousers and a well ironed black shirt, supported up by a large amount of self esteem. He turns to one of the blonde women in the back and asks her 'up' with a mixture of a flirty eye-gaze and a few select English words. As she gets up on the

138 *New Sociologies of Sex Work*

floor, a little embarrassed, he gently puts his arms around her back and asks her to close her eyes. As the slow moving dance set ends he discretely offers her his card and explains to her that he is a *tango taxi dancer*.

Tango Tourism: An Intimate Industry

A growing body of research on gender and globalization has been dedicated to exploring sexual-economic exchanges. In the developing world this research has tended to focus on prostitution (Truong 1990, Bales 2003, Hardy this volume, Rivers-Moore this volume). However, recently there has been a shift to focusing more broadly on the complex nexus between cash/sex in contexts in the developing world (Meisch 1995, Pruitt and LaFont 1995, Ebron 1997, Kempadoo 1999, Brennan 2003, Sanchez Taylor 2006). Such studies have argued that transactions are often more diffuse and complicated than is traditionally acknowledged in literature that has concentrated on prostitution. O'Connell Davidson and Sanchez Taylor note, for example, the ways in which 'women, men, and children enter into fairly open-ended relationships with tourists in the hope of securing some material benefits' (2005: 20) arguing that these should be considered as much part of sex tourism as the phenomenon of brothel or street prostitution in tourist areas. This approach opens up the potential for considering new subjects, practices and life-trajectories. For example, it becomes clear that in these transactions, the consumer is not always a man, the currency is not always money and the acts are not always limited to heterosexual intercourse. As such, in troubling these traditional conceptualizations, it becomes possible to understand other actors, such as taxi dancers, as being engaged in sexual-economic exchange and therefore as performing sex work.

This chapter considers the nature of a particular sexual-economic exchange, between taxi dancers and their customers, in the context of the global tourist industry. It draws on ideas about romance tourism, sex work, intimate labour and body work to explore the phenomenon of taxi dancers. Taxi dancers sell tango dance experiences to tourists in Buenos Aires, Argentina, as part of a broader tango-tourism industry. They are for the most part, male and Argentinean, selling dances to female tourists, although there are also female workers in the market. By examining these encounters and exchanges, the chapter explores the grey-zones of global commercialized intimacy, spaces which have previously been hidden by the more explicit and stereotypical forms of sexual commerce. Importantly, it looks at an area in which gendered assumptions are reversed, as men rather than women become the workers in the interaction. To do so, the chapter draws on comprehensive ethnographic field-work inside the tango scene of Buenos Aires. It includes participant observations, interviews and informal conversations with both tourists and Argentineans engaged in the dance scene, as well as an analysis of popular representations and narratives of tango dancing (novels, discussions on virtual home pages for tango dancers and advertisements for classes and clubs).

In what follows, we offer some social, historical and political background on the context in which taxi dancers are working. This section locates taxi dancing in Argentina's economic and social history and offers information about taxi dancing itself. The substantive part of the chapter is split into two sections. The first explores the ways in which the labour of the taxi dancers can be understood, specifically looking at two different working conditions in which taxi dancing takes place: free-lancers and agency workers. The second examines which types of labour are being performed in taxi dancing and how these might be conceptualized. We conclude with some comments about the relationships between sex work and commercialization of intimacy in late capitalism.

Background: The Intimate Market of Taxi Dancing

The Argentine tango scene is a diverse economy of dance schools, tango clubs, shoe and clothes shops, tango profiled guest houses, bars and restaurants, as well as tourist companies offering special packages for tango dancers. Within this scene multiple actors and subjects play distinct roles across a variety of sites and spaces. City guides, clothing vendors and tango hostel owners sell their wares far beyond the walls of the *milonga*, instead using shops, the street and the internet to attract customers. Although this market also caters for Argentinean tango dancers, it is increasingly tailored towards international guests. Ninety per cent of the Buenos Aires tango scene income comes from abroad, primarily from European and North-American tourists. The extraordinary economic crisis in 2001 which eroded avenues for income generation for millions in Argentina (Fiszbein et al. 2002, Whitson 2007) means that tango has become one of a decreasing number of viable means of making a living. Depending on foreign revenue is a far safer and more remunerative strategy for guaranteeing income in a country whose currency and domestic possibilities for income generation have proven in the past to be decidedly unstable.

Taxi dancers are thus only one of many groups of actors seeking to make a living through tango tourism. The dancers offering their services as dance partners to tourists in exchange for money are generally argentine men from their thirties into their seventies. This demographic is changing however, as younger men and women are also entering the scene, seeing the work as part of a longer-term career in tango. Some hope to become performers or teachers and view the money and experience of working with tourists as useful skills to collect along the way. Others see the contact with foreign dancers as offering possible contacts for future dance teaching jobs in Europe and North-America.

Sometimes *taxistas* meet their clients, who are predominantly beginner foreign dancers, in the clubs where they dance for three or four hours. However, they may also offer tango classes and private practice settings, helping clients to learn steps and movements with a more advanced dancer. For foreigners on a short two- or three-week stay, taxi dancers can also act as invaluable companions, offering

140   *New Sociologies of Sex Work*

local knowledge about an often complex and closed cultural scene of tango. Taxi dancers can navigate their way through a city scattered with many – and at times difficult to find – *milongas*. Furthermore, the strict rules of conduct of the dance scene are difficult to understand. Most Argentinean tango clubs adhere to a tradition in which men ask women to dance through the *cabaceo*, a complicated play of eye-gazes. Rigid tango hierarchies make it difficult for beginner dancers to get asked to dance – or get dance invitations accepted – without access to the social network of local dancers. Taxi dancers thus provide an alternative for those who find it difficult to play 'the game', but still wish to throw themselves into the romance of the dance-floors.

Freelancers

Although there are many forms of taxi dancers, the predominant form of work is as an independent, informal worker. As such, as with other transactions in the informal economy (see for example Thomas 1995, Bigsten et al. 2004), it is difficult to estimate the volume and size of the population working as taxi dancers. However, each evening, approximately one or two taxi dancers can be found in each of the larger tango clubs in Buenos Aires. These spaces are used not only for accompanying clients, but also for promoting their business and finding new customers. Such informality, and the fact that many of the dancers danced for leisure, as well as for business, means it is not always easy to discern who is working and who is not. There are however, a number of features that make taxi dancers distinguishable. The identity of the dance partner is one such way in which dancers become identifiable. Leisure dancers would generally select someone of equal skill and if they were a male dancer, perhaps a younger and attractive dancer. As Nicolas, an Argentinean acquaintance, asked me rhetorically when he spotted a taxi dancer on a regular night out in the club *Salon Canning*: 'Do you really think a guy like that would go out with a woman who cannot dance and who is old enough to be his mother?'

Miguel, a man in his mid- to late forties, work informally as a taxi dancer in Buenos Aires. He charged eight dollars an hour for his company. He was outspoken and proudly identified as a 'free-lancing' taxi dancer. He talked warmly about the evenings at work, cheerfully describing his clients as *pasajeros* – passengers – who he showed a good time. From his perspective he was helping foreign women who did not get asked to dance or who needed a guide to local clubs, whilst at the same time as he was making a bit of money out of his passion for tango. He added that the women normally turned out to be pleasant company and moreover often bought him his entrance ticket (around three dollars), a drink in the bar and on occasion, paid for his taxi ride home. Although he was unable to make a living from tango escorting, unlike some of the Argentinean top dancers who toured Europe and North-America giving dance classes, it did not appear to bother him. He had a job as a vendor in a telephone store and earned a decent salary. The taxi dancing was mostly for fun, although it had also become an important source of income during the difficult times of the economic crises. Other freelancing taxi dancers talk of their job in similar terms. Indeed, many of them did not depend financially on the income and talked of it as a 'fun way' to combine their hobby and passion – tango – with the possibility of making some extra money.

Freelancers such as Miguel said that their work gave them a great deal of freedom, unlike other professions. In working for himself, he did not have a manager instructing him about what to do, with whom, or when. Rather, independent *taxistas* decided to whom they would provide services and thus the responsibility fell on them to search for new clients on their own accord. Some sought to attract clients at tourist venues known for hosting large international events such as *Confiteria Ideal* and *Niño Bien* and approached potential customers with business cards and verbal invitations. Others were more discrete, trying to make sure that a 'real' connection was established, meeting their clients in night-clubs before offering to share their dancing skills through private dance classes. As well as recruiting business in the clubs, Miguel ran his own webpage and advertised in the freely distributed tango papers, *El Tangauta* and *B.A. Tango* (with articles published in both Spanish and English and a large section of publicity from small scale tango enterprises), found in all clubs and dance schools. The independence of freelance dancing produced a particular ambivalence for dancers such as Miguel. Although they were not economically dependent on the work in the tango clubs and saw it as a joyful means of connecting with new people who were similarly passionate about tango, the uncertainty of independent work necessitated constant adaptation to the vagaries of the market and tourists' demands and desires.

Agency Taxi Dancers

Although it is more common for taxi dancers to work independently in the informal economy, more organized businesses have emerged in response to the increasing number of international guests interested in tango. These businesses are often small-scale and not only offered dance companions, but full tango travel packages; including accommodation in hostels and hotels, guided tours, dance lessons and guaranteed dancing in the clubs provided by taxi dancers. It was not only Argentines who have taken advantage of this boom in tango tourism. An East Coast North American couple, Monique and Steve, ran 'Hotel Tango' an all inclusive tango tourism business. Monique emphasized the easier access to tango clubs as important part of the tango, in particular the value of 'speeding things up', rather than attempting to figure everything out on your own. Connecting tourists with taxi dancers are amongst the services they offer. They state that the agency offers a 'quality mark', protecting tourists from 'tango tricksters', such as freelancing taxi dancers who do not possess decent dancing skills or who wooed the women through flattery and flirtation:

> **Steve:** The line is this "you dance quite nicely, I could really help you dance a lot better. Let me help you, I can improve you a lot. How long will you be here?"

"Two weeks". "I can really make a good dancer in two weeks". [And the tourists say] "Really? Really? Really?"

Part of the service Monique and Steve pertain to offer therefore not only guarantees access to the tango world, but also protection for tourists, who they saw as emotionally vulnerable. Another agency, *Taxi Tango*, was a fairly recent addition to the scene. However, the manager, Ezequiel, had considerable experience in the industry. With his clothing, trendy hair-style and polished English, he was quite the modern entrepreneur, eager to discover and explore new markets. Unlike Miguel's emphasis on pleasure and enjoyment, Ezequiel stated unequivocally that taxi dancing was strictly business. In fact, it was good business. Ezequiel had plans to expand, making the agency international and cleaning up what he saw as its 'poor reputation'. 'I have a 20-year perspective', he said. 'This is going to become an international business. We are going to send out employees to tango festivals in the US and Europe and make the tango accessible to even more people'. At the time of the field-work, *Taxi Tango* had approximately 25 employees. The majority fitted the usual demographic, but there were also a couple of female dancers. The working hours they received varied, depending on season and demand. Most of the taxi dancers worked no more than one or two nights a week. However, at approximately ten dollars per hour and with a minimum booking fee of three hours dancing, this offered a good remunerative form of employment. Yet most of them had other sources of income as well, such as work in bars and restaurants. Just as Miguel valued the freedom of freelance dancing, many of the female dancers were willing to sacrifice the independence for the safety that the agency offered. As such, many dancers' decisions to work independently or for an agency were based on the degrees of constraint and freedom they sought, held in tension with ensuring safety and stability. Loss of freedom over choice of clients, behaviour and work-hours was balanced for agency workers by the extra security, both personal and financial, that the agency offered.

Labouring on the Tango Scene: Intimacy and Authenticity in Emotional Bodywork

The types of labour that taxi dancers performed in their encounters with international tourists varied and were shaped by a number of factors. We argue here that these were constituted not only by social and verbal skills, but moreover on the dancers' performance of *emotional labour* (Hochschild 1983, 2003), as the work necessitates the transmission of emotions and feelings and is performed in exchange for a wage,[1]

---

1   Hochschild defines *emotional labour* as, 'the management of feeling to create a publicly observable facial and bodily display; emotional labour is sold for a wage and therefore has exchange value. I use the synonymous terms *emotion work* or *emotion management* to refer to these same acts done in a private context where they have *use*

and also by intimate *body work* (Wolkowitz 2006) due to the closeness of bodies. These were often held in acute tension with each other, as the types of labour dancers were required to perform were shaped by those desired by clients and for agency workers, those that managers wanted to encourage.

Managers of agencies were keen to stress that taxi dancing was a *service*. Agencies often used methods frequently employed by other service sector employees in order to instill this value in their workers. For example, training days held by agencies used managerial practices such as team-building activities often used in other workplaces and business recruitment centres. The aim was to guide dancers towards becoming accomplished and most importantly, professionalized, taxi dancers. The key, one trainer said, was not to become an excellent dancer, but an excellent service worker in the tourist sector. This included speaking English, being socially competent in order to manage and respond to the particular demands and habits of a variety of new customers. As one trainee taxi dancer commented, somewhat disparagingly, the training he received from the agency was not at all dissimilar from a job he'd just left – in a call centre.

Despite the emphasis on professionalism and service skills, the agency owners also emphasized a certain degree of *personal expression*. In many service jobs, such as hotel work or food service, discussing a workers' personal matters with clients is considered inappropriate. Taxi dancers, however, tended to report that the job necessitated the sale of more than dancing, it also required the transmittance of a particular personality and emotional labour. Some lone tourists desire social company outside the tango embrace, others expect to receive unique tango knowledge through the close presence of an 'authentic' Argentinean dancer. Santi, a free-lancer, explained that anyone who wished to retain a client for an entire week could not depend on dancing skills alone, but that they also needed to establish a personal connection. Dancers needed not only to make clients feel comfortable on the dance floor, but also during dance breaks. Ezequiel agreed. He encouraged his staff to engage in informal discussions with their clients, an element which some dancers in his staff found difficult for several reasons. Primarily, because it demanded advanced English ability, secondly because it required a number of social skills and even particular knowledge about the tourists' home countries. Indeed, Martin, a participant in a trainee day at the *Taxi Tango* agency, was 'headhunted' for his ability to easily make contact with new people and his good level of English. Yet he was unsure if he would take the job, due to the fact they had not yet seen him dance, he said that 'there is something weird about a dancing job where you're not employed for your actual dancing.'

Various cultural representations and dance narratives portray tango as a mixture of passion, sensuality, nostalgia and intimacy. Many international visitors come to Buenos Aires to search for what some people refer to as the *tango feeling*, a strong

---

value' (Hochschild 1983/2003: 7). She adds, 'the emotional style of offering the service is part of the service itself' (1983/2003: 5), and that, 'what was once a private act of emotion management is now sold as labour in public-contact jobs' (ibid.: 186).

emotional experience with a dance partner involving promises of intimacy and connection. Others talk of it in terms of 'flow'; those moments when the bodily, emotional and musical communication with a partner makes you lose track of time and space. As such, transmitting such feelings is partly the job of a taxi dancer. This implies creating a flow in the dance that allows for the client to loosen up and be carried away by the music and the atmosphere. In some cases it involves chivalry and flirting aimed making a client feel confident in her dancing and hence more susceptible to sensuality and romantic feelings. However, the emotional aspects of tango do not demand taxi dancers' transmittance of feelings to their clients, but often, rather the opposite. The intention, instead, is often to hide their own feelings. During a trainee day, Ezequiel asked the workers to think of ways to disguise unwanted feelings such as irritation and frustration towards their clients. Many customers would be beginner dancers who would make mistakes and possibly make the taxi dancers 'look bad' on the dance-floor. If working for the agency, such personal queries needed to be managed for the requirements of the job. Thus, the emotion work of taxi dancers is not only about producing feelings in their clients (reliance, intimacy, sensuality), but perhaps more importantly, also about managing their own feelings (Hochschild 1983, 2003) in order to produce a romantic or sexualized experience for the client.

Such acting is a complex and demanding task, but one which is complicated further by the physicality and closeness of the dancer to the client. Indeed, the labour performed by taxi dancers differs from many other service jobs such as call centre employees, hotel receptionists and food service staff. The very nature of dancing implies that workers are involved in a very particular type of labour that we might interpret as *body work* (Wolkowitz 2006). This refers to paid work that involves 'the care, pleasure, adornment, discipline and cure of others' bodies', and more precisely an 'employment that takes the body as its immediate site of labour, involving intimate, messy contact with the body, its orifices or products through touch or close proximity' (Wolkowitz 2006: 147). The fact that tango is an improvised couple dance implies that all movements are communicated corporeally, body-to-body and without choreographic figures. The sensual moves, the heart-to-heart contact between the worker and client and sensing movement through a partners' body, require a particular type of bodily presence and ways of bodily engagement with the work tasks. For a taxi dancer this includes skills in how to complete the tight dance embrace of the traditional tango styles (as different from the open embrace dancing in *tango nuevo*) with a client, in which the intimate bodily communication of marks and lead is transferred chest-to-chest. This implies adjusting the taxi dancers and the clients' bodily comportment through careful placement of chest and hands; judging how close to go to make a client feel comfortable – and feel comfortable oneself; and how to use the body to accommodate the customer across the dance floor. Some taxi dancers describe every new meeting with a client as forcing a difficult line to be drawn between *too* much distance and *too* intimate an encounter. The 'tango feeling' demands close proximity – although a too intimate embrace might evoke feelings of intimidation:

both for the client and the taxi dancer. Some taxi dancers described how they managed the level of intimacy step by step, through a careful process of finding out how close to go. Some also used the *cortina*, the break between dance-sets, as a means to re-establish physical distance with a client.

Although the taxi dancers putatively sell dances, companionship and time, with all the emotional and bodily interaction this embodies, connotations of both the term 'taxi dancer' and their actions have sexual associations. Argentinean male sex workers are often referred to by the term 'taxi boys' and the myths and legends of tango itself claim that it emerged from the brothels of Buenos Aires (Guy 1995). Newspaper documentation from the early 19th century describes the new music halls, cafés and night clubs of Buenos Aires as venues where female dancers attracted and excited male clients in order to offer sexual transactions through bought dances (Guy 1995). Such points of semblance, association and metonym help to produce the *taxistas* as exotic and curious. However, as an American study from 1932, *The Taxi-Dance Hall*, demonstrates the concept of dance escorting might actually also stem from an institution found in some larger North-American cities during the depression. Cressey (2003, 1932: 3) describes the taxi dancer in the United States as 'like the taxi-driver with his cab, she is for public hire and is paid in proportion to the time spent and the services rendered'.

Indeed, the effectivity of the emotional labour and body work deployed by taxi dancers is significant in that it is designed to manage these very associations between taxi dancing and sex work. Responding to the sexualized nature of tango, which has sometimes been interpreted as if dancing is a form of foreplay to sex, Ezequiel, for instance, emphasized that *Taxi Tango* was not an agency for 'Latin lovers'. He stipulated that no flirting with clients was allowed and that romantic or sexual invitations were not to be accepted. Even though he admitted that he had got a lot of international press attention from the associations with sex and that it therefore boosted business, he sought to disassociate his agency from sex work. This not only related to the reputation of the company, however, but also related to clients' desires for non-overtly sexualized dancers. Many female tourists stated that they felt more comfortable with teachers and taxi dancers who upheld a professional profile, that is, tango workers who clearly separated dancing from flirting. Yet taxi dancers managed the connotations in different ways. For some male dancers, a sexualization of the situation became a way of dissociating the relation with a client from that of worker and consumer – with which they felt uncomfortable – to man and woman. Pablo explained that this was a way of making the work a little bit more interesting, although he underscored that this only happened when the connection was right. In this sense, using flirty manners and engaging in a heterosexual play was a way of reinstalling oneself as an active subject, in place of the passive worker bending to the desires of clients and management.

In this respect, male and female taxi dancers clearly differed. Fears about the risks that associations with sex work could pose were particularly expressed by female dancers. Although none of the taxi dancers I met had experiences of clients with outspoken expectations of a continuation of the sexual interaction established on the dance floor, the associations of taxi dancing with prostitution made some of them cautious and they emphasized on the importance of maintaining a professional distance. They took measures to avoid unsafe situations, such as meeting customers inside the tango clubs and taking friends along. A group of female taxi dancers I met explained they had developed some means for dealing with possibly 'sleazy' or 'pushy' clients. They would 'stop going' with a client who was acting too intimately and made sure that one or several friends were out dancing in the same club. Even if nothing normally happened, meeting a stranger in a night club, made some, especially new dancers, nervous. Gabi, a twenty-five year old dancer who just joined the *Taxi Tango* described her first meetings with clients as 'weird dates'. She said that the arrangement was similar to that of a romantic blind date in that you are given a name, some physical attributes, a time and a place, with the difference being that an exchange of money will take place at the end of the night. Though her experiences with customers were exclusively positive she still felt that she was subject to a different kind of vulnerability than the male dancers.

The Twists and Turns of Tango Labour

The labour of the commercialized intimacy of taxi dancing twists and turns like the steps of the tango itself and as such, the case of tango taxi dancing opens up the research field of sex work and sex tourism to involve broader questions of how to approach a global commercialization of intimacy. Like the sensual tango, these interactions and encounters demand a complex understanding of sex, intimacy and labour. This is reflected in the intricate interaction between emotional labour and bodywork and their relationship with sex work. The impact of performing these entangled forms labour mean that, contrary to the wishes of some of the dancers and more specifically, the management, taxi dancing differs to standard service work in particular ways. Instead, it is more appropriate to draw comparisons between professions such as nurses and masseurs in which the body is the site of labour, or rather, in which a physical intimate relation between provider and client is created through touch. Still, this comparison has a number of obvious limitations. First, in terms of spatial settings: the dimly lit *milonga* is a far cry from the well-lit, sterile, institutional rooms of hospitals and health care centres. Night clubs, in contrast, are venues where romantic and sexual relations tend to occur, while sexuality tends to be written out of the spatial script of the hospital. Second, the intense emotionality of the tango sometimes demands a performance of romance and intimacy, within which dancers must walk a tightrope between embracing the association with sex work, and distinguishing taxi dancers from escorts who sell sex more directly.

Such complexities suggest a need to move beyond simplistic comparisons with the service workers or sex workers. Furthermore, while the conceptual

Taxi Dancers 147

framework of female sex tourism or romance tourism reveals certain aspects of the taxi dancer-client interaction, it is not sufficient to make complete sense of the labour and consumption of the intimate tango dance. Taxi dancing should be understood as a complex entanglement of various acts of labour and consumption that involve the body and emotions, that allude to romance and sex and sometimes deliver them, thus escaping easy categorization. Sex is present, not through the presence of naked bodies, kissing or sexual intercourse, but instead in the use of certain manners (sexual aesthetics, flirtations) and an exclusion of others (a sexual continuation outside the dance floor).

Despite its contextual specificity, taxi dancers' complex labour cannot be solely understood in the context of the history of the tango and the nationhood of Argentina. Instead, it must also be understood in the context of ongoing processes of globalization. The 'new gold' of love and affection in contemporary capitalism (Hochschild and Ehrenreich 2003), epitomized in the sex work and international care chains, has generally been associated with the labour of women. Women have previously been represented as the primary links and actors in these chains. Yet through this examination of taxi dancers, it is possible to see the ways in which men are also deeply integrated into them, offering care and comfort, affection and acts of romance in exchange for a wage. As such, considering the case of taxi dancers, not only integrates the idea of sex workers in international care chains (Rivers-Moore 2009), but also challenges representations of women as the sole workers in these chains. Recognizing men as intimate labourers challenges gendered assumptions about the exploitation of care, sex and love and suggests further complexity to the ways in which love, affection and sex are commodified and integrated into the global marketplace.

References

Bales, K. (2003). 'Because She Looks Like a Child', in B. Ehrenreich and A.R. Hochschild (eds) *Global Woman: Nannies, Maids and Sex Workers in the New Economy*. New York: Metropolitan Books.

Bigsten, A., Kimuyu, P. and Lundvall, K. (2004). 'What to Do with the Informal Sector?', *Development Policy Review* 22(6): 701–15.

Brennan, D. (2003). 'Selling Sex for Visas: Sex Tourism as a Stepping-stone to International Migration', in B. Ehrenreich and A.R. Hochschild (eds) *Global Woman: Nannies, Maids and Sex Workers in the New Economy*. New York: Metropolitan Books.

Cressey, P. (1932/2003). *The Taxi-Dance Hall: A Sociological Study in Commercialized Recreation and City Life*. New York: Routledge.

Douglas, M. (1991). *Purity and Danger: An Analysis of the Concepts of Pollution and Taboo*. London: Routledge.

Ebron, P. (1997). 'Traffic in Men', in M. Grosz-Ngaté and O. Kokole (eds) *Gendered Encounters: Challenging Cultural Boundaries and Social Hierarchies in Africa*. New York: Routledge.

Ehrenreich, B. and Hochschild, A.R. (2003). *Global Woman: Nannies, Maids and Sex Workers in the New Economy*. New York: Metropolitan Books.

Fiszbein, A., Giovagnoli, P. and Aduriz, I. (2002). 'Argentina's Crisis and Its Impact on Household Welfare', *Argentina Poverty Update*. Washington, D.C.: The World Bank.

Guy, D.J. (1995). *Sex and Danger in Buenos Aires: Prostitution, Family and Nation in Argentina*. Nebraska: University of Nebraska Press.

Hochschild, A. (1983/2003). *The Managed Heart: Commercialization of Human Feeling*. Berkeley: University of California Press.

Holm, B. (2004). *Pardans*. Stockholm: Bonnier Förlag.

Jamieson, L. (1998). *Intimacy: Personal Relationships in Modern Societies*. Cambridge: Polity Press.

Kempadoo, K. (ed.) (1999). *Sun, Sex, and Gold: Tourism and Sex Work in the Caribbean*. Lanham: Rowman & Littlefield.

Malkki, L.H. (1995). *Purity and Exile: Violence, Memory, and National Cosmology among Hutu Refugees in Tanzania*. Chicago: The University of Chicago Press.

Meisch, L.A. (1995). 'Gringas and Otavaleños: Changing Tourist Relations', *Annals of Tourism Research*, 22(2): 441–62.

Nagel, J. (2003). *Race, Ethnicity and Sexuality: Intimate Intersections, Forbidden Frontiers*. Oxford: Oxford University Press.

O'Connell Davidson, J. and Sanchez Taylor, J. (2005). 'Travel and taboo: heterosexual sex tourism to the Carribean', in L. Schaffner and E. Bernstein (eds) *Regulating Sex: The Politics of Intimacy and Identity*. London: Routledge.

Pruitt, D. and LaFont, S. (1995). 'For Love and Money: Romance Tourism in Jamaica', *Annals of Tourism Research*, 22(2): 422–40.

Rivers-Moore, M. (2009). 'Getting Ahead in Gringo Gulch', unpublished PhD thesis. Cambridge: Murray Edwards, University of Cambridge.

Sanchez Taylor, J. (2006). 'Female Sex Tourism: a Contradiction in Terms?', *Feminist Review*, 83(1): 42–59.

Shilling, C. (2004). 'Physical capital and situated action: a new direction for corporeal sociology', *British Journal of Sociology of Education*, 25(4): 473–87.

Thomas, J.J. (1995). *Surviving in the City: the Urban Informal Sector in Latin America*. London: Pluto.

Truong, T.D. (1990). *Sex, Money and Morality: Prostitution and Tourism in Southeast Asia*. London: Zed Books.

Urry, J. (1990). *The Tourist Gaze: Leisure and Travel in Contemporary Societies*. London: Sage.

Whitson, R. (2007). 'Beyond the crisis: economic globalization and informal work in urban Argentina', *Journal of Latin American Geography* 6(2): 122–36.

Wolkowiz, C. (2006). *Bodies at Work*. London: Sage.

Yuval-Davis, N. (1997). *Gender and Nation*. London: Sage.

Chapter 10

Temporal Dimensions of Cabaret Dancers' Circular Migration to Switzerland

Romaric Thiévent

Introduction

The production and consumption of sex work services is intimately linked to the mobility of different categories of people. On the one hand, there are many examples in which the individuals purchasing sex workers' services are international travellers (Thorbek 2002, Kempadoo 1998). These may include the highly mobile male entrepreneurs and executives who are known to purchase sexual services when travelling abroad (Yeoh 2005, Truong 1996) and the thousands who flock to 'hot' spots such as Thailand or the Dominican Republic where they consume erotic bodies of exotic Others (Wonders and Michalowski 2001, Truong 1990). On the other hand, sex work is often performed by – international or internal – migrants (Oso Casas 2009 and 2003, Agustin 2006, Spanger 2002, Sardi and Froidevaux 2003, Van Blerk 2000, Lim 1998, Tyner 1996). Sex workers constitute a mobile population not only because they have migrated, but also because many of them are constantly on the move. In that respect, Agustin (2006: 32) argues that in Europe the migration of sex workers is:

> a migration form that rarely 'settles down': the phenomenon is called, in Europe, 'migrant prostitution' because many workers tend to stay only a few weeks or months in a site and then move on, in a circuit that crosses national borders. These workers are migrant not only because they left home and came to Europe, but because they keep on migrating.

Many sex workers are, in fact, involved in circular migration which is a continuing and repetitive form of mobility 'characterized by a pattern of coming and going between a "home" place and a destination place' (Hugo 2009: 167). The circular mobility in which sex workers are involved may be local, regional national and/or international. They are driven by different rationalities and sometimes managed by sex workers themselves or organized by other people (Sardi and Froidevaux 2003, Morokvasic 1999). Constant circulation is sometimes a strategy designed to avoid illegality or detection. Some women circulate between European countries following the expiration of their tourist visa (Agustin 2006) and others move within national contexts between night clubs (Oso Casas 2003) and districts

(Agustin 2003), avoiding foretold police raids. International circulation can also be driven by the temporary nature of exotic dancers' permits issued by countries like Canada (Macklin 2003), Cyprus (Philaretou 2005) or Switzerland (Thiévent 2010). Circulation between towns and/or countries can also be a way for sex workers to compartmentalize their lives and a means of avoiding their relatives discovering their involvement in the sex industry (Spanger 2002). Finally, this ongoing mobility is sometimes the result of the very functioning of particular sectors of the sex industry as shown by Oso Casas (2003) in the case of the 'plaza system' in Spain, which involves a permanent rotation of sex workers between night-clubs or apartments.

Despite the fact that several sectors of the sex industry function due to the extensive employment of female migrants, and that mobility is a central feature of many sex workers' lives and activity, migrants who sell sex have been overlooked in migration and mobility studies. Instead, the mobility patterns of migrant sex workers are still mostly considered and analysed through the prism of trafficking and, as a consequence, sex workers are often constructed as passive objects and victims without agency (Agustin 2006, Thorbek 2002). I consider that trafficking as an *a priori* analytical lens is incompatible with the study of sex workers' mobility patterns. A migration approach seems more suitable to allow researchers and policymakers to develop an appropriate and subtle understanding of the different elements at work in shaping and constraining sex workers' mobility and, by extension, their working conditions.

In this chapter, I use a migration framework to analyse the international circulation of a particular group of migrant sex workers, namely cabaret dancers in Switzerland, who come to the country under 'L' permits. 'L' permits allow cabaret dancers to work legally in Switzerland for a period no longer than eight months during a twelve months period. These foreign women working in the cabaret industry are constantly on the move and involved in circulation processes at two different scales. Given the temporary nature of their permit, cabaret dancers circulate at an international scale, mainly between Switzerland and their home country. Furthermore, during their stay in Switzerland, cabaret dancers usually change workplace several times, generally each month (see also Thiévent forthcoming). Cabaret dancers' activity is thus marked by a high degree of mobility and characterized by transferability defined by Psimmenos (2000: 84) as the situations where workers are '... transferred across places or labour procedures according to market necessities.'

I analyse the international circulation of cabaret dancers from a temporal perspective, focusing on three temporal dimensions of their circulation patterns:

1. the *periods of work*, corresponding to the period of the year during which a cabaret dancer comes to work in Swiss cabarets;
2. the *duration of the work periods,* corresponding to the number of months during which a cabaret dancer works in Swiss cabarets;

3. the *career*, corresponding to the number of years of involvement in cabaret dancing.

As this chapter will demonstrate there are significant differences in these three temporal patterns of circulation. I will show how each of these temporal dimensions is structured and constrained by an entanglement of factors operating at different levels. These include dancers' familial, academic or professional commitments in their country of origin; the Swiss and cantonal[1] immigration policies; the working conditions; the ability to get hired; patrons' demands for young women; debts due to financial irregularities in the recruitment process; and cabaret dancers' migratory projects.

The first section lays out the methodology used to understand the temporal dimensions of cabaret dancer's international circulation. I will then present the cabaret dancing context in Switzerland focusing on the legal framework and the description of cabaret dancers' activity. In the third part I will examine the different factors shaping and constraining the temporalities of cabaret dancers' circular migration.

Methodology

The data used in this chapter was collected through semi-structured interviews, observation in cabarets and informal discussions. Semi-structured interviews were conducted with two categories of informants. The first included individuals professionally involved in the Swiss cabaret industry: nineteen current and former cabaret dancers of various origins, eleven agents, seven cabaret owners and two waiters.[2] The second category of interviewees comprised of four NGO representatives and ten members of the federal or cantonal administration. In addition, I have conducted several rounds of observation in night-clubs, whereby I watched the shows, offered champagne to dancers in order to talk to them, had several informal discussions with waiters, dancers and agents, and observed interactions between dancers and customers. This allowed me to define and continually refine the questions asked during semi-structured interviews as well as to generate further information about cabaret dancers' circulation.

---

1   Switzerland is a confederation made up of 26 cantons. The related adjective is 'cantonal'.

2   In order to facilitate access to this hard-to-reach population, I gave 50 Swiss francs (about 46 USD) to every dancer who took part in an interview.

The Context of Cabaret Dancing in Switzerland

The majority of women working in approximately three hundred cabarets of Switzerland come from countries outside the European Union (EU) and the European Free Trade Association (EFTA), and hold the 'L' permit for cabaret dancers. In December 2008, 1257 dancers came from 16 different countries. The majority of dancers (72.3 per cent) came from Eastern European countries and Latin America (20 per cent) (see Table 10.1).

Swiss immigration policy stipulates that people from countries which are not part of EU/EFTA are generally not allowed to work in the country if they are not highly qualified. As such, the 'L' permit for cabaret dancers constitutes an exception. 'L' permit holders can only work as cabaret dancers and are subject to expulsion from Switzerland if they remain unemployed for a period exceeding one month. The characteristics of this permit have been criticized by many non-governmental organizations (NGOs), politicians and scholars as they are thought to make dancers reliant on cabaret owners and agents and may increase the risk of exploitation (Dahinden and Stants 2006, FIZ 2006, Franzi-Föllmi 1997, Caroni 1996). But at the same time however, it has been suggested that the eradication

Table 10.1   Origin and number of cabaret dancers holding an 'L' permit in December 2008

Origin	Number	(%)
Eastern Europe	*909*	*72.3*
Ukraine	496	39.4
Russia	156	12.3
Romania	84	6.7
Moldova	73	5.8
Belarus	60	4.8
Uzbekistan	33	2.7
Bulgaria	5	0.4
Others	2	0.2
Latin America	*252*	*20.0*
Dominican Republic	225	17.9
Brazil	26	2.1
Paraguay	1	0.1
Southeast Asia	*55*	*4.4*
Thailand	55	4.4
Africa	*40*	*3.2*
Morocco	37	3.0
Ivory Coast	3	0.2
Stateless persons	*1*	*0.1*
Total	1,257	100

of this permit may place dancers in a more vulnerable position as they would no longer be afforded any legal protection (FIZ 2006).

Cabaret dancers come to work in Switzerland through recruitment agencies. These Switzerland based agencies recruit dancers in many countries through various means: some travel to different countries to find women willing to work in Swiss cabarets, while others collaborate with foreign agencies or local recruiters. Most of the recruitment is 'passive' and done through mouth-to-mouth networking (Poli and Thiévent 2009, Dahinden and Stants 2006). In addition, Swiss agents take care of the administrative tasks required for the delivery of a visa and establish contracts with cabaret owners. In exchange for their intermediation work, they earn 8 per cent of a dancer's gross income.

According to the legal definition of dancers' activity, cabaret dancers are strippers, and only strippers. However, the reality is quite different. Even if the legal definition of cabaret dancing is limited to this, stripping does not constitute the central part of the job. Rather, the main activity of dancers is to talk with clients and encourage them to consume alcohol, mainly champagne. Given that the entrance to a cabaret is free, the only source of income for cabaret owners stems from alcohol consumption. Dancers have also an interest in encouraging clients to consume alcohol because they earn a commission on the total amount of drinks they 'sell' over the month.[3] Some cabaret dancers also provide sexual services inside and/or outside the cabarets. Although these are explicitly forbidden by law, in most cabarets one can find '*séparés*', that is, little spaces separated from the rest of the cabaret by opaque curtains, allowing intimacy between a dancer and a customer. In order to access these private spaces, customers have to pay for a certain amount of champagne that varies according to the cabaret. Then, the dancer negotiates the kind of sexual service performed and its price and, usually, the money she receives from clients is hers. Patrons may also take dancers out of the cabaret by paying a certain amount of champagne for their exit.

Temporal Dimensions of Cabaret Dancers' International Circulation

In the next section I will focus on the different factors shaping and constraining the three temporal dimensions of cabaret dancers' circulation.

Periods of Work

For very few dancers the period of work is not important. It is irrelevant whether the period is from January to May or from February to August as they just want to earn a living. The majority of dancers, however, attach importance to the time of

---

3   Cabaret dancers have to reach a threshold which can vary from 8,000 to 15,000 Swiss francs (about 13,850 USD) per month according to the cabaret. If they reach the threshold, they earn between 8 to 15 per cent of the total amount sold.

year during which they come to work in Swiss cabarets and as such, try to choose them carefully. For these women, it appears that preferences for particular periods are determined and constrained by the connections they have with their country of origin. They try to balance work as a cabaret dancer with relationships with family members and/or friends, as well with the different kinds of activities in which they are involved in their home country, such as employment or education. Cabaret dancers are simultaneously embedded in different places around the globe. Like many migrants, especially circular migrants, cabaret dancers maintain associations with their countries of origin (Hugo 2009, Morokvasic 2003, 1999). Borrowing Morokvasic's statement about East European transnational migrant women, we can consider that cabaret dancers '... are not connecting to their home community from abroad, but genuinely living in/between two worlds, one foot there another here, with their base being their home' (Morokvasic 2003: 112). In the following section I will explore the factors that inform cabaret dancers living 'in/between two worlds' and show how they constrain their choice over work periods.

Social and familial bonds   Social and family bonds often inform cabaret dancers' circulation patterns in the time of the year in which they work in Switzerland. Eight of the nineteen interviewees had children and were involved in familial arrangements characterized by alternation between periods of spatial separation and of co-presence. Many dancers who left their children behind had ambivalent feelings. On the one hand, they felt guilty for leaving their children at home. On the other, they manifested pride for being able to offer them a better life. One way for dancers to cope with these feelings of guilt was to be present for specific events such as Christmas, or at times when they can be with their children, such as school holidays. Rather than transforming the traditional meaning of motherhood to fit their situation, as Hondagneu-Soleto and Avila (1997) found when they explored the lives of live-in domestic workers in the United States, cabaret dancers try to manage their circulation to match their ideas of 'motherhood'. As an agent who was in this business for more than 20 years explained, this strategy was widespread and affected recruitment practices:

> It is sometimes difficult to find girls. There are months where girls are missing and others where there are too many girls. During specific periods like October to November and March to May there are always too many girls. And during other periods like December to January or June to September the girls are missing. Because for Christmas, they want to be with their family. You know, a lot of them have children. During the summer their children are on holidays and they can stay with them.

The tendency of some cabaret dancers to take family obligations, such as childcare into consideration when deciding when to work abroad reflects other studies which have shown that, amongst other reasons, caring for family often was a determining factor in structuring female circular migration (Morokvasic 2003, Ellis et al. 1996).

This demonstrates the strong links between transnational migration and family, and shows how '... migration as a life-changing decision and process is deeply embedded, and must be understood, in the context of family norms, relations, and politics' (Yeoh 2005: 63).

Apart from family obligations, the maintenance of bonds with friends was also mentioned by a Russian dancer as a reason underlying her choice over work periods:

> I never came to work in Switzerland in the summer. In the summer, I prefer to stay at home in Russia, in my town. In winter it's very cold ... People stay inside. But in summer it is hot. It is the occasion to see friends and have parties in the parks. That's why I always come in Switzerland between October and May.

The example of this dancer, who wants to be at home during specific periods in order to maintain ties with friends, is particularly interesting because friendship, contrarily to family bonds, is rarely considered as a factor structuring circular migration patterns.

Academic and professional involvement The professional or academic commitments of some dancers also seemed to structure their periods of circulation. For example, two dancers have professional commitments in their home country. A 27-year-old Ukrainian woman, for instance, worked part time as a lab-assistant in a hospital and enjoyed her job but, from her point of view, her salary was not sufficient enough to have a decent life. After hearing of the possibility to work in Swiss cabarets, she made an arrangement with her employer and had been working in Swiss cabarets from January to June for three years while she continued to work as a lab assistant in Kiev from July to December. This arrangement allowed her to keep a job that provided her with 'a social status', but which was badly paid, yet also increase her income substantially through dancing in Swiss cabarets.

A further six dancers came to Switzerland to finance their University degree despite finding it difficult to reconcile their activity as cabaret dancers with their academic education. As a 24-year-old Romanian who had been dancing in Swiss cabarets for four years described, 'I'm here to finance my university studies. So I always try to come during the university summer break. But it is not always possible and sometimes I miss a lot of courses'.

The above examples demonstrate how the involvement in the country of origin informs cabaret dancers' choice of circulation period because they have to try to conciliate and synchronize their activity as cabaret dancers with familial, professional, academic and/or social obligations in their home country.

The Duration of Work Periods

While all of these factors shaped women's choices in when they worked, a number of other factors influenced how long they worked during specific periods. These

156 *New Sociologies of Sex Work*

included Swiss and cantonal immigration policies, working conditions and ability to be hired.

Swiss and cantonal immigration policies The Swiss immigration policy represents the general and legal framework determining the length of stay of 'L' permit holders'. Theoretically, the minimum length of stay is three months because, in order to obtain their visa at the Swiss embassy, cabaret dancers have to prove that they already have contracts for a period of three months in a row. 'L' permit holders are allowed to stay for a maximum of eight months. While the national immigration policy clearly shapes the length of time of cabaret dancers' stay, the cantonal immigration policies further constrain the duration of work periods.

Whereas the general conditions related to the possession of the L permit, like rights and duties, are defined at a national level, the permits are issued by the Swiss cantons which have power in this process. Seven Swiss cantons (Saint-Gall, Thurgovie, Zoug, Appenzell Rhodes-Intérieures, Valais, Jura and Vaud) decided to deliver 'L' permits for dancers only to citizens of countries which are part of the EU/EFTA. All of which have justified their decision by invoking the particularly poor working conditions for cabaret dancers coming from non UE/EFTA countries, and the recurrent suspicions regarding the trafficking of women originating from these countries.

These legal modifications at the cantonal level have influenced the duration of cabaret dancers' periods of work by making the competition for jobs more intense. The intensification of competition stems from the fact that, for women from non EU/EFTA countries, there are now fewer possibilities to work, while the number of women from these countries willing to work in Swiss cabaret remains high. With the reduction of available workplaces for non EU/AELE women in the cabaret industry, it has become more difficult for agents to establish the 'three months in a row' contracts required to obtain visas for dancers. As a result, dancers are increasingly faced with uncertainty, as they never know when or whether they will be able to obtain a visa to work in Switzerland. This increase in competition seems to be the cause of a lengthening of work periods. For example, several dancers who previously worked for between four to six months have reported extending their stay for eight months in a row in order to keep their stay profitable. As one 29-year-old Russian woman who had been dancing for six years explained:

> For six years, I used to spend four months in Switzerland and then went back to Russia for four months, and so forth. But now, there is more competition and it becomes harder to find a visa. The competition is now harder because some cantons do not issue 'L' permits to non-European women anymore. It is more and more difficult to establish contracts. So when X (her agent) finds me a three-months contract required to enter Switzerland, I try to stay for eight months.

The extension of work periods is not always solely the result of cabaret dancers' choice, but can also be due to pressure from their agent. For agents who

Temporal Dimensions of Cabaret Dancers' Circular Migration to Switzerland   157

previously worked with cabarets located in cantons where the 'L' permits have been suppressed, it has become more difficult for them to find the three months contracts that cabaret dancers require to enter Switzerland. As a consequence, the regularity of their income was no longer secure. As this agent reported one way to cope with this new situation and reduce its impact on his income was to ask dancers to stay for the maximum of months they are allowed:

> The hard part of the job is to find the contract for three months in a row. You have to make a lot of calls, to travel, and so on. With the suppression of the L permit it is now even harder to establish theses contracts. That's why I now tell my dancers that they have to stay for eight months. I have to eat too, you know. The only money we earn is when a cabaret dancer has a contract. So when I find the three-months contracts, I want to make my work profitable.

By doing so, many dancers felt under pressure to stay for longer periods than they had planned, which sometimes placed strain on their family or professional commitments in their home country.

Managing working conditions   The hard working conditions which often characterize cabaret dancers' activity have been frequently cited. Diverse NGO publications (FIZ 2006, Fondation Scelles 2002), Swiss federal office reports (OFJ 2001) and scientific studies (Chimenti 2009, Dahinden and Stants 2006, Franzi Föllmi 1997) have highlighted the particularly harsh and potentially harmful working conditions these women face. These are mainly due to high levels of compulsory alcohol consumption, long periods of night work and pressures to sell sex and can lead some dancers to develop alcoholism, sleeping and eating disorders, anxious states or depression.

These working conditions have an effect on the duration of cabaret dancers work periods. Chimenti (2009) has shown how some dancers did not work for the eight months they were allowed to, but instead worked for shorter periods in order to be able take a break in their country of origin. Several dancers were involved in such mobility patterns aiming to limit the effects cabaret dancing could have on their health. Some women determine the duration of their stay on a day to day basis depending on their resilience to working conditions. Other dancers who know the heavy burden of working in the Swiss cabaret industry, like this Ukrainian woman, determine a maximal duration of stay in advance of arriving in Switzerland:

> **D:** This year I will stay for maximum five or six months. I always have worked for a maximum of six months.
> **I:** Why?
> **D:** It is very exhausting. It is good to have a break of two or three months after six months. Sleeping during the night or during the day is a very different thing, you know. After a period of time, you have to sleep during the night or you become crazy. You have to rest.

158   *New Sociologies of Sex Work*

Therefore, the length of cabaret dancers stay in Switzerland is also, to some extent, informed by their will to manage the sometimes very harsh working conditions that they face. For many women these harsh conditions pose a threat to the mental and physical well-being which has led some to cut short their stay and return home to rest.

Ability to be hired   A further factor that shaped dancers' duration of stay was their ability to find work. Most of the time dancers entered Switzerland with only the certainty of being hired for three months in a row. For dancers who wanted to work longer than three months, extending their stay depended on their ability to get hired. I have argued elsewhere that the acquisition of 'circulatory competences' allowed dancers to secure employment and to gain control over the spatial and temporal dimensions of their circulation (Thiévent 2010). As cabaret dancers' activity cannot be separated from the high mobility which characterizes it – we can say that mobility is consubstantial of this activity – these competences have been named circulatory. These competences are composed by three interrelated dimensions: a certain 'knowhow', information and social networks. The 'knowhow' is principally related to the ability and skill necessary to sell a lot of champagne. Dancers who have this 'knowhow' are identified as 'good dancers' by cabaret owners and are more likely to be hired. The information needed to secure regular employment, is for example, knowing which agents are able to secure regular employment. Finally, the building of social relations based on friendship and/or trust with actors of the cabaret industry, like cabaret owners, offer dancers a security over future employment. Dancers who have and use these competences can have greater control over the duration of their work periods.

Length of Involvement in Cabaret Dancing

In this section I explore the factors influencing the length of involvement in the Swiss cabaret industry. These included patrons' demand for young women, debts contracted during the recruitment process and cabaret dancers' migratory project.

Nature of the demand   Physical appearance is of great importance for cabaret dancers. As patrons want to be surrounded by young women, it is rare for a dancer to continue to work in cabarets beyond the age of 30 or 35. As this agent who was working in Geneva for 13 years explains:

> There is not a clear cut age limit to hire a dancer. But at the same time it is true that age is an important criterion. Cabaret owners want young women, because patrons want young women. That's how it goes. For example, in Geneva, when a dancer reaches the age of 30 you can almost consider her retired. But it is not specific to the cabaret industry. It is the same for fashion models, careers are short.

Data from the Federal office for migration confirm this tendency not to engage women aged over 35. In December 2008, among the 1257 cabaret dancers working in Switzerland with an L permit, 76.3 per cent were aged between 20 (which is the minimum age for dancers) and 30 years old, while 20.6 per cent were between 31 to 35 and only 0.1 per cent were over 35.[4]

Dancers cannot compete with patrons' preference for young women and those who are over 30 have to think about a change of activity or, if they still want to work in cabarets, are pushed to accept work in less lucrative cabarets or in night clubs offering bad working conditions. This Romanian dancer explained to me how her age was not only limiting her ability to find work, but also lowering her working conditions:

> I am already 32 and I think it won't last long (her work in cabarets). I still want to work in cabarets for a few years if the cabaret owners allow me to, but it becomes difficult when you are 32. Even if I look after my body, I cannot look like a 20 or 25-year-old. Some cabaret owners do not want to employ me anymore. I cannot choose anymore and have to work in dirty places.

As such, the nature of demand is an important factor which determines whether or not a dancer is hired and for how long they are able to work in the industry.

Debts due to financial irregularities during the recruitment process   Many women become indebted to agencies and employers through illegal administration fees; this also informed how long dancers worked in the Swiss cabaret industry. Debts seem to have a strong impact on the duration of cabaret dancers' involvement in this activity as they have sometimes to work for many years in order to repay their loans. The recruitment of cabaret dancers is sustained by an 'immigration industry' composed of Swiss and foreign agencies, local recruiters and cabaret dancers. The recruitment process is marked by a high degree of financial irregularity. Legally, the agency commission, which is deducted from cabaret dancers' wages, must not represent more than 8 per cent of their gross salary, even if several agencies are involved. Nevertheless, many dancers pay huge and illegal fees to different intermediaries.

As many migrant dancers believed it was common and legal practice, some dancers had paid Swiss agents up to 4,000 Swiss francs to obtain contracts to enter Switzerland, and others had given up to 5,000 Swiss francs to foreign agencies to be put in contact with a Swiss agent (called the double commission). This was the case of this Moroccan dancer, who was 25 and was in Switzerland for the first time when I met her:

> A woman, a Moroccan woman offered for me to come to Switzerland and I said 'yes'. To come here, I paid 6,000 Swiss francs to this woman. I had to pay

---

4   Federal Office for Migration, SYMIC (2008).

160   *New Sociologies of Sex Work*

> for the agent's address in Switzerland and for the journey. To pay her, I have borrowed money from my family and friends... When I came here, I understood that everything this woman told me was false. She told me that I could earn a lot and that I could reimburse all my credits in two or three months. It is not true. I earn less than she told me. So now I am like trapped. I have to do this work for a longer period than I had previously thought.

Women deeply in debt were trapped in the cabaret industry and had little control over the ways in which they worked, including the duration. Furthermore, as shown in other contexts, it seems that 'greater social and labour precariousness affects indebted immigrant women – they have to work more intensively in order to repay loans, they are forced to accept poorer working conditions that may put their health at risk' (Oso Casas 2009: 63–4). The situations of women misled by different kinds of intermediaries, who prey on their desire to earn money and their lack of information about legal practices, demonstrate the effects of these actors' activities on the immigration industry (Lim and Oishi 1996). On the one hand, recruitment agencies make it possible for women to work in Swiss cabarets, but on the other hand they often are the very cause of the vulnerability of these women which limits their autonomy and decision making capacity.

Migratory project   Apart from the exception of a woman who reported a desire to see the world and learn about a different culture as the main reasons for working in the Swiss cabaret industry, economic improvement is the common denominator of all cabaret dancers' migratory project. Nevertheless, behind this apparent unity are significant differences. As shown by Dahinden and Stants (2006), these migratory projects can be divided into two categories: the individual and the collective. This distinction is important to draw, because the nature of the migratory projects influences the duration of dancers' involvement in cabaret dancing.

For some cabaret dancers the migratory project tends to be individualistic as they seek to improve their own economic situation and often have a precise goal, such as financing a university degree, buying an apartment or opening a shop. Women whose migration decision is based on their own individual needs tend to stay in the cabaret industry for one to four years depending on their personal project, and cease this activity once they have reached their objectives. Some dancers have clearly manifested their intention to completely cease this activity once they have enough money to achieve their goals. For other dancers the decision to work in Swiss cabarets had a strong collective nature and cannot be considered as the result of a decision aimed simply at improving individual economic needs. On the contrary, migration has to be considered as a family or household strategy intended to improve the economic wellbeing of larger units of related people. Women involved in collective migration projects in which the decision to migrate was based on household needs, tended to work in cabarets as long as possible, sometimes more than ten years with only little breaks between each period of work, because the wellbeing, and sometimes the survival, of entire families depend upon their income.

Conclusion

In this chapter, I have analysed three different temporal dimensions of cabaret dancers' circular migration to Switzerland (the periods of work, the duration of work periods and the length of involvement in cabaret dancing) and have shown how they were structured and shaped by an entanglement of factors operating at different analytical levels. While some of these factors are closely related to cabaret dancers' involvement in the industry, others like the financial pressure of the transnational household or migration policies are common to different category of migrants. From the point of view of the women involved, the elements shaping and constraining their circulation are often contradictory forces. For example, the lengthening circulation periods induced by cantonal legislative modifications runs contrary to the desires of some cabaret dancers to take a rest in their country of origin after short periods of work. Furthermore, cabaret dancers face several barriers in their attempt to synchronize and coordinate their work in the Swiss cabaret industry with social and familial obligations, professional or academic involvement and migratory projects. They 'weigh' the different possibilities available to them, which often means a sacrifice of one part of their life either in their home country or in terms of working conditions. The focus on different temporal dimensions allows an identification of specific factors which influence dancers' decisions on their circulation, that could not have been otherwise underlined. The results demonstrate that paying particular attention to temporal dimensions can add to our understanding of circular flows. The case study also shows how the working conditions of cabaret dancers were related to their mobility patterns, which were shaped in similar ways to other migrants.

Acknowledgement

I would like to thank Laurence Crot and Etienne Piguet from the Institute of Geographie of the University of Neuchâtel as well as Graeme Hugo from the Department of Geographical and Environmental Studies of the University of Adelaide for their important and helpful comments on earlier versions of this text.

References

Agustin, L.M. (2003). 'A migrant world of services', *Social Politics*, 10(3): 377–96.

Agustin, L.M (2006). 'The Disappearing of a Migration Category: Migrants Who Sell Sex', *Journal of Ethnic and Migration Studies*, 32(1): 29–47.

Caroni, M. (1996). *Danseuses et candidates au mariage: aspects juridiques de la traite en Suisse*. Lucerne: Caritas.

Chimenti, M. (2009). 'Selling sex in order to migrate: the end of the migratory dream?', *Journal of Ethnic and Migration Studies*, 36(1): 27–45.

Dahinden, J. and Stants, F. (2006). *Arbeits- und Lebenbedingungen von Cabaret-Tänzerinnen in der Schweiz*. Neuchâtel: SFM.

Ellis, M., Conway, D. and Bailey, A.J. (1996). 'The circular Migration of Puerto Rican Women: Towards a Gendered Explanation', *International Migration Quarterly Review*, 34(1): 31–62.

FIZ (2006). *Champagne, strass et travail précaire. Conditions de travail et de vie des danseuses de cabaret en Suisse*. Zurich: FIZ.

Fondation Scelles (2002). *La prostitution adulte en Europe*. Ramonville St-Agne: Érès.

Franzi Föllmi, M. (1997). *Flies in the Spider's Web or Spiderwoman? Mail-order Brides and Migrant Sex Workers in Switzerland*. The Hague: Institute of Social Studies.

Hondagneu Soleto, P. and Avila, E. (1997). '"I'm here, but i'm there": The meanings of Latina transnational motherhood', *Gender and Society*, 11(5): 548–71.

Hugo, G. (2009). 'Circular migration and development: an Asia-Pacific perspective', in O. Hofirek et al. (eds) *Boundaries in Motion: Rethinking Contemporary Migration Events*. Brno: Centre for the Study of Democracy and Culture, 190–265.

Kempadoo, K. (1998). 'Introduction: Globalizing sex workers' rights', in K. Kempadoo and J. Doezema (eds) *Global Sex Workers: Rights, Resistance, and Redefinition*. New York and London: Routledge, 1–28.

Lim, L.L. (1998). *The Sex Sector: The Economic and Social Bases of Prostitution in Southeast Asia*. Geneva: ILO.

Lim, L.L. and Oishi, N. (1996). 'International labor migration of Asian women: distinctive characteristics and policy concerns', *Asian and Pacific Migration Journal*, 5(1): 85–116.

Macklin, A. (2003). 'Dancing across borders: 'exotic dancers', trafficking and Canadian immigration policy', *International Migration Review*, 37(2): 464–500.

Morokvasic, M. (1999). 'La mobilité transnationale comme ressource: le cas des migrants de l'Europe de l'Est', *Cultures & Conflits*, 33–34(printemps-été): 105–22.

Morokvasic, M. (2003). 'Transnational mobility and gender: a view from post-wall Europe', in M. Morokvasic et al. (eds) *Crossing Borders and Shifting Boundaries, Vol. 1: Gender on the Move*. Opladen: Leske + Budrich, 101–33.

OFJ (2001). *Traite des êtres humains en Suisse. Rapport du groupe de travail interdépartemental traite des êtres humains au Département fédéral de justice et police*. Berne: Office fédéral de la justice.

Oso Casas, L. (2003). 'The new migratory space in Southern Europe: the case of Colombian sex workers in Spain', in M. Morokvasic et al. (eds) *Crossing*

Borders and Shifting Boundaries, Vol. 1: Gender on the Move. Opladen: Leske+Budrich, 207–27.

Oso Casas, L. (2009). 'Money, sex, love and the family: economic and affective strategies of Latin American sex workers in Spain', *Journal of Ethnic and Migration Studies*, 36(1): 47–65.

Philaretou, A. (2005). 'Eastern-European Sex workers in Greek-Cypriot cabarets', *Sexual Addiction and Compulsivity*, 12(1): 45–64.

Poli, R. and Thiévent, R. (2009). 'Agents de migrations: les intermédiaire sur le marché suisse des footballeurs et des danseuses de cabaret', *Revue économique et sociale*, 67(2): 107–12.

Psimmenos, I. (2000). 'The making of periphratic spaces: the case of Albanian undocumented female migrants in the sex industry in Athens', in F. Anthias and G. Lazaridis (eds) *Migration in Southern Europe: Women on the Move*. Oxford: Berg, 81–102.

Sardi, M. and Froidevaux, D. (2003). *'Le monde de la nuit': Milieu de la prostitution, affaires et 'crime organisé'*. Geneva: Erasm SA.

Spanger, M. (2002). 'Black prostitutes in Denmark', in S. Thorbek and B. Pattanaik (eds) *Transnational Prostitution: Changing Global Patterns*. London and New York: Zed Books, 121–36.

Thiévent, R. (2010). 'Les compétences circulatoires des danseuses de cabaret extra-européennes', in M. Liber et al. (eds) *Cachez ce travail que je ne saurais voir: Ethnographies du travail du sexe*.Lausanne: Antipodes, 137–54.

Thiévent, R. (forthcoming). 'Emotion, international division of labor and circulation: the case of cabaret dancers in Switzerland', in E. Heikkilä and B. Yeoh (eds) *International Marriages in the Time of Globalization*. New York: Nova Science Publishers.

Thorbek, S. (2002). 'Introduction – Prostitution in a global context: changing patterns', in S. Thorbek and B. Pattanaik (eds) *Transnational Prostitution: Changing Global Patterns*. London and New York: Zed Books, 1–9.

Truong, T.D. (1990). *Sex, Money and Morality: Prostitution and Tourism in South-East Asia*. London: Zed Books.

Truong, T.D. (1996). 'Gender, international migration and social reproduction: implications for theory, policy, research and networking', *Asian and Pacific Migration Journal*, 5(1): 27–52.

Tyner, J. (1996). 'Constructions of Filipina migrant entertainers', *Gender, Place and Culture*, 3(1): 77–93.

Van Blerk, L. (2008). 'Poverty, migration and sex work: youth transition in Ethiopia', *Area*, 40(2): 245–53.

Wonders, N. and Michalowski, R. (2001). 'Bodies, borders, and sex tourism in a globalised world: a tale of two cities – Amsterdam and Havana', *Social Problems*, 48(4): 545–71.

Yeoh, B. (2005). 'Transnational mobilitites and challenges', in L. Nelson and J. Seager (eds) *A Companion to Feminist Geography*. Oxford: Blackwell, 60–73.

PART IV
Sex Work:
Organizing, Resistance and Culture

Chapter 11

'If you shut up, they kill you':
Sex Worker Resistance in Argentina

Kate Hardy

Introduction

Sex work has long been subject to intense political struggles over its definition, practice and the language used to describe it (see for example Jeffreys 1997, Kesler 2002, Overall 1992, Pateman 1983, Pheterson 1996, Weitzer 2007). Yet within these debates sex workers' own political activity has largely been ignored, with the focus falling instead on discussion within the academy, between feminists' groups and in spaces of policy making. This is somewhat surprising considering that sex workers have been self-organizing and expressing themselves in the political arena in varying forms and with diverse political positions for over a hundred years. Ever since Polish sex workers protested about maltreatment and poor conditions in Costa Rica at the end of the nineteenth century (Hardy 2010), sex workers have engaged in lively political protest and contention, yet they have received relatively little attention for doing so.

Recently, however, there has been a renewed focus on sex worker organizing, as sex workers' movements have intensified, particularly over during the last 30 years (Jenness 1998, Kempadoo and Doezema 1998, Kempadoo 2002, Gall 2006 and 2007). In addition to the growing number and visibility of sex workers' organization, another important shift in sex workers' organizing is the move from their constitution as social movements to trade unions (Gall 2006), bringing sex workers into more institutionally recognized forms of political contention. Although most of the research on this has to date focused on Western organizations, and analyses have generally been pessimistic about the actual and potential gains of sex workers' organizations (see for example Mathieu 2003, Hubbard 1999, Gall 2006 and 2007), less attention has been paid to organizing in the global South where sex workers find themselves in profoundly different conditions to those in the West and global North (for a notable exception see Kempadoo and Doezema 1998).

This chapter explores a group of sex workers in Argentina who have made important headway in gaining power and making their voices heard across multiple institutions and spaces. It argues that in contrast to the pessimistic analyses of other scholars AMMAR, a union of sex workers in Argentina, represents a case in which sex worker organizing has been successful. In doing so, the piece asks

168   *New Sociologies of Sex Work*

why sex worker organizing may have been more successful in Argentina than elsewhere by examining the demographic make-up of the workers and activists, the conditions in which they live and work, the challenges they have faced and the strategies they have used to overcome seemingly insurmountable obstacles. It argues that the discourse of sex work as work has been particularly important for the union, but, importantly, that this has been grounded within a broader politics of social change. Additionally, it suggests that the cultural, historical and spatial specificity of particular places should be taken into account when assessing sex worker organizing, as the particular challenges and obstacles they contend with are grounded in and shaped by specific local contexts.

The chapter draws on research undertaken in 2007 and 2008 in Argentina with the sex workers' union, AMMAR (*la Asociación de Mujeres Meretrices de la Argentina* – The Argentine Female Sex Workers' Union), using a variety of methods including participant observation, interviews and a survey of almost three hundred questionnaires. It first offers a short history of AMMAR and the primary ideas, politics and ideologies on which it is founded. Next, it examines the challenges that AMMAR have faced, focusing first on obstacles that arise from the conditions in which sex workers work that are shared with a number of other groups of workers and second, on challenges relating to the specific nature of sex work. In light of these intense difficulties, the strategies that AMMAR has used to confront them are presented next, alongside some reflection on why they have been successful in Argentina. The chapter ends with some conclusions about how to understand and assess sex worker organizing.

AMMAR

AMMAR is the female sex workers union of Argentina. '*Meretrices*' has no direct translation into English and is an old fashioned word that translates closer to 'courtesan' than to sex worker ('*trabajadora sexual*'). However, AMMAR's discursive adoption of '*trabajo sexual*' (sex work) makes the translation a fair representation of their political position. The organization was founded in 1994 in response to constant police harassment of sex workers. They currently have between 1,500 and 2,000 members across the country in ten provincial branches, making it one of the largest movements of sex workers in the world, behind India. Membership is premised on three factors: that women work independently, that they work from their own free choice and that they are over 18 – the legal age of consent. Although the identities of AMMAR members are founded on 'free choice' in entering and working in the sex industry, AMMAR recognize that notions of choice and consent are extremely complex in the sex industry, as they are more broadly in all contexts in which people are forced to sell their labour. However, the notion of choice is used to separate women who select sex work as an economic strategy from victims of trafficking or endentured servitude and in order to assert labour rights rather than 'rescue' as their main political strategy.

AMMAR focus almost exclusively on street sex workers, in part because they believe that it is only street workers who are fully independent. In contrast, other workers who work indoors, in *casas* (houses), *privados* (flats), *whiskerias* and *boliches* (night clubs or bars) pay 50 per cent to owners and do not have control over hours of work and selection of clients. Although AMMAR's services frequently extend to women working in houses, flats and clubs, the organization often avoids direct involvement with women working in these conditions. This is firstly due to a moral rejection of the exploitation of labour, and particularly women's sexual labour, for the profit of others. However, it also relates to a more practical concern in that the involvement of organized crime in indoor sex work can make intervention in this sector extremely dangerous. It is claimed that networks of powerful individuals, including important members of the police and judiciary, are often involved in running indoor sex work. The seriousness of the potential consequences of interference with indoor work was demonstrated most poignantly in 2004, when Sandra Cabrera, Branch Secretary in the province of Santa Fé, was murdered by a bullet to the neck. Cabrera had been denouncing police brutality against sex workers and the involvement of powerful individuals in the prostitution of minors and sexual exploitation of women and children.

AMMAR members tend to work full time in sex work as their only form of income generation. Unlike in other contexts, where it has been claimed that sex work is a transient occupation, the majority of women had worked in sex work for over five years and almost 40 per cent had worked for more than ten years. Sex work also tended to be the only economic activity in which they were engaged, as only 17 per cent had other jobs, the largest proportion of whom were domestic servants. Their other jobs were made up of low skilled, low paid labour such as community work, ambulant sales and food preparation. Most cited lack of education and job opportunities as the reasons for their entry into sex work. Seventy-seven per cent of the women either had only primary school education or had completed no education at all. In a context of ongoing economic crisis in Argentina since the 1990s, there were few opportunities for remuneration for women without education. An additionally striking feature was the responsibilities the women shouldered towards children and other familial dependents. Survey findings showed that 40 per cent of respondents were living alone with their children, while only 17 per cent lived with both their partner and their children. Although living with a partner did not guarantee additional financial or economic support from that partner, it demonstrates that a large number of women were left in an extremely vulnerable economic situation, without the support of other wages.

As such, the need to perform unpaid childcare alongside generating income to support their families was a foundational reason for many of the women's decisions to enter sex work, either because the flexible hours meant they could look after their children or because the relatively higher rates of pay meant they could spend less time working and more on childcare.

Ideologies

Understanding the structural conditions and ideological context in which women interpret and understand their struggle is essential for understanding any social conflict (Stephens 2002). In the case of sex work this is particularly pertinent due to the intense ideological battle that has contextualized the politics of sex work (or 'prostitution'). AMMAR activists state that they are triply oppressed; as women in a patriarchal society, as members of the working class in an unjust and unequal capitalist world and as sex workers in a hypocritical society with a double morality in which men's and women's sexuality is differentially defined. As such, they analyse the roots of their oppression and social exclusion around a triple axis of gender, class and sexuality. With regard to the debates surrounding the question of understanding sex work as a labour strategy, they position themselves as 'women who without opportunities, chose to sustain our families by doing this work' (AMMAR website, www.ammar.org.ar). This emphasis on choice, but choice within structural limitations, is significant in bridging the polarized sex work/prostitution debate and introducing a more structural analysis of sex work, but one which allows for sex workers' agency. AMMAR also locate themselves firmly within the working class, stating that, 'we recognize ourselves as part of the working class because our work feeds our families'.

The discourse of work is important for the AMMAR's identity, strategies and alliances, but it was only a strategy at which they arrived after lengthy discussion between themselves and with activists from the *Central de Trabajadores Argentinos* (Argentine Workers' Centre) (CTA), the trade union confederation to which they belong (Hardy 2010). Above all, they adopted the language of work as a strategy for demanding the protection of the law and the rights enshrined in it, which protect all other workers and citizens. The assertion of parity with others meant that AMMAR had both the moral and material basis from which they were able to demand the equal application of the law and could access benefits that other workers are able to, such as pensions and social benefits, documentation, housing and healthcare. Due to the lack of recognition of sex work as work and also due to its stigmatized nature, sex workers are currently unable to access all of these through the normal avenues such as via the state and also trade unions.

Beyond these material implications, the discourse of sex work also had broader political relevance. In identifying as workers and as part of the working class, the women of AMMAR located themselves as part of a 'historic majority' of working people with a long history of struggle against marginalization and exploitation. This not only had symbolic relevance, but has also enabled them to ally themselves with others in the CTA, including teachers, state workers and the unemployed, as well as pensioners and neighbourhood groups. In doing so, they have linked their work and their struggle to all forms of exploitation, whether in the *maquiladora*, the *bordello* or on the street, but they argue that the answer to ending exploitation is not simply demanding an end to prostitution. Instead they assert the importance

Sex Worker Resistance in Argentina 171

of allowing, enabling and supporting the exploited to organize themselves, giving them the tools to follow their own path to self-organization.

AMMAR's primary objective is 'that one day there are no more women that exercise this work for necessity' (www.ammar.org.ar, 10 November 2008), but they add to this that, 'as we are not owners of the truth we leave open the discussion as to whether – in the future that we dream of – there will be women that all the same want to do this work' (www.ammar.org.ar, 10 November 2008). With this, they do not defend sex work as desirable work necessarily, but as something which should not be attacked and that may or may not exist in a fairer, more equal world. In arguing for this, they locate their struggle in a much broader political project, demanding greater opportunities and freedoms for women and for the poor and for a more equitable world. In doing so they argue that it is structural violence that is inherent to sex work: the violence of the absence of choice, and violence from the state, rather than a generalized violence against women inherent in the act of selling sex. It is often asserted that strategies around sex work must decide between unionization – on the one hand – and on struggling for its elimination on the other (Pritchard 2010). However, AMMAR's approach demonstrates that the unionization and self-organization of sex workers is not contrary to, but in fact works best when embedded in a wider struggle for the transformation of economic and social relations.

Challenges to Sex Work Organizing

Although AMMAR have successfully argued that sex work is work and have, in doing so, established a place for themselves within the CTA (Hardy 2010), they still face a number of challenges in organizing as workers. In order to understand the relevance of AMMAR's successes and the strategies they have developed to achieve them, it is necessary to contextualize these in light of the multiple challenges these women have faced in organizing.

Shared Challenges

Organizing any type of workers presents a number of significant challenges. However, as both a form of *bodywork* (Wolkowitz 2002) and also as a type of *informal labour* (Basu and Thomas 2008; Kapoor 2007), sex workers face a number of challenges to organizing that are not encountered by more traditionally organized sectors. First, bodywork, defined as work in which the primary site of labour is the body of another person, is labour intensive (only one body can be worked on at any time); the work is also therefore immobile. Sex workers who directly sell sex to a client must be in the same space as the client when the service is delivered. This often results in spatially dispersed working environments, making it hard to recognize and make contact with other workers. Secondly, the nature of such personal services means that there is no single shared employer to whom to direct demands and grievances. As many traditional trade union tactics have been based on the concept of multiple numbers of workers in a shared, concentrated workplace, with a mutual employer to whom to direct demands (Cobble 2007), this creates a number of difficulties for sex worker organization. Thirdly, the informality of sex work presents its own problems. Informal workers have proven elsewhere to be a similarly 'hard to organize' group. Craske (1999) argues that a major challenge posed is that employment in the informal sector undermines workers' potential for collective action and the development of a political subjectivity. Mitter (1994) elaborates further, arguing that this absence of collective identity is due to their invisibility and their geographical isolation. However, it is informal workers' lack of work contracts and their invisibility in official spaces and institutions of industrial relations that present the biggest challenges in asserting any claim and demands for improving working conditions. These often deny them the right to organize as workers, as well as blocking access to traditional avenues of collective bargaining and minimum labour standards frameworks (Goldman 2003).

Specific Challenges to Sex Worker Organizing

Many of the challenges in organizing sex workers are thus similar to efforts to organize all workers and particularly workers who have irregular employment relations, such as informal workers. However, there are also a number of factors specific to sex work, and particularly specific to street sex work, that present major barriers to union organizing. These revolve first around the structural and social conditions of sex workers' lives; second, in relation to stigma; and third, with regards to the resistance that sex workers face from various groups.

The vast majority of women in the study had very low levels of education. Only 23 per cent had completed secondary education and 11 per cent had not completed any sort of education at all, including at primary level. The low educational level of most of the women not only disadvantaged them in the labour market but also created problems for organizing, which can often necessitate written forms of communication, including emails, leaflets, official documentation and letter writing to officials and state actors.

In addition to lack of education, the women were also commonly lone heads of households with sole responsibility for the provision of childcare, domestic labour and income. Women tended to have between one and six children and they often supported other dependents, either older relatives or young children who had been sent to live with them. These intense pressures on women's time and energy often confounded their ability to participate in union activities, even when they had the will to do so. Lack of childcare was one of the most widely cited reasons for their inability to participate more to a greater degree in the organization. Twenty-three per cent of women said that they would be more likely to participate in the organization if they had someone to take care of their children. Thirty-seven per cent stated that they would be encouraged to participate if they had more time, reflecting the multiple strains on women's time.

Lack of education, low income and multiple pressures on women's time often led to high levels of ill-health. Other than by AMMAR, many women had never been offered information about safe sex and sexual health more generally. Accessing healthcare was also extremely complex for many women. Due to the lack of recognition of sex work as sex work, women could not access union healthcare and thus had to navigate the chronically under-funded public healthcare system. Their hours of work also clashed with the timings of hospital appointments, meaning that women had to make difficult decisions about taking their children with them to seek medical attention and missing a day of work and therefore income. Additionally, many women faced serious discrimination at the hands of health professionals. An activist in Córdoba explained that these experiences of discrimination and shame frequently meant that women self-selected out from seeking medical care:

> We've been saying to [the workers] that they will be attended to properly, that they aren't going to be discriminated against, that they're not going to treat them as if they were a dog … because that's what they were scared of, you see? [Scared that] they would say "I work on the street" [and they'd say] "ahh don't touch me".

Poor health reduced women's capacity to participate in and contribute regularly to the organization, and their experiences in the health system often reinforced and multiplied their sense of exclusion.

Alongside these structural conditions, it is hard to underestimate the effects of stigma on sex workers' ability to organize. Stigma presented myriad challenges to forming and participating in the trade union. Many types of bodywork, such as care for the elderly or for children, are devalued and undermined (Dyer et al. 2008), yet sex work is arguably the most highly stigmatized form of bodywork. Sex workers are often denoted as illegitimate subjects, and therefore they do not have recourse to the full rights of citizenship. In Argentina, this is reflected nowhere more strongly than in the apathy of the police in responding to violence against sex workers and the response of one particular provincial governor, who during an ongoing series of murders of sex workers, stated that this was simply an 'occupational hazard' of sex work. Such lack of recognition by the state and other authorities, impacts both on sex workers' ability to act as political actors in formal institutional spaces, but also on sex workers' self-esteem and confidence in raising their voices to make their demands heard.

Additionally, stigma has a significant impact on sex workers' sense of self. Low self-esteem was the most significant indicator of this. Many women felt as if they did not have the legitimacy to speak and that even if they did, they would not be listened to. Furthermore, many women faced severe difficulty in 'coming out' as sex workers, as it often resulted in ostracization and possibly violence from friends, families and the communities in which they lived. This profoundly complicated their ability to act in the public sphere, with similarly significant

174 *New Sociologies of Sex Work*

consequences for the possibility of building a movement and gaining recognition. As working through the media is of central importance to most contemporary struggles, it was necessary for the women to find a manner in which they were able to communicate with the media without revealing their identities.

The difficulty involved in 'coming out' or appearing in the media therefore complicated their ability to be involved in an organization in which it was necessary to identify as a sex worker. This often led to further marginalization and high personal costs for participating in the organization:

> The first marches we did, we went out with masks on so that no-one would recognize us, until one good day we realised that this didn't make sense. If no-one recognized us, what on earth were we going on marches for? So we said "no, we have to take them off and take responsibility for who we are, for what we do" and one day, we took them off. We were front page of Clarin [Argentina's biggest selling newspaper]. In 1997 I took off the mask for the first time and Clarin turned up! The most important newspaper in the country! And they took a photo of us and we were on the front page. And my family did not talk to me for two years. My sisters said that I was the shame of the family, but it didn't matter. It was worth it. (Reynaga, General Secretary, AMMAR)

Third, the quasi-legal nature of sex work and the accompanying behaviour of the police in such conditions presented serious challenges to organizing. Sex work is not constitutionally illegal, but was governed by provincial codes, which punish 'scandalous behaviour'. These are frequently exploited by the police who elicit bribes, sexual favours and detain women arbitrarily. Many women reported being arrested while taking their children to school or eating in restaurants. Miranda, a worker in her sixties, reflected that:

> They've taken me for nothing before. I was sitting outside a mattress shop with another woman on the corner, I don't know if the owner called, or what but ... they came took me away. I was just sitting there talking. They say that you're causing a scandal. What a lie! How can I, an old woman, cause a scandal? With what?

In Córdoba alone, in the three years between 2004 and 2007, 557 women were arrested under the *Codigo de Faltas*, the local provincial code. Detention in torrid conditions increases health problems and reduces women's income, both by removing their ability to work while they are detained and in order to pay fines back once they are released. All of the women had stories of police brutality and harassment. Maria, a Dominican woman who did not participate in the union, told of a time in which she went to her corner of work:

> there was a policeman who was always hassling me. He pushed me. He pushed
> me and he knew that I was going to be hit by the passing buses, but he didn't
> care, he threw me out [into the road] anyway.

Activists have also faced increased harassment when they have become active in AMMAR. In Jujuy, activists have been targeted for arrest simply because of their activism. Jorgelina Sosa, Deputy Secretary of AMMAR, emphasized that 'there can be ten girls standing there on the corner, but they only take those who are involved in activism'. Sandra Cabrera's murder is perhaps the most striking example of police corruption, harassment and violence against sex workers. To cover up Cabrera's death, police reported that the murder had been a 'crime of passion' by a former lover. In response, AMMAR released a short film documenting the lack of justice and impunity surrounding her death. They entitled the film '*Si te callas, te matan*' (if you shut up, they kill you). Although Cabrera had been silenced because she would not shut up, the film implored the women to carry on their struggle, emphasizing that although militancy in AMMAR could cost them their lives, it was much more dangerous to keep quiet.

Alongside violent resistance and brutality from the police, AMMAR have also encountered resistance from other groups. Some feminist groups have been extremely resistant to the idea of sex worker self-organization and in the early years of their formation AMMAR were refused access to the famous women's *encuentros*, yearly meetings in which women's groups and organizations from all over Argentina meet together for a week to talk, protest and debate. In addition, the Evangelical and Catholic Churches have often resisted AMMAR's right to self-organize. For example, when the Entre-Ríos provincial legislature retracted Article 45 of Provincial Law 3815 of the *Código Contravencionales*, which had penalized women working in sex work, the local Evangelical Church resisted this move, claiming that it would sanctify sin.

Strategizing Inside AMMAR

The multitude of challenges faced by sex worker activists confound many orthodox forms of labour organizing, and as such, the mobilization of sex workers demanded strategic and tactical innovation and the creation of new approaches. AMMAR have responded to this in a number of important ways and have developed multiple strategies for doing so. These strategies have been formulated around legislative change, recognition, resubjectification and redistribution.

In 1994, when AMMAR was first being formed, their first struggle sought legislative change in order to challenge and alter the legal framework within which sex work was regulated in Argentina, their first aim was to overturn the *Edictos Policiales* (Police Edicts), which enabled police in the city to detain women in the metropolitan city of Buenos Aires. By allying with other groups, such as the *Madres de la Plaza de Mayo*, the group of mothers who fought against the dictatorship to demand the return of their children who were disappeared during the military *junta*, in 1998, AMMAR won the repeal of the *Edictos*. Since that date, no woman in Buenos Aires has been detained for practicing sex work. Additionally, local codes were repealed in the provinces of Entre Ríos and Santa Fé in 2003 and 2010, respectively, meaning that women are now able to practice sex work freely in those areas without constant fear of police intervention and harassment.

The repeal of these laws should not, however, be understood simply as a form of strategic legalism. Indeed, their repeal shifted the legal context in which women worked, but more importantly, it transformed sex workers' work in more material ways by establishing safer and more just conditions for women. By removing the threat of arrest and detention that women had previously faced, this also reduced the risk presented by the detrimental economic and health effects of incarceration and forced unprotected sex with police officers. Although such change has been geographically uneven and limited to two provinces and one metropolitan area, this is significant, particularly when compared to the achievements of other sex workers movements. Decriminalization has been at the heart of many movements, yet alongside New Zealand, Argentina is one of the few other places in which this has been achieved and in both cases it would not have been achieved without strong sex worker organization.

In addition to seeking redress from the state in terms of formal law change, AMMAR has also sought recognition from the state, both as an organization and as individual workers. The discourse of sex *work* has been profoundly important for achieving these gains. AMMAR has been able to institutionalize itself as a leading voice in state policy making. It is now hard to imagine decisions being made on sex work, or indeed HIV/AIDS more generally, without reference or consultation with AMMAR. AMMAR have also received more formal recognition in the form of *Personería Juridica*, state recognition as a not-for-profit organization. Perhaps more importantly, the language of sex work has also been essential for challenging the intense stigma that has tended to undermine women's propensity to get involved in collective practices, including political action. AMMAR have been extraordinarily successful in challenging feelings of stigma amongst sex workers. When questioned about the importance of AMMAR, rather than referencing material advantages such as healthcare, women repeatedly returned to themes of self-esteem, recognition and pride. In Rio Negro, in the South of Argentina, Maria said that:

> Now, the rest of society respects us and values us as women and as mothers.
> Never again as *"putas de la calle"* (street whores).

Similarly, Isabel stated that it was not only about how they were treated, but also in shifts in ways that they had begun to imagine and relate to themselves:

> AMMAR is important because it teaches us to look after ourselves and to be better every day, to value ourselves more as people and not to let them treat us as prostitutes, because we are sex workers.

As Isabel implies, much of the increased self-esteem experienced by the women has been drawn from the shift from the stigmatized identity of 'prostitute' to a more respected shared identity of 'worker'. Identities formulated around themselves as sex workers rather than as 'prostitutes' has a number of important connotations. Firstly, it recognizes the economic element of activity and the fact that many of the women worked in sex work in order to support families, just – as they emphasized – like all other workers. Secondly, it allowed the women to locate in a broader historical community, that of the working class.

The extent to which AMMAR have been successful in shifting these identifications amongst the women was reflected strongly in survey data. When asked how they identified, 85 per cent identify as sex workers, while 13 per cent identified as 'women in the situation of prostitution'. The creation of this political subjectivity based on work identities was necessary for sex workers to be able to enact social change by reinvigorating their sense of self. It is hard to overestimate the importance of this in making sex workers confident and strong enough to act in their own interests and speak on their own behalf. These new subjectivities, which were founded on their identities as workers, thus helped to build the movement by generating a body of individuals who feel legitimated to demand their rights. Mathieu (2003: 48) finalizes her analysis of sex workers' (or 'prostitutes') organizations by stating that, 'as long as prostitutes' relation to their condition remains ambivalent, social movements fighting for the recognition of prostitutes' rights will face huge difficulties to mobilize them, and will remain marginal'. It is clear from the response of these women, that in the cities in which AMMAR works, this ambivalence has been transformed by offering an alternative identity to sex workers.

Beyond recognizing and transforming sex workers' subjectivities, AMMAR also sought to redistribute public goods to sex workers in order to improve their standard of living. In order to achieve this, rather than focusing on universal policies which would enshrine access to state resources for sex workers, AMMAR branches have tended to focus on establishing accords and deals with individual state actors. In terms of health services, activists have established an agreement with the Rawson Hospital in centre of Córdoba, so that sex workers can access appointments to be tested for Sexually Transmitted Infections (STIs) and to receive non-judgemental medical treatment for other conditions. The Sandra Cabrera Health Centre, which was established due to collaboration between AMMAR activists and the municipal government of La Plata, has ensured that sex workers and their children can be treated for any medical conditions. Additionally, although AMMAR have generally shied away from claiming social benefits, such as welfare payments, they have been successful in enabling some women to access income support. In Córdoba, the CENPA-AMMAR primary school opened in

178   *New Sociologies of Sex Work*

2003. It offers primary education to sex workers and their children, as well as to other women from the communities in which they live.

All of these strategies have enabled sex workers to better access public services and public goods, significantly improving not only their physical well-being, health and standard of living but also challenging their previous alienation and exclusion from such spaces. Yet these processes have necessitated ongoing labour from AMMAR activists in order to establish and maintain arrangements with individuals and organizations and they remain decidedly unstable as they continue to depend on the goodwill of particular state and government figures.

Why Success in Argentina?

Although AMMAR still have a long way to go to achieving full civil, human and labour rights and social inclusion for sex workers, I argue that Argentina has been a success story in sex worker organizing and suggest that specific conditions have engendered such success. The first reason relates to the political history and landscape of Argentina. There is a strong tradition of trade union affiliation in the country, due in part to the institutionalization of organized labour under Juan Peron in the 1940s (James 1988, Levitsky 2003). Due to this history, the category of 'worker' carries valuable symbolic weight in Argentina's social landscape (Sitrin 2006). As such, it is an identity to which people feel more compelled to align and it has more symbolic power than in other places and contexts.

The second reason relates to the demographic characteristics of AMMAR's membership and representatives. AMMAR has achieved a level of legitimacy – both amongst its members, within the sex worker community and on the wider political scene – that has not been possible elsewhere. Its activists are seen as 'legitimate voices' in speaking about the street working sector of the sex industry in multiple spaces from the National Board on HIV/AIDS to legislative debates on legal change. This has not been achieved in many places, including places in the West, where sex worker activists may have access to higher levels of education and larger pools of resources, yet have been unable to develop the recognition that AMMAR has established. I suggest that this is due to the fact that both activists and non-participants were characterized by the same demographic characteristics. The shared class positions and low levels of education counter the criticisms of critics who have charged other sex workers organizations elsewhere of being constituted by 'white, middle-class and college-educated happy hookers' (Bernstein 1999). It is argued that this disqualifies them from representing the views of the entire sex industry, as they are seen to be the most empowered, disguising the voices and opinions of the more vulnerable. Although these accusations were drawn from analyses of Western movements and mainly those emanating from the United States, they have been used to argue that sex workers' movements generally have not represented the voices of the most powerless or most marginalized. This is patently not true in the case of AMMAR. Additionally AMMAR has only focused on one sector of the sex industry: female street sex work. By focusing almost exclusively on street work, they have focused on the area in which they have worked themselves. This has meant that they are more representative of the women they represent and having worked in the same working conditions, understand the reality, the complications and the experience.

Conclusion

In contrast to claims that sex worker organizing has tended to be unsuccessful or limited, this chapter has shown that through a multiplicity of strategies AMMAR have been successful in improving working and living conditions for sex workers. It demonstrates that the specific nature of sex work, its labour process and relations, necessitates innovative and complex approaches to improving sex workers' lives on an immediate and practical basis, as well as struggling for broader social change. It is only by paying closer attention to the specific challenges faced by sex workers in their particular local context that it is possible to judge their success, or otherwise. The labour relations of sex work also differ across the sex industry, between and within places. As such, sex worker organizations may work best when they focus on one particular sector or set of labour relations within the industry and are lead by sex workers who have direct experience of those sectors. Such an approach offers activists an opportunity to connect with workers with whom they have shared experiences and to gain greater legitimacy in speaking and representing the sector with whom their conditions most align.

References

Basu, R. and Thomas, M.D. (2008). 'Exploring women's daily lives and participation in the informal labour market in Mumbai, India', *Gender and Development*, 17(2): 231–42.

Cobble, D.S. (2007). *The Sex of Class: Women Transforming American Labor*. Cornell: ILR Press.

Craske, N. (1999). *Women and Politics in Latin America*. New Brunswick: Rutgers University Press.

Dyer, S., McDowell, L. and Batnitzky, A. (2008). 'Emotional labour/body work: The caring labours of migrants in the UK's National Health Service', *Geoforum*, 39: 2030–8.

Gall, G. (2006). *Sex Worker Union Organizing: An International Study*. Basingstoke: Palgrave.

Gall, G. (2007). 'Sex Worker Unionisation: an exploratory study of emerging collective organisation', *Industrial Relations Journal*, 38(1): 70–88.

Goldman, T. (2003). *Organizing in South Africa's Informal Economy: An Overview of Four Sectoral Case Studies*. Working Paper 60. Series on Representation and Organization Building. ILO.

Hardy, K. (2010). 'Incorporating Sex Workers into the Argentine Labor Movement', *International Labor and Working-Class History*, 77(1): 89–108.

Hubbard, P. (1999). *Sex and the City: Geographies of Prostitution in the Urban West*. Aldershot: Ashgate Publishing.

Jeffreys, S. (1997). *The Idea of Prostitution*. Melbourne: Spinifex Pres.

Jenness, V. (1998). *Making it Work: The Prostitutes' Rights Movement in Perspective*. New York: Aldine de Gruyter.

Kapoor, A. (2007). 'The SEWA way: Shaping another future for informal labour', *Futures*, 39: 554–68.

Kempadoo, K. (2002). 'Globalizing Sex Workers' Rights', in N. Holmstrom (ed.) *The Socialist-Feminist Project: A Contemporary Reader in Theory and Politics*, 211–13. New York: Monthly Review Press.

Kempadoo, K., and Doezema, J. (eds) (1998). *Global Sex Workers: Rights, Resistance, and Redefinition*. London and New York: Routledge.

Kesler, K. (2002). 'Is a feminist stance in favour of prostitution possible: an exploration of current trend', *Sexualities* 5(2): 219–35.

Mathieu, L. (2003). 'The Emergence and Uncertain Outcomes of Prostitutes' Social Movements', *The European Journal of Women's Studies*, 10(1): 29–50.

Mitter, S. (1994). 'A comparative survey', in M.H. Martens and S. Mitter (eds) *Women in Trade Unions: Organising the Unorganised*. Geneva: ILO, 3–14.

Overall, C. (1992). 'What's wrong with prostitution? Evaluating sex work', *Signs*, 17: 705–24.

Pateman, C. (1983). 'Defending prostitution: charges against Ericsson', *Ethics*, 93(3): 561–5.

Pheterson, G. (1996). *The Prostitution Prism*. Amsterdam: Amsterdam University Press.

Pritchard, J. (2010). 'The Sex Work Debate', *International Socialism Journal*, 125: 81–102.

Stephens, L. (2002). 'Women in Mexico's Popular Movements: Survivial Strategies Against Ecological and Economic Impoverishment', in K. Abbassi and S.L. Lutjens (eds) *Rereading Women in Latin America and the Caribbean: The Political Economy of Gender*. Lanham: Rowman and Littlefield. 91–111.

Weitzer, R. (2007). 'Prostitution as a form of work', *Sociology Compass* 1(1): 143–55.

Wolkowitz, C. (2002). 'The social relations of bodywork', *Work, Employment & Society*, 16(3): 497–510.

Chapter 12

'Just get pissed and enjoy yourself':
Understanding Lap-dancing as 'Anti-work'

Rachela Colosi

... I was standing by the DJ booth with Danny (a barman) watching the other dancers work the floor. It was a Saturday night and approaching midnight. On this particular evening I had pushed the 'researcher' part of me to the back of my mind and been seduced by the 'dancer' in me. I decided to have a few drinks (or at least, looking back, perhaps a few too many). Danny and I were drinking bottles of Corona, cautiously, as Gerard (manager) would not have been happy seeing one of the dancer's glugging lager from a bottle! Another dancer, Davina, had been instrumental in my slip into 'dancer mode', and in my pursuit of inebriation which inevitably followed. She had been encouraging me all night, insisting: 'just get pissed and enjoy yourself; you only live once!' How could I refuse; it is perhaps difficult to explain unless you are in the presence of other dancers in a lap-dancing club environment. Davina was always having fun at work, laughing with the girls, chatting to the customers and getting drunk. For her like many of the other girls, coming to work was not about 'working' ridiculously hard, it was about so much more...[1] (Field Diary: June 2004)

Introduction

Lap-dancing clubs are part of a global industry. 'Gentlemen's clubs', as they are increasingly known, are becoming a central feature of the night-time economy across much of the United Kingdom (hereafter, UK) (Chatterton and Hollands 2003), although there has been some disagreement about the numbers of clubs currently in the UK.[2] The lap-dancing industry was estimated, in part due to the rapid expansion of chains such as 'Spearmint Rhino' and 'For Your Eyes Only', to be worth in the region of £300 million in the early 2000s (Jones et al. 2003). However, this industry is still in its infancy in the UK, as the first club of its kind

---

1   All observational and interview data presented in this chapter was recorded between November 2003 and February 2006. Pseudonyms have been used to protect the identities of those involved.

2   Claims made by groups such as 'Object' and the 'Fawcett Society' suggest there are in the region of 300 lap-dancing clubs in the UK. This however, is disputed by the 'Lap-dancing Association' who argue the figures are much lower.

did not open until the mid 1990s (Jones et al. 2003), while the industry in United States (US) and Canada evolved in the 1980s (Egan 2006a).

Despite the fact that these venues are increasingly viable places of employment within the night-time leisure economy, lap-dancing is still very much stigmatized (Colosi 2010b forthcoming). It is acknowledged as risqué (Hanna 2003) and 'deviant' (Carey et al. 1974, Forsythe and Deshotels 1998a) and continues to be morally judged (Scott 1996).Therefore this occupation is seen as distinct from many other modes of work. General definitions of 'work' are diverse and do not necessarily refer to paid employment. However, for the purpose of this chapter, I draw on Grint's (2005: 10) definition of work as the opposite of leisure and 'something we have to do, something we may prefer not to do and something we tend to get paid for'. 'Leisure', like work, despite having various definitions (Furnam 1990), is defined here as the experience, enjoyment and personal autonomy which can be experienced in any situation (Shaw 1985). In this sense, the concept of leisure focuses on the 'fun' dancers engage in whilst at work. Having fun in the work place is often discussed in relation to the use of humour (see Linstead 1985, Taylor and Bain 2003, Sanders 2004). However, the fun engaged with in the lap-dancing club often goes beyond the use of humour and involves leisure activities that might be associated with a night out, including drinking alcohol and taking drugs making it quite distinctive (see Colosi 2010b forthcoming). This is not to suggest that those in more mainstream work places such as office environments, for example, never consume alcohol or drugs in the work-place to experience pleasure. However, it is perhaps more unusual in these settings and therefore unlikely to become part of the workers' communal rituals, as can be seen in the lap-dancing club. Such patterns of behaviour are what additionally identify lap-dancing as a distinct mode of work.

Furthermore lap-dancing can be described as a form 'anti-work'. 'Anti-work', as well as being tied with the ritualistic pursuit of fun, is also described as 'anti' on the basis that dancers frequently make attempts to resist management and the work rules they are given. Having fun is not the only reason why dancers continue to dance, but it plays an important role in their resistance as workers. This chapter will explore how having fun takes priority in the lap-dancing club, fuelling motivation, helping build social relationships, improving dancer status, and also how it plays an important role in dancer resistance, helping to shape lap-dancing as a form of 'anti-work'.

Dancing, Working and Resisting

Erotic dance, thus far, has attracted significant attention from academics and practitioners in the US and Canada where the industry is more prolific. Conversely there has been very little material produced about European and UK lap-dancing markets (for exceptions see Bott 2006, and Bindel 2004). The strip club literature produced in the US and Canada, which first emerged in the late 1960s,

Understanding Lap-dancing as 'Anti-work' 183

has traditionally explored broad areas such as dancer motivation, exploitation/ empowerment, the stigma associated with erotic dance, and dancer-customer interactions. Emerging from these wider themes, research has focused on specific areas concerned with the impact of dancing on the dancers' lives (Wesely 2002, Deshotels and Forsythe 2005, Barton 2006); dancer identities (Rambo-Ronai 1992, Reid et al. 1994, Wesely 2003); 'counterfeit intimacy' (Boles and Garbin 1974b, Enck and Preston 1988, Pasko 2002); dancer interaction strategies (Rambo-Ronai and Ellis 1989, Pasko 2002); customer and dancer relations (Frank 2002, Egan 2006a); working conditions (Holsopple 1998, Maticka-Tyndale et al. 1999 and 2000, Lewis et al. 2005); the emotional labour of dancing (Frank 1998, Barton 2007); gender-power relations (Wood 2000, Wesely 2002, Murphy 2003, Bott 2006); customer and dancer typologies[3] (Brewster 2003, Enck and Preston 1988, Ericson and Tewksbury 2000, Montemurro et al. 2003) and stigma management strategies (Thompson and Harred 1992 and 2003, Bradley 2007).

Within these themes there has been some acknowledgement of the pleasurable experiences women derive from lap-dancing (Bell et al. 1998, Egan 2006a). Although these pleasurable experiences are often related to performance, there is little emphasis placed on the pleasures derived from some of the dominant processes of socialization between dancers through engaging with social rituals, as discussed in this chapter. Discussions which relate to the pleasures gained from dancing also emphasize how dancers are able to negotiate some control in their workplace (see Wood 2000, Pasko 2002, Spivey 2005), in particular through creating their own informal codes of conduct (see Price 2000). It is argued, for instance, that dancers are able to influence their regulation through a process of informal training. Workers teach one another how to dance whilst on-the-job and in doing so make new dancers familiar with the special code of ethics by which they work (Price 2000). Egan (2006b) develops discussions around resistance further and contends that dancers use music to resist management and customers. Egan argues that through music selection during stage performances dancers enact a 'lyrical form of protest in their jobs' (2006b: 201). She argues that managers are disturbed by some of the messages produced by certain types of rap music used, which attacks white, middle-class culture (Egan 2006b). Meanwhile, Spivey (2005) contends that workers utilize front and backstage resistance strategies involving individual and collective techniques mainly directed at customers. These techniques vary but the common objective is to distance the dancer from the customer and de-sexualize her body.

Workplace resistance can never be absolute, but 'employees will constantly find ways of evading and subverting managerial organization and direction at work' (Ackroyd and Thompson 1999: 47; see also Hodson 1995, Martinez Lucio and Stewart 1997, Mulholland 2004, Roscigno et al. 2004). In other workplaces beyond lap dancing, worker resistance has been shown to take the form of gossip;

---

3   This only gives examples of the most common sub-themes to emerge from the general body of literature.

184 *New Sociologies of Sex Work*

confrontation; resignation; toleration; theft; sabotage; noncooperation; collective action; formal complaints; use of law and violence (Tucker 1993). The use of humour, particularly satire and teasing directed at managers and team leaders is also argued to play an important role (see Collinson 1988, Linstead 1985, Rodrigues and Collinson 1995, Taylor and Bain 2003). According to Taylor and Bain 'taking the piss' (2003: 1496) for example, involved workers sometimes viciously gossiping about team leaders and making their behaviour the topic of a joke. Furthermore, Holmes and Marra (2002) suggest that humour helps shape workplace culture not only by resisting management, but also in developing solidarity between workers. This occurs when worker 'alliances develop organically when workers identify with one another, and acting together they collude, collaborate and co-operate over challenges to management practice' (Mullholland 2004: 710).

In what follows I argue that lap-dancing is a form of 'anti-work' in which dancers prioritize having fun. Firstly I will argue that the pursuit of fun is central to dancer motivation, both in terms of their initial entry and continued participation as lap-dancers. Secondly, the main ways in which fun is practiced through engagement in social rituals will also be explored. Thirdly, the social rituals through which fun is practiced is argued to represent a form of anti-work. Finally, I will argue that dancers maintain collective forms of resistance and self-regulation by ensuring all dancers adhere to an ethos of fun and anti-work.

Research Background

This chapter is based on an ethnographic study about the relationships between lap-dancers and the occupational culture with which they engaged in a UK chain-operated lap-dancing club named as 'Starlets'. Data was generated through extensive participant observation over approximately a two year period,[4] along with a small number of unstructured interviews conducted with lap-dancers. The fieldwork was carried out whilst I worked as a lap-dancer and was therefore actively engaged as a member of the 'culture' being observed. Prior to initiating this study I had been a lap-dancer in Starlets for almost two years. Further discussion of the complexities of my positionality can be found elsewhere (Colosi 2010b forthcoming).

Starlets

Starlets was a medium-sized lap-dancing club situated on the fringe of a busy northern city centre. It was regulated and had a similar physical appearance to other UK-based chain-operated lap-dancing clubs (see Colosi 2010b forthcoming). The club had two floors on which the dancers interacted with customers, offered

---

4   Observations were predominantly conducted inside 'Starlets', although a number of observations were made outside of this setting whilst both socializing and living with dancers.

private dances and performed stage shows. Other significant areas of the club included the dancers' changing room and managers' office. As is usual in most clubs there was a décor which aimed to bring about an atmosphere of sensuality. The use of colours such as rich crimsons and gold set off by soft lighting helped to create what has been described as a landscape of desire (Liepe-Levinson 2002). At the time of this ethnography the club operated a strict 'topless only' policy, which was a limit placed upon the extent of nakedness by the local authority licensing board[5] who issued the establishment's license.[6] The club was operated by two main (male) managers, and, as well as dancers other occupational roles in Starlets included security staff, waitresses, bar staff, DJs, receptionists and hosts.[7] The number of dancers working at this venue per night was variable, and depended upon factors such as day of the week and time of year, but could be as few as 10 and as many as 35 dancers. Many of the dancers had worked in other lap-dancing clubs or as agency strippers[8] prior to working in Starlets. Others had no or minimal experience of the stripping industry. Dancers were expected to perform regular stage shows and generated their earnings from lap-dances (private dances) and sit-downs.[9] Each dancer paid commission (also known as a 'house fee') to the club managers to conduct business on the premises. The amount of commission paid to the club varied and frequently changed over the time fieldwork was conducted, but on average dancers paid between £40 and £80 per shift.

For Love of Fun, Not Just Money

As well as citing money as an important motivational factor, early 'motivation' literature tended to favour pathological explanations for women's involvement in stripping, signifying it as a result of their 'deviancy' (see for example Skipper and McCaghy 1970, Boles and Garbin 1974a, Carey et al. 1974). What has remained consistent is the contention that women's involvement in stripping is predominantly financially motivated (see for example Forsythe and Deshotels 1998a, Barton 2006). With the exception of Forsythe and Deshotels (1998a), this explanation seems to have been taken at face value by most researchers who are

---

5   This has since changed with dancers based at 'Starlets' now able to offer customers both topless and fully nude private dances.

6   In England and Wales lap-dancing clubs, as of April 2010, were re-licensed as 'Sexual Entertainment Establishments'. This is outlined in the Policing and Crime Act 2009. Prior to this lap-dancing club were regulated under the Licensing Act 2003.

7   Hosts were employed to show customers to seats as they entered the club.

8   This refers to women who find work through a stripping agency and are hired out as strippers to perform nude and semi nude stage shows in pubs, night clubs and social clubs. Furthermore, these workers may also be hired as 'strip-o-grams' for private parties.

9   This refers to when a customer pays for the company of a dancer for 30 minutes or more; customers would be charged at an hourly rate.

186 New Sociologies of Sex Work

unaware, or do not acknowledge the ways in which this account is at odds with the actual actions and behaviour of these women in the lap-dancing club environment, but also by the fact that these workers sometimes offer more than one reason for lap-dancing (see Colosi 2010b forthcoming). Indeed, there is a wider literature on work motivation which stresses that economic considerations are often wrongly assumed to be paramount in determining people's work choices, and that moral beliefs or the pursuit of pleasure are often more important considerations (Duncan and Edwards 1999, Bradley et al. 2000, Dunn 2010a and 2010b forthcoming).

Forsythe and Deshotels (1998a) argue that choosing to be a dancer and continuing to work in the stripping industry is perhaps more complex than it would first appear, without clearly offering an alternative set of explanations and yet they still conclude that money is a dominant motivation. I argue here that although, as established by earlier studies, there was an indication that the financial reward of dancing was important in explaining dancers' entry and continued participation in this job, many of the women who participated in this ethnography appeared to be equally, if not more, motivated by the excitement and fun associated with stripping than the financial reward. I have argued elsewhere that entry routes into dancing and continued participation are complex, as dancer motivation is tied with practical reasons, such as making money, but simultaneously connected with more emotionally driven reasons such as experiencing pleasure through having fun (see Colosi 2010b forthcoming).

It is perhaps this complexity that sometimes made it difficult for dancers to articulate their own motivation for dancing. As Karen, a dancer, stated 'I don't think it's straightforward, as in "I need money, I need a job". It's hard to put your finger on'. Furthermore, although Ruby, a dancer, stated that the money was her motivation for lap-dancing, on a number of separate occasions she said that 'the money isn't enough to keep me here'. Despite the emotional as well as physical labour lap-dancing involves (Barton 2007) workers stressed the intense pleasure they gained both from dancing and from social interaction with the other dancers. Nelly summed up how working at Starlets could be positively experienced: 'Like being on a night out but getting fuck loads of money'.

Forsythe and Deshotels (1998a) suggest that at times erotic dancers appeared to be more concerned by the social relationships they shared with other dancers than the 'work' they were expected to engage with. For instance, it is pointed out that on leaving this job, dancers 'reported that they missed the membership groups and participating in the subculture of dancers. Many dancers attempt to leave the occupation only to return after a short hiatus' (Forsythe and Deshotels 1998a: 90). Forsythe and Deshotels (1998a) do not elaborate much further. However, this was corroborated in my own research as membership and camaraderie between the dancers working in Starlets also appeared to draw women back after a period of short retirement (see Colosi 2010b forthcoming).

The spirit of 'anti-work', in having 'fun', which was observed amongst many of the dancers at Starlets is again further suggested by dancer Karen who explained to me 'you're going to work, having a laugh, having a good time, I'm not arsed if

I don't make any money ... just having a laugh, thinking I may as well just have a laugh'. It is important not to take Karen's statement completely at face value, after all, she did want to make money and it is doubtful she would have worked for free. However, what Karen was perhaps trying to stress is that having fun is an important part of her job that keeps her there. Importantly, the money earned in the lap-dancing club is not just about making enough to ensure survival; it also enables dancers to engage with a particular lifestyle and with the various social rituals that were witnessed in Starlets.

Understanding Fun Through Social Rituals

To further understand the anti-work ethos and the type of fun had in Starlets, it is necessary to make sense of the 'social rituals' engaged in by the dancers. Dancers were intensely socialized into understanding the tacit rules of the club through their regular and active engagement with social rituals. Such rituals included drinking alcohol and sometimes taking recreational drugs (see also Boles and Garbin 1974b, Maticka-Tyndale et al. 2000, Montemurro 2001, Barton 2006, Bott 2006). At the beginning of a shift at Starlets, it was common for dancers to sit in groups in the main work areas, talking and drinking alcohol. Similarly, dancers who used drugs would enter the toilet cubicle at intervals during a shift, sometimes in groups of twos or threes, to take cocaine, ecstasy or amphetamine. The following field diary extract highlights a set of behaviours regularly observed amongst dancers on the main work floor:

> ...The doors of the club were about to open and most of the dancers were already on the main floor waiting for their vodka cranberries or white wine to start the night with. Every night dancers took advantage of the 'two drinks for a fiver' offer. Once served it was an opportunity, before customers arrived, for the dancers to sit around with one another and gossip about various events inside and outside the club...

This was a common scene and it was the regularity and the meaning behind these social activities that made them ritualistic. It was necessary to engage in these social rituals in order to be popular and respected in the lap-dancing club environment, something which is important for these workers. Acceptance and respect of other dancers were brought about by the dancers' tolerance of, and active engagement in, these social rituals. This helped improve relations between workers and ensured they were in synchronicity with the dominant anti-work ethic.

In Starlets there was a clear hierarchy of dancers which was produced, controlled and maintained by the dancers, not by management. This represented the workers' very own unofficial career structure. Other dancer hierarchies have been implicit in discussions of lap-dancers elsewhere (Price 2000, Barton 2006). The one identified in Starlets is more comparable to the subculture of taxi-dancers identified by Cressey (1932) in which dancers were part of their unique 'social world' with their own rituals and code of conduct (see Colosi 2010a). The hierarchy identified in Starlets comprised of three status roles: 'new girl', 'transition' and 'old school'; with the 'new girl' possessing the least status and 'old school' carrying the highest level of status. The transition stage was a period in which a dancer was in the process of becoming established, though considered neither new nor acclaimed. Rather than just being defined by dancing skills and income generation, these statuses were marked by the respect of other dancers, personal autonomy and control within the club.

Developing relationships through the engagement with social rituals sometimes meant dancers would partake in activities they would not have ordinarily considered before working as dancers. Lisa, for example, described how her social behaviour changed after starting work at Starlets:

> ...When I first started I never ever touched anything [drugs]. And then just started taking it [cocaine] at work. Had a little bit of a dip where I'd like take it quite a lot at work ... It was a lot of things that started it. But mainly, I think coz [sic] I started hanging with Charley (dancer); she'd give us it for free. I think a lot of it starts coz they (dancer) want to be in this circle, in this gang. It's kinda [sic] like you smoke to be in the cool gang. That sort of thing...

This was not uncommon. Kat, for example, had never consumed alcohol let alone drugs before she started dancing. This changed as Kat gradually became immersed in some of the dominant patterns of social behaviour evident in Starlets. Kat's transformation is described in the following field diary extract:

> Kat was known for having a good time and making the most of her freedom to drink. She was also known to regularly take cocaine at work. As I have noted before in previous field notes, Kat has changed from the unconfident and somewhat anti-social dancer when she started out here. She used to sit alone drinking coke but now she's never seen without a vodka cranberry out of her hand.

Although the focus here is on the use of alcohol, Kat regularly used cocaine, like many other dancers. Other popular drugs used by the dancers in Starlets included ephedrine,[10] amphetamine (speed) and ecstasy. The use of ephedrine was considered different from the other recreational drugs used and was regularly compared to caffeine supplements or energy drinks. Nelly, for instance, when on one occasion offered me an ephedrine tablet and assured me: 'It's just like Proplus.[11] It's not bad for you'. Dancers, perhaps because of the prolific and accepted use of drugs

---

10   A drug used clinically for asthma, however it is taken recreationally for its stimulant effects. Recreational use of ephedrine is currently illegal in the UK.

11   Non-prescription fatigue relief caffeine tablets.

Understanding Lap-dancing as 'Anti-work' 189

in Starlets, were desensitized to these activities. This in some ways also mirrors a wider process of drug normalization in which the use of certain drugs is argued to have become socially accepted (Parker et al. 1998). Dancers would sometimes openly use drugs in communal areas such as the changing room, or casually offer them to fellow workers. On a number of occasions I was also offered cocaine. On one occasion three dancers casually divided up three lines of cocaine on the dressing room counter. After they left, I asked Stacey, another dancer who was sitting near me what she thought about it. She simply shrugged and smiled, explaining to me, 'it's not the first time I've seen that and it won't be the last'.

Rather than interpreting the social rituals described as a process of socialization and hedonistic pursuit, some researchers have pointed to the use of drugs and alcohol as being part of an effort to numb the 'emotional toll of stripping' and stigma neutralization (Barton 2007, Maticka-Tyndale et al. 2000). Drugs and alcohol are indeed used by lap-dancers as a coping strategy for emotional stresses and strains brought about by their job (see Colosi 2010b forthcoming); yet beyond this, dancers also engage in these activities in the pursuit of pleasure and in order to enhance the social experience of lap-dancing. Unlike in more mainstream occupations, the use of alcohol whilst on duty is considered acceptable and even encouraged. The consumption of drugs and alcohol within the industry is indicative of the difference between how fun is both manifested and experienced in lap dancing compared to that identified in more mainstream office-based workplaces (see Holmes and Marra 2002, Taylor and Bain 2003).

Resistance, Regulation and Hierarchy

Although lap-dancers are governed by the 'house rules'[12] of the club, which were created by managers and owners, dancers also developed and maintained their own 'tacit rules'. This has been identified in other lap-dancing clubs (see Rambo-Ronai and Ellis 1989, Price 2000) and in other modes of work (see Holmes 2000, Taylor and Bain 2003). In Starlets the tacit rules were not as straightforward as the formal house rules and not presented as a list of 'dos and don'ts'. Each status role was subject to a different code of conduct directing their behaviour. For instance, new girls were likely to be chastised by co-workers for making physical contact with a customer during a private dance. However, this type of conduct was more acceptable and tended to be overlooked when carried out by an old school dancer (see Colosi 2010b forthcoming). Beyond dancer conduct, the tacit rules enabled dancers to manipulate and override some of the club's powers as articulated through the house rules. For example, informal rules provided them with the means to use drugs, consume alcohol to get intoxicated and transform their work experience into anti-work, as a form of resistance against discipline. Formal rules which prohibit the excessive use of alcohol and drugs are ignored and undermined

---

12   A list of rules governing the conduct of dancers and customers.

and prioritizing fun represents a protest against the management's emphasis on making money and maintaining control.

In Starlets although the tacit rules were not fixed and frequently changed in response to the input and influence of different dancers, one theme did remain consistent: personal autonomy. A desire for personal autonomy underpinned the tacit rules and therefore part of their self-regulation. In Starlets maintaining self-regulation required some negotiation between the workers and managers. Dancers, particularly those of high status, such as old school dancers, would sometimes employ various bargaining strategies. As Leanne suggests in the following extract, some dancers, despite their dislike of the managers, were willing to provide sexual favours in order to gain some control in the club:

> ...I sat at the bar and talked to Leanne as the day shift came to a close...We got into a conversation about Gerard [manager] and his relationships with other dancers. He'd dated a few dancers; Princess and a couple of European dancers who no longer worked... Leanne suggested that some dancers were quite happy to sleep with Gerard despite the widespread dislike of him. 'I've walked in on a couple of lasses shagging him in the office. I'm not mentioning any names, but all I'm saying is that they get away with stuff'...

Although dancers did at times have 'serious' relationships with managers, Leanne was quite clear during our conversation that more often than not the sexual relations between a dancer and a manager was, in her mind, usually related to a dancer's desire for power in the club. Other examples have included dancers using the supply of drugs such as cocaine. Linda, for example, told me how other dancers were known to slip managers wraps of cocaine in an attempt to keep the commission payment down. Although these actions might seem more about their own personal gain, these bargaining strategies inevitably have a roll-on effect and impact on the other dancers. As well as helping bring about dancer autonomy, these actions present managers as easy targets for manipulation and further reduce their image of professionalism, deepening the dancers' lack of respect for club 'authority' and the need to comply with house rules. The disrespect for managers was apparent in the regular verbal mockery directed at them by the dancers, often witnessed in the changing room (see also Taylor and Bain 2003), along with the display of nonchalance presented by dancers in the monthly meetings held by mangers. Respect, instead of being directed at the managers at Starlets was turned inward, with dancers admiring the established old school workers more than the managers and club owners, in part due to their manipulation of them.

Spreading the Gospel of Anti-work

Dancers at Starlets were keen to maintain the anti-work ethos that was articulated through the various social rituals. This was because maintaining commitment to anti-work ultimately sustained collective practices of resistance. As suggested earlier, although income generation played an important role in the dancers' occupation, not just as a matter of survival, but also to ensure the maintenance of their leisure and lifestyle; it is the pursuit of fun and excitement in which dancers encouraged each other to participate. As indicated earlier, engaging with various social rituals was crucial in climbing the 'career ladder' of lap-dancing. There were consequences for those who continually distanced themselves from, refused to engage in, or outwardly opposed the social rituals. While those who accepted and complied with the anti-work ethic were rewarded with increased popularity and an elevated status in the dancer hierarchy. This did not mean that dancers had to drink alcohol and/or consume drugs, but it was necessary for those workers to accept this behaviour from others, and strive to have fun by socializing with other dancers. In order for resistance to be effective and to maintain self-regulation, it was important for other workers to be united and for a consensus about informal (tacit) rules and regulations to be accomplished (Mulholland 2004). It was therefore in a dancer's interests to adhere to these rules if she wanted to be accepted by her fellow workers.

The story of Kate, a new girl at Starlets, helps highlight how challenging the tacit rules, through non-adherence to the social rituals, can lead to ostracization. During Kate's limited time at Starlets, other dancers regularly complained about how she repeatedly breached tacit rules despite being corrected by her more experienced co-workers. Despite her new girl status, as well as making open contact with customers, Kate regularly consumed vast amounts of alcohol and or drugs such as amphetamine and ephedrine to the extent that she was often so intoxicated that she could barely speak or stand. Consequently her behaviour was reported to managers and she was quickly dismissed. Although the use of alcohol and drugs is accepted and encouraged in the pursuit of having fun, there are rules that govern exactly how these social rituals are practiced. For instance, the indiscrete use of drugs and heavy consumption of alcohol amongst new girls is seen as problematic. This indicates that there were limits for new workers. The widespread contempt for Kate was articulated by one of her colleagues Sally, who, in response to Kate's dismissal told her 'What do you expect, you fucking weirdo! Don't expect to get any sympathy from us'. Other dancers too, after failing to adhere to the tacit rules faced opposition from established old school dancers. Tiger, for example, isolated herself from other dancers, refusing to partake in communal social rituals. She explained to me: 'I'm not here to make friends. I'm here to make money'. In this way Tiger shunned the tacit rules and more widely the anti-work philosophy other dancers adopted. As well as causing resentment, this led to her being repeatedly taunted by some of the other dancers, some of whom directed verbal, and sometimes more physical forms of abuse at her. On one occasion, following a disagreement, a physical fight broke out between Tiger and Davina. Following this incident, Charley, an old school dancer, intentionally damaged some of Tiger's personal property, including a stereo and clothing, which had been stored in the changing room.

New Sociologies of Sex Work

As well as weeding out non-conformists, dancers attempted to sustain their anti-work philosophy through their mentoring of new girls. High status dancers, for example, would often take it upon themselves to offer their mentorship to new starters. Price (2000) also acknowledges that established dancers mentor new workers, teaching them about the dancer code of conduct. In Starlets this involved guiding dancers through acceptable customer-dancer interaction and improving private dance and stage performances. However, more crucially they would be taught about the importance of social engagement with other dancers. In addition, in being made aware of the more negative relationships that could emerge between dancers, such as the ones shared by both Kate and Tiger with the other dancers, new girls soon learned the importance of building positive relationships with the existing dancers, by accepting and partaking in social rituals, putting them in tune with the anti-work ethos.

Conclusion

This chapter has demonstrated how lap-dancers, to some extent, prioritize fun in the workplace not only to experience pleasure but also in order to resist management's rules and regulations. Furthermore, what is suggested is that despite claims that women's long-term engagement with lap-dancing is fundamentally motivated by money, the pursuit of pleasure through having fun was equally as important in Starlets. Processes of socialization evident amongst dancers were underpinned by their engagement in various social rituals. Tacit rules placed having fun as a lap-dancing priority and shaped the dominant anti-work ethos promoted amongst the dancers. Workers attempted to circulate this ethos amongst dancers, simultaneously increasing solidarity and ensuring subtle forms of resistance. Although in many ways lap-dancing conforms with other types of work it is nonetheless distinctive. This is evident by the availability of alcohol and use of drugs. The practice of fun and resistance is also different from that experienced in many other work environments. For instance, some of the wider work literature suggests that workers resist through the use of humour, however, this is distinct from the pursuit of fun as resistance outlined in Starlets, which goes beyond having a laugh. This is perhaps because the work-places under study are largely office-based (see Taylor and Bain 2003), where the social practices associated with the lap-dancing club are less common or simply impossible. Furthermore, in the lap-dancing literature, although dancer control and resistance are discussed, the role fun plays in this process, as described in this chapter, is absent. As such, this chapter therefore develops existing arguments about lap-dancing and integrates them with wider work place resistance by identifying numerous strategies of resistance in lap-dancing which are expressed through an ethic of 'anti work'.

References

Ackroyd, S. and Thompson, P. (1999). *Organisational Misbehaviour*. London: Sage.

Barton, B. (2002). 'Dancing on the Mobius strip: Challenging the Sex War Paradigm', *Gender and Society*, 16(5): 585–602.

Barton, B. (2006). *Stripped: Inside the Lives of Exotic Dancers*. London: New York University Press.

Barton, B. (2007). 'Managing the Toll of Stripping: Boundary setting among exotic dancers', *Journal of Contemporary Ethnography*, 36(5): 571–96.

Bell, H., Sloan, L. and Stickling, C. (1998). 'Exploiter or Exploited: Topless Dancers Reflect on their Experiences', *Journal of Women and Social Work*, 13(3): 352–68.

Bindel, J. (2004). *Possible Exploits: Lap Dancing in the UK*. Glasgow: Glasgow City Council.

Boles, J. and Garbin, A. (1974a). 'The Choice of Stripping for a Living: An Occupational Study of the Night Club Stripper', *Sociology of Work and Occupations*, 1(1): 4–17.

Boles, J. and Garbin, A. (1974b). 'Strip Club and Stripper-Customer Patterns of Interaction', *Sociology and Social Research*, 18: 136–44.

Bott, E. (2006). 'Pole Position: Migrant British Women Producing "Selves" Through Lap Dancing Work', *Feminist Review*, 83: 23–41.

Bradley, H., Erickson, M., Stephenson, C. and Williams, S. (2000), *Myths at Work*. Cambridge: Polity Press.

Bradley, M. (2007). 'Girlfriends, wives and strippers: Managing stigma in exotic dancer romantic relationships', *Deviant Behaviour*, 28: 399–406.

Brewster, Z. (2003). 'Behavioural and Interactional Patrons: tipping techniques and club attendance', *Deviant Behaviour*, 24: 221–43.

Carey, S.H., Peterson, R.A, and Sharpe, L.K. (1974). 'A Study of Recruitment and Socialization in Two Deviant Female Occupations'. *Sociological Symposium*, 11: 11–24.

Chatterton, P. and Hollands, R. (2003). *Urban Nightscapes: Youth Cultures, Pleasure Spaces and Corporate Power*. London: Routledge.

Collinson. D. (1988). 'Engineering humour: Masculinity, joking and conflict in shop floor relations', *Organization Studies*, 9(2): 181–99.

Colosi, R. (2010a). 'A return to the Chicago School? From the "subculture" of taxi-dancers to the contemporary lap-dancer', *Journal of Youth Studies*, 13(1): 1–16.

Colosi, R. (2010b, forthcoming). *Dirty Dancing? An Ethnography of Lap-dancing*. Devon: Willan.

Cressey, P. (1932). *The Taxi-Dance Hall*. Chicago: Chicago University Press.

Deshotels, T. and Forsythe, C. (2005). 'Strategic Flirting and the Emotional tab of Exotic Dancing', *Deviant Behaviour*, 27: 223–41.

Duncan, S. and Edwards, R. (1999). *Lone Mothers, Paid Work and Gendered Moral Rationalities*. London: MacMillan.

Dunn, A. (2010a). 'The "Dole or Drudgery" dilemma: education, the work ethic and unemployment', *Social Policy and Administration*, 44(1): 1–19.

Dunn, A. (2010b, forthcoming). 'Welfare conditionality, inequality, and unemployed people with alternative values', *Social Policy and Society*, 9(4).

Egan, D. (2006a). *Dancing for Dollars and Paying for Love: The Relationships Between Exotic Dancers and their Regulars*. Basingstoke: Palgrave.

Egan, D. (2006b). 'Resistance under the Black Light: Exploring the Use of Music in Two Exotic Dance Clubs', *Journal of Contemporary Ethnography*, 35(2): 201–19.

Enck, G.E. and Preston, J. (1988). 'Counterfeit Intimacy: Dramaturgical Analysis of an Erotic Performance', *Deviant Behaviour*, 9: 369–81.

Ephedrine Legal Advice (2004). *What is Ephedrine?* Available at: http://www.ephedrine-ephedra.com/pages/what_is_ephedrine_1234.html [accessed 20 August 2004].

Erickson, J. and Tewksbury, R. (2000). 'The "gentlemen" in the Club: a typology of strip club patrons', *Deviant Behaviour*, 21: 271–93.

Forsyth, C.J. and Deshotels, T. (1998a). 'A Deviant Process: The Sojourn of the Stripper', *Sociological Spectrum*, 18(1): 77–92.

Forsyth, C.J. and Deshotels, T. (1998b), 'The Occupational Milieu of the Nude Dancer', *Deviant Behaviour*, 18: 125–42.

Frank, K. (1998). 'The Production of Identity and the Negotiation of Intimacy in a "Gentleman's Club"', *Sexualities*, 1(2): 175–202.

Frank, K. (2002). *G-Strings and Sympathy: Strip Club Regulars and Male Desire*. London: Duke University Press.

Frank, K. (2007). 'Thinking Critically about Strip Club Research', *Sexualities*, 10(4): 501–17.

Furnham, A. (1990). *The Protestant Work Ethic: The Psychology of Work-Related Beliefs and Behaviours*. London: Routledge.

Grint, K. (2005). *The Sociology of Work, Third Edition*. Cambridge: Polity Press.

Hannah, J. (2003). 'Exotic Dance Adult Entertainment: ethnography challenges false mythology', *City and Society*, 2: 165–93.

Hodson, R. (1995). 'Worker Resistance: An Underdeveloped Concept in the Sociology of Work', *Economic and Industrial Democracy*, 16(1): 79–110.

Holsopple, K. (1999). 'Stripclubs according to strippers: Exposing workplace sexual violence', in D. Hughes and C. Roche (eds) *Making the Harm Visible: Global Sexual Exploitation of Women and Girls, Speaking Out and Providing Services*. Kingston: Coalition Against Trafficking in Women.

Jones, P., Shears, P. and Hillier, D. (2003). 'Retailing and the regulatory state: A case study of lapdancing clubs in the UK', *International Journal of Retail and Distribution Management*, 31(4): 214–19.

Lewis, J. (1998). 'Learning to Strip: The Socialization Experiences of Exotic Dancers', *The Canadian Journal of Human Sexuality*, 7(1): 51–66.

Lewis, J., Maticka-Tyndale, E., Shaver, F. and Schramm, H. (2005). 'Managing Risk and Safety on the Job: The Experiences of Canadian Sex Workers', *Journal of Psychology and Human Sex Work*, 17(1/2): 147–67.

Liepe-Levinson, K. (2002). *Strip Show: Performances of Gender and Desire.* London: Routledge.

Linstead, S. (1985). 'Jokers wild: The importance of humour and the maintenance of organisational culture', *Sociological Review*, 33(4): 741–67.

Martinez Lucio, M. And Stewart, P. (1997). 'The Paradox of Contemporary Labour Process Theory: The Rediscovery of Labour and the Disappearance of Collectivism', *Capital and Class*, 62(2): 49–78.

Maticka-Tyndale, E, Lewis, J. and Clark, J. (1999). 'Social and Cultural Vulnerability to Sexually Transmitted Infection: The Work of Exotic Dancers', *Canadian Journal of Public Health*, January–February: 19–22.

Maticka-Tyndale, E, Lewis, J. and Clark, J. (2000). 'Exotic Dancing and Health', *Women and Health*, 31(1): 87–108.

Montemurro, B. (2001). 'Strippers and Screamers: The Emergence of Social Control in a Noninstitutionalized Setting', *Journal of Contemporary Ethnography*, 2(3): 275–304.

Montemurro, B., Bloom, C. and Madell, K. (2003). 'Ladies Night Out: a typology of women patrons of a strip club', *Deviant Behaviour*, 24: 333–52.

Mullholland, K. (2004). 'Workplace resistance in an Irish call centre: slammin', scammin' smokin' an' levin'', *Work, Employment and Society*, 18(4): 709–24.

Mumby, D. (2005). 'Theorizing Resistance in Organization Studies: A Dialectical Approach', *Management Communication Quarterly*, 19(1): 19–44.

Murphy, A. (2003). 'The Dialectical Gaze: Exploring the Subject-Object Tension in Performances of Women who Strip', *Journal of Contemporary Ethnography*, 32(3): 305–35.

Parker, H., Aldridge, J. and Measham, F. (1998), *Illegal Leisure: Normalization of Adolescent Recreational Drug Use (Adolescence and Society Series)*. London: Routledge.

Pasko, L. (2002). 'Naked Power: The Practice of Stripping as a Confidence Game', *Sexualities*, 5(1): 49–66.

Price, K. (2000). 'Stripping Women: Workers control in strip clubs', *Current Research on Occupation and Research*, 11: 3–33.

Rambo-Ronai, C. (1992). 'The Reflexive Self Through Narrative: A Night in the Life of an Erotic Dancer/Researcher', in C. Ellis and G. Flaherty (eds) *Investigating Subjectivity: Research on Lived Experience.* London: Sage.

Rambo-Ronai, C. and Ellis, C. (1989). 'Turn-Ons For Money: Interactional Strategies of the Table Dancer', *Journal of Contemporary Ethnography*, 18, 271–98.

Reid, S., Epstein, J. and Benson, D. (1994). 'Role Identity in a Devalued Occupation: The case of female exotic dancers', *Sociological Focus*, 1, 1–15.

Rodrigues, S. and Collinson, D. (1995). '"Having fun?" Humour as resistance in Brazil', *Organizations*, 18(5): 739–68.

Roscigno, V. and Hodson, R. (2004). 'The Organizational and Social Foundations of Worker Resistance', *American Sociological Review*, 69: 14–39.

Sanders, T. (2004). 'Controllable Laughter: Managing Sex Work Through Humour', *Sociology*, 38(2): 273–91.

Scott, D. (1996). *Behind the G-Strings*. North Carolina: McFarland.

Shaw, S. (1985). 'The meaning of leisure in everyday life', *Leisure Sciences*, 7(1): 1–24.

Skipper, J. and McCaghy, C. (1970). 'Stripteasers: The Anatomy and Career Contingencies of a Deviant Occupation', *Social Problems*, 1: 391–405.

Spivey, S. (2005). 'Distancing and solidarity as resistance to sexual objectification in a nude dancing bar', *Deviant Behaviour*, 26: 417–37.

Taylor, P. and Bain, P. (2004). '"Subterranean Worksick Blues": Humour as Subversion in Two Call Centres', *Organization Studies*, 24(9): 1487–1509.

Thompson, W. and Harred, L.J. (1992). 'Topless dancers: Managing Stigma in a Deviant Occupation', *Deviant Behaviour*, 13: 291–311.

Thompson, W. and Harred, L.J. (2003). 'Managing the stigma of topless dancing: a decade later', *Deviant Behaviour*, 24(6): 551–70.

Wesely, J.K. (2002). 'Growing up Sexualised: Issues of Power and Violence in the Lives of Female Exotic Dancers', *Violence Against Women*, 8(10): 1182–207.

Wesely, J.K. (2003). 'Exotic Dancing and the Negotiation of Identity: The Multiple Uses of Body Technologies', *Journal of Contemporary Ethnography*, 32(6): 643–69.

Williams, L. and Parker, H. (2001). 'Alcohol, cannabis, ecstasy and cocaine: drugs of reasoned choice amongst young adult recreational drug users in England', *The International Journal of Drug Policy*, 12(5): 397–413.

Wood, E.A. (2000). 'Working in the Fantasy Factory', *Journal of Contemporary Ethnography*, 29: 1–31.

Chapter 13

The Diverse Vulnerabilities of Lesbian, Gay, Bisexual and Trans Sex Workers in the UK

Kath Browne, Mark Cull and Phil Hubbard

Introduction

It is now abundantly clear that the dominant myths which portray sex work as gendered exploitation do not accommodate the lived realities of all of those who sell sex. After all, sex workers do not solely sell sexual services exclusively to the opposite sex and it is possible for women to sell sex to women or men to sell sex to men, whether occasionally or habitually. Furthermore, the existence of Lesbian Gay Bisexual and Trans (LGBT) identified individuals in sex work markets undermines the idea that there is an inevitably gendered and hetero-patriarchal relationship at the heart of sex work. Moreover, the spaces in which these individuals sell sex are potentially very different from the spaces of 'traditional' on-street and off-street prostitution where women have sold sex to men. Existing work on men who sell sex to men, for example, notes that sex may be exchanged for money in public sex environments and 'cottage' venues such as public urinals (Gaffney 2007), while in towns with more sizeable 'scenes' sex may be exchanged through gay male saunas and bath-houses (Connell 2009). It is also widely understood that sex may be sold in gay clubs and venues, though not always openly, while the importance of escort work in gay scenes is evidenced by the proliferation of adverts for out-calling sex workers in LGBT papers, magazines and on the web (especially via gaydar – see Ashford 2009). Awareness of, and engagement in, these spaces may obviously encourage particular routes into, through and out of sex work: how forms of intimacy and economy entwine in such spaces is something that may fundamentally determine people's experiences of sex work.

In this chapter, we thus aim to prise open debates around sex work and gender by focusing on the prevalence, and spatially-differentiated nature, of sex work among LGBT-identified individuals in the UK. While it has long been noted that female sex workers can identify as lesbian but engage in transactional heterosex, allowing for a spatial and emotional separation of home and work (Hart 1995, Nagel 1996), there is little exploration of whether they sell sex within LGBT communities or on the 'scene'. Knowledge regarding gay male, bisexual and trans sex workers are similarly partial and patchy, despite increasing numbers of commentators highlighting this lacuna (Ashford 2009, Connell 2009). This chapter accordingly represents a first cut through the thorny issues of identity, taking payment for sex,

198 *New Sociologies of Sex Work*

vulnerabilities and empowerment, drawing on two community-university research projects, *Count Me In Too* and *Out On My Own*, both of which worked with community and university partners and which, among other questions, explored experiences of sex working among LGBT communities.

Given our contention that investigations of sex work always need to examine the place of sex work and to recognize the existence of diverse routes into and out of sex work, shaped by the distinctive socialities that played out within LGBT spaces, this chapter focuses on the city of Brighton & Hove. Using empirical evidence produced by the *Count Me In Too* project we firstly explore who within the LGBT community identifies as selling sex, whom sex is sold to and how this sex work is narrated and understood. We also draw on the *Out On My Own* study, which focused on housing and homelessness amongst LGBT young people. Drawing on this we argue that the cost of housing in Brighton & Hove and the desire to migrate to this 'gay mecca' frames sex work in this city for LGBT people. As a specific local exploration into the geographies of male sex work, we use this chapter to flag up a range of issues relating to both vulnerability and empowerment that could form the basis for future research into new sociologies of male sex work, in the UK and beyond. In doing so, we want to highlight that sex work is not always best understood as an issue of gendered exploitation, and argue that further nuanced explorations of empowerment are needed to acknowledge the choices facing sex workers and LGBT communities in varied circumstances.

LGBT Sex/Work in the 'Gay Capital' of Brighton & Hove

Starting from the perspective that sex work needs to be understood contextually and geographically, our investigation of sex working among LGBT-identified individuals focuses on Brighton & Hove, a large town (granted city status in 2000) on the south coast of England. Long associated with the ludic and liminal (see Shields 1991), Brighton has always enjoyed a certain notoriety as a place of illicit sexual liaison, captured in the notion of the 'dirty weekend' and the traditions of 'kiss-me-quick' seaside lasciviousness. The reputation of Brighton as a place of adulterous liaison was established in the inter-war years, and has remained stubbornly recalcitrant despite many attempts to reimage the resort (Hemingway 2006). Some clues as to the prevalence of sex working among LGBT communities in Brighton & Hove can be gauged through anecdotal and published accounts which argue that young men exchange sexual services in public spaces, often frequenting the Bushes cruising area or the pier/seafront area (Harris and Robinson 2007). Elsewhere, Ashford (2009) has analysed Gaydar adverts for sexual services, suggesting that, outside London, Brighton & Hove is the UK city with the largest number of men advertising sexual services to other men.

The dominant place myth of Brighton as 'historically embodying the genitals, rather than the heart' (Munt 1995: 114) has undoubtedly played a role in its establishment as Britain's best-known LGBT resort, for many the UK's

The Diverse Vulnerabilities of Lesbian, Gay, Bisexual and Trans Sex Workers   199

'gay capital'. Its reputation as a relatively safe space town in which to be 'out' has contributed to it having a large and vibrant 'scene', becoming a key site in the political struggle for LGBT citizenship (Browne 2007). Yet evidence from grassroots research shows that over 90 per cent of LGBT people in Brighton & Hove were not from the city and move there because of its LGBT communities and the support this is perceived to offer them to live LGBT lives (Zorro 1998, Webb and Wright 2000, Browne and Davis 2008). The city offers a wide variety of services that are either directly targeted at LGBT communities (for example Mind Out, LGBT Switchboard) or cater for LGBT – or at least gay male – populations (Terrence Higgins Trust, Sussex Beacon).[1] In this context Brighton & Hove is read, and sells itself as accepting, open, supportive of, and celebrating alternative, particularly gay, sexualities. However, the lack of knowledge of LGBT sex working in Brighton & Hove (see Potter 2004) means that formal service provision in the main remains focused on sex working women through the Oasis project (which focuses on substance abuse and sexual health issues).

The idea that men selling sex are less needy of support services than women clearly informs this uneven provision. Yet to assume that men are more capable of making informed choices, practice sex safely or capable of dealing with 'dodgy punters' is to ignore the different circumstances under which men sell sex. In some circumstances, male sex workers may be prepared to sell sex in unsafe places, to accept poor pay or treatment, or make themselves vulnerable to rape and violence. The drift of vulnerable young people (including those leaving the care system) towards Brighton may create a context which needs further examination in relation to sex work. The city has a potentially large transient and homeless population, many of whom may have left their previous home because of issues relating to their sexual and/or gender identity (Cull et al. 2006). These issues were explored in *Out On My Own* (Cull et al. 2006), a partnership research project between Hove YMCA and the University of Brighton that studied the experiences and needs of homeless Lesbian, Gay, Bisexual and Transgender young people in Brighton & Hove. Thirty-three young people were interviewed using a biographical topic guide, which explored their life experiences and sought to understand what had led them to become homeless. A further ten young people completed a paper questionnaire. Most of the young people who participated in the study were recruited through the Hove YMCA's Housing Advice drop-in centre. Others were referred by different young peoples' services providers, or recruited through advertising and through outreach to gay venues and known public sex environments. The participants were aged between 16 and 25 years, 23 were young men, 17 young women, and three identified as transgender. Nearly all the young people in the study reported a history of mental health problems and/or substance misuse, with over two thirds having a history of attempting suicide. Two-thirds had been bullied at school, and

---

1   Mind Out is a mental health organisation that caters for LGBT people and is part of the charity Mind. Switchboard is an information service for LGBT people similar to that offered nationwide. Terrance Higgins Trust and Sussex Beacon are both HIV charities.

a similar number were 'not in education, employment or training' (NEET) at the time.

Although the study was specifically investigating homelessness in Brighton & Hove, the young peoples' experiences of selling or exchanging sex were explored in the interviews and via a tick box question included in the questionnaires. Eight young people identified themselves as having exchanged or sold sex, five of these through an in-depth interview, whilst the other three had completed the paper questionnaire. All eight who disclosed their engagement in selling or exchanging sex had slept rough. The five young people interviewed by the researcher had several common vulnerabilities, disclosing mental health related issues: four of the five had attempted suicide. They all discussed problematic drug use or addiction, and four of them also described harmful levels of alcohol use. Furthermore, four of the five had lived in local authority care.

Count Me In Too chronologically followed *Out on My Own. Count Me In Too* is a research project where lesbian, gay, bisexual and trans (LGBT) people shared their views and experiences, and worked with service providers and others to gather and present evidence promoting positive changes for LGBT people. The project has produced ten detailed reports, including eight with local service providers, on a range of themes (all available at www.countmeintoo.co.uk). These include recommendations identified from the 819 questionnaires completed by respondents and testimonies of 69 people who took part in 19 focus groups in 2006 (see Browne 2007). Of significance for this chapter, the questionnaire included a section on payment for sex. This was a routed section (i.e. only those who answered yes to the question were asked for further details) and contained quantitative and qualitative questions. The questions for this section (as with the research more broadly) came from community groups and statutory services. The payment for sex section was devised by the female sex working project (Oasis), who provided both the opening question and questions for the routed section. A further question on offering or engaging in sex for somewhere to stay emerged from the *Out On My Own* research as a key issue. This data was analysed as part of the housing and general health analyses groups (see Browne and Davis 2008, Browne and Lim 2008).

Integrating these studies enables insights into the city of Brighton & Hove's sex markets from a variety of perspectives. In the sections that follow these projects overlap and intersect to explore a range of nuanced lived experiences of sex work. The chapter will initially explore the statistical data regarding who sells sex to whom, questioning hetero-gendered assumptions, before exploring the diverse motivations for engaging in sex work, challenging the predominance of the gender exploitation paradigm, whilst noting the role of vulnerability in shaping decisions to engage in sex work.

Lesbian, Gay, Bisexual and Trans Sex Work: Evidence from *Count Me In Too* and *Out On My Own*

In order to address the lack of knowledge regarding payment for sex amongst those who identify with/as LGBT, the *Count Me In Too* research asked 'have you ever taken payment for sexual acts?'. This revealed that 10 per cent (n. 81) of all participants had taken payment for sex. As a figure, this is difficult to compare with heterosexually-identifying populations given the lack of questions about such issues in successive UK National Sexual Attitudes Surveys. Nevertheless, this indicates that there may be a sizeable overlap between sex working and LGBT communities in Brighton & Hove. Further exploration of this data revealed very particular gendered distinctions, both in terms of who was selling sex and who they were selling sex to. 14 per cent of men (n. 61) and 5 per cent (n. 18) of women said that they have taken payment for sexual acts ($p < 0.05$). However, trans people are just as likely as non-trans people to have taken payment for sex.[2] In terms of the purchase of sex, 93 per cent (n. 73) of those who exchanged sex did so with men, 14 per cent (n. 11) with women.

When these categories are broken down by gender (Tables 13.1 and 13.2), there are clear differences between who men and women sold sex to. This research clearly indicates a gender differential: 97 per cent (n. 61) of men who had sold sex, sold it to men, with just 7 per cent (n. 4) selling or exchanging sex with women. In *Count Me In Too* 78 per cent (n. 14) of women took payment from men, with 44 per cent (n. 8) taking payment from women. Although this reiterates the contention that lesbians engage in sex work with other women as well as men, they suggest that sex work by men for other men is the most prevalent form of sex work for LGBT people. In this sense, these figures are extremely important for disrupting some of the key ideas regarding the gendered stereotyping, and associated assumption of patriarchal exploitation within sex work – which is not just about men buying sex from women.

When taking payment for sex is broken down by sexual identity (as chosen by participants), the research found that lesbians/gay women are the least likely to have taken payments for sexual acts and gay men, bisexuals and those who are queer or otherwise coded in relation to their sexual identification are more likely to have taken payment for sex ($p = 0.01$) (see Table 13.3). It could then be contended that within the LGBT community, those other than lesbians are more likely to enter into sex work or at least take payment for sexual acts. While further work is needed to investigate the intersections between LGBT identities and women's engagement with sex work, there appears a more substantial overlap in terms of

---

2   Although it is common for theorists to explore trans people as fluid and transgressive (e.g. Butler 1990), we do not have sufficient scope to make any inferences in this chapter (but see Browne and Lim forthcoming, Lim and Browne 2009). Here it is suffice to note that trans theorists have contested the use of trans identity in ways that do not actually engage with trans people and their experiences.

Table 13.1 When you sold or exchanged sex who did you have sex with? – Men by gender (*Count Me In Too*, missing data excluded)[*]

		Male	Female	Total
Not men	No.	2	4	6
	%	3.2	22.2	7.4
Men	No.	61	14	75
	%	96.8	77.8	92.6
Total	No.	63	18	81
	%	100.0	100.0	100.0

[*] Unless otherwise stated all tables only include those who had taken payment for sex.

Table 13.2 When you sold or exchanged sex who did you have sex with? – Women by gender (*Count Me In Too*, missing data excluded)

		Male	Female	Total
Not women	No.	58	10	68
	%	93.5	55.6	85
Women	No.	4	8	12
	%	6.5	44.4	15
Total	No.	62	18	80
	%	100.0	100.0	100.0

Table 13.3 Payment for sexual acts by sexual identity (*Count Me In Too*, missing data excluded)

		Lesbian/gay woman	Gay	Bisexual	Queer	Otherwise coded	Total
Yes	No.	10	55	5	5	4	79
	%	3.7	13	10.6	17.9	12.9	9.8
No	No.	263	369	42	23	27	724
	%	96.3	87	89.4	82.1	87.1	90.2
Total	No.	273	424	47	28	31	803
	%	100.0	100.0	100.0	100.0	100.0	100.0

male sex work and gay/bisexual/queer identification. Nonetheless, and as widely recognized across the sexual health literature, not all men selling sex to men necessarily define within the category 'gay' (Hall 2007).

As is clear from our discussion above, conceptualizing sex work requires a nuanced understanding of practices, payment and spatialities, this includes the temporalities of sex work. Table 13.4 shows that for the majority of those in

Table 13.4   Frequency of selling or exchanging sex (*Count Me In Too*, missing data excluded)

		Total
It is a regular source of income	No.	3
	%	3.7
Very occasionally, when I have to	No.	10
	%	12.3
It was just a one-off	No.	21
	%	25.9
I don't do it any more	No.	47
	%	58
Total	No.	81
	%	100.0

the *Count Me In Too* survey, sex work was a 'one-off' or something that they located in their past rather than a regular source of income (4 per cent, n. 3) or that they take payment for sex occasionally when they have to (12 per cent, n. 10).[3] One-off experiences of sex work within LGBT communities questions the presumed permanence or longevity of sex work, and problematizes assumptions that individuals become 'trapped' in sex work.

Between Vulnerability and Empowerment: Why Sell Sex in Brighton & Hove?

New sociologies of sex work suggest that the reasons for selling sex vary, and challenge the antithesis of pleasure and prostitution. As Brewis and Linstead (2000) point out, it is important to acknowledge that sex workers can take pleasure from their work, and that for some it is also a way of seizing power rather than acceptance of exploitation. In our study, almost all participants who had exchanged sex sold sex for money (95 per cent, n. 75), with 18 per cent (n. 14) exchanging sex for accommodation or shelter (see Table 13.5). Furthermore 23 per cent (n. 18) said that the reason they sold sex was because they needed money for housing (see Table 13.6 below), suggesting that financial need and housing need entwine. Supporting this *Count Me In Too* also found that those who have been homeless are more than three times as likely to have exchanged sex for payment (22 per cent) than those who have never experienced homelessness (7 per cent).

In order to understand the link between homelessness and sex work it is useful to explore the local context of Brighton & Hove. In the *Out On My Own* research,

---

3   While it is impossible to know if this is an effect of the method of data collection, uncovering these 'one off' experiences is an important finding.

Table 13.5 What have you ever exchanged sex for? (Multiple responses allowed, *Count Me In Too*)

	Frequency	Per cent
Money	75	94.9
Somewhere to stay	14	17.7
Drugs	12	15.2
Alcohol	6	7.6
Other	3	3.8

and supporting other research regarding Brighton & Hove (see Zorro 1998, Webb and Wright 2001), two-thirds of the participants had migrated to the city. This was mostly due to its reputation as a safe place for LGBT people to live. Yet Brighton can be expensive: in 2005, Brighton & Hove was assessed as having the highest affordability gap outside of London, and the floor[4] of the owner-occupier housing market was assessed as requiring a household income of £29,200 (DCA 2005 cited in Brighton & Hove 2005), excluding around 60 per cent of the city's population (see Browne and Davis 2008). Likewise, the floor[5] of the private rented market (£14,400) is, according to the 2005 Housing Needs Survey (DCA 2005), well beyond the means of many households. Rates of 'local housing allowance' also do not cover much beyond the very bottom end of the rental market in any property size. Thus, many who come to the Brighton & Hove struggle to live within the city. Moreover, as with all local governments in the UK, Brighton & Hove City Council operate a 'local connection' policy that targets city services towards 'local people', and seeks to reduce migration of vulnerable homeless people into the city. This requires that those claiming housing/income support have a 'local connection' to the area through employment or family, failing to recognize the specific support that LGBT people might need (Browne and Davis 2008). This leads to a variety of strategies for finding somewhere to stay. The necessity of shelter and food can therefore lead to various forms of sex work:

> **Joshua:** I've been a prostitute many times in my life, and we (boyfriend) went off to Amsterdam last year. It was better than sleeping in the park (in Brighton), and we went to work for an (escort) agency [Later in the interview] That's when (whilst rough sleeping in Brighton) he (boyfriend) started to become an escort down the Bushes...and we ended up living in a Brighton park. (*Out on My Own*) I was living on the streets and needed to eat (aged 14 years, *Count Me In Too* Questionnaire 70)

---

4   Household income required to buy the cheapest single-bedroom accommodation in the cheapest area of the city at 95 per cent mortgage.

5   Household income required to rent the cheapest single-bedroom accommodation in the cheapest area of the city with rent accounting for 30 per cent of net household income.

The Diverse Vulnerabilities of Lesbian, Gay, Bisexual and Trans Sex Workers 205

Building on the findings from the *Out On My Own* study, whether someone had offered sex for somewhere to stay was a question in the *Count Me In Too* questionnaire, which found that 4 per cent of LGBT people (n. 31) have had sex or made themselves available to have sex in order to have somewhere to stay in the past five years. A further 4 per cent (n. 28) had done so in the period before the last five years. Such findings reiterate that the decision to take payment for sex is one that is not necessarily about men exploiting women but about economic vulnerabilities that are associated with both marginalized men and women.

In addition to economic factors, both studies found links between homelessness, sexual abuse/domestic violence and exchanging sex for payment. For example, one respondent stated they 'needed money because I needed to pay rent to avoid an abusive home' (*Count Me In Too* questionnaire 185). For some, sex work offered the ability to stay in Brighton & Hove, away from abusive families elsewhere, despite having no local connections or employment. Thus, whilst these individuals are vulnerable, sex work offered a source of income that enabled them to address and counter the abuse that they might otherwise have been subject to.

Luke, having disclosed sexual abuse to his family who then threw him out at the age of 20, Luke became homeless and moved in with an older gay man, who lived in Brighton and whom offered to help him out:

> Luke: He wanted a relationship from me, which was something I didn't want. There was nothing that attracted me to him and to be truthful if you're not attracted to a person there's no chemistry is there? I got kicked out of my sister's, he was basically around at the time and, well, he said he'd help me. I had to trust him I had no-one else to turn to and he fucked me over. We had a sexual contact...but it weren't of a frequent occurrence (*Out On My Own*)

The experience of being thrown out of family homes or leaving because of a lack of acceptance or sexual bigotry, was one that resulted in LGBT people leaving their accommodation without anywhere to stay. Because they did not want to return to family homes where participants had experienced rejection, and at times abuse, they sought housing and employment in Brighton & Hove. Homeless young people in *Out On My Own* often found housing solutions that were inappropriate. This left them vulnerable to other men,[6] because they did not receive appropriate local authority support for their housing. Thus, housing and the need for somewhere to stay is clearly a significant factor when considering LGBT sex work in Brighton & Hove. This can be seen as relating to the expense of living in Brighton & Hove, as well as the 'pull' of the city for LGBT people (Browne 2007).

Questions of vulnerability were, however, differently negotiated and Anthony speaks of working with his friends, advertising his services and in many ways maintaining control of his business:

---

6   In *Out on My Own* only older men were identified as taking advantage of participants in these situations.

Anthony: I've been in a few dodgy escapades, let's put it that way. One of them was to a certain degree I was a male escort and to a certain degree I was a rent boy.

Interviewer: So that would be how you would say it, as a male escort?

Anthony: Yeah, even though I was under the age of 18. Yeah I was looking for a sugar daddy.

Interviewer: Did you find one?

Anthony: No I didn't actually. Well kind of, actually, I found a lot of people who were willing to pay, let's put it that way.

Interviewer: And did you advertise or did you work through an agency?

Anthony: Advertised but a different way. Instead of just putting up little things in phone boxes, it was more leaflets that we designed ourselves, and stuff like that.

Interviewer: So was there a group of you?

Anthony: Yeah, um, only a couple of us though would go, obviously make business.

Interviewer: So you'd get a phone call would you?

Anthony: Make a call, but we were our own pimps, none of us cared. Life was that shit.

Interviewer: Do you think you were doing it for the money at the time, or was it just because life was shit?

Anthony: Life was shit, and money. For example, one night one bloke paid me £310.

Interviewer: So when you said you wanted the money, was that just to sort of get by because you didn't have enough money generally, or did you want it for something that was expensive, like your drugs?

Anthony: It was more for buying shitloads of bud. I'm just going to be blunt. I am very, very heavily addicted to cannabis. I've had too many champagne tastes, and trust me that champagne taste is expensive...none of us cared if we were stoned. What happens when you are stoned. Your body becomes very relaxed... it's easier to work (*Out On My Own*).

Vulnerabilities identified in *Out On My Own* also related to drug use. In *Count Me In Too* 12 per cent of those who exchanged sex did it for drugs/alcohol. Anthony's discussion nonetheless points to the complexity of addiction in sex work, where his addiction to cannabis meant that he engaged in sex work to fund his habit and being stoned made it easier to work. Shifting between discourses of want and need, Anthony points to how it is misleading to only see LGBT sex work within a paradigm of vulnerability and need. Instead there is a complexity to conceptualizing LGBT sex work that moves between empowerment/exploitation. Table 13.6 highlights the multiple reasons that LGBT people engage in sex work. These range from being forced to do so, the possibilities of this form of working for providing 'easy' money, a lack of other available forms of employment and the flexibility of working hours.

The Diverse Vulnerabilities of Lesbian, Gay, Bisexual and Trans Sex Workers   207

Table 13.6   What were/are your reasons for selling sex? (Multiple responses allowed, *Count Me In Too***)**

	Frequency	Per cent
Other	36	45.6
I needed money for housing	18	22.8
I wanted to work in the sex industry	12	15.2
I needed money for drugs/alcohol	12	15.2
The hours/money suited me better than other jobs	12	15.2
I couldn't get any other job	8	10.1
Someone else forced me to do it	5	6.3

Table 13.7   Major categories from qualitative data: What were/are your reasons for selling sex?

Categories	No. of responses
I wanted to experience it/I enjoy(ed) it	7
Need(ed) extra money (in addition to other employment)	7
Needed money for:	
Housing/rent/shelter	4
Food	2
Bills	1
Study fees	1
I like extra spending power/gifts/going places I couldn't otherwise afford	4
Someone offered payment or gifts	4
Opportunity/because I could	3
It was a one off	2
Mental health difficulties	2
Of which: Unable to work	1
Self-harm	1

1. Where responses fall into more than one category they are counted in each category that they fall into.
2. Subsets of a major category (marked by 'Of Which') enumerate responses where respondents have specified a kind or type of the major category.
3. In this table, subsets of a major category (marked by 'Of Which') are mutually exclusive.

46 per cent (n. 36) of those who had taken payment for sex did so for reasons other than those listed in this study (see Table 13.6). Table 13.7 illustrates the qualitative data which has been thematically coded and offers other reasons offered by those who said 'other' in Table 13.5 ('What were/are your reasons for selling sex?') there are a variety of responses that once again move across the pleasure/vulnerability binary suggesting that LGBT sex work needs to be theorized in ways that account for an array of experiences, motivations, problems and potentials. Here, respondents' motivations can be located along a continuum between vulnerability – for example, mental health difficulties – and the pleasure-seeking dimensions of sex work.

Engaging in sex work as a 'one-off', some respondents also pointed to the experience of 'try[ing] it once!' (questionnaire 286). This questions the necessary stigmatization or embarrassment regarding sex work within LGBT communities, and instead points to the need to consider the range of acceptance of sex work within marginalized and disenfranchised groupings. Moreover, and continuous with other research that has questioned exploitation paradigms (e.g. Bernstein 2007, Mai 2009), participants pointed to enabling desires to be fulfilled as well as exploration of diverse sexual expressions. As such, sex work may enable LGBT people to enact sexual identities that might be repressed or regulated were they to occur in other spheres or spaces.

Conclusion

Although queer and LGBT sex work is often occluded in international discussions of prostitution and sexual commerce, this chapter suggests that selling sex may be relatively common amongst LGBT individuals (or at least those living, working and/or socializing in Brighton & Hove). While the dominant form of sex work discussed here involves men selling sex to men, the studies reported here revealed a varied array of experiences, motivations, and problems that demand further exploration. Many questions remain to be answered about the overlap between, and movement within, the spaces where sex work is negotiated and transacted (such as leisure venues within the LGBT scene, local listing magazines), and the extent to which these enable different forms of sex work, whether one-off or repeated. Yet the fact that many of those who sold or exchanged sex did so because they could, because they enjoyed it or simply because it facilitated a sexual encounter poses interesting questions about the relations of intimacy, exploitation and work, confirming Zelizer's (2004) view that the distinction between paid-for sex and sex 'freely' transacted is a very blurred one. This does not mean we can ignore the ways that selling sex can be related to and reiterate vulnerabilities, abuse and poverty, but neither does it reduce discussions to an empowered client/disempowered sex worker dichotomy set within solely patriarchical or quasi-patriarchal structures (cf. Jeffreys 2008).

The Diverse Vulnerabilities of Lesbian, Gay, Bisexual and Trans Sex Workers 209

As suggested at the outset of this chapter, studying sex working amongst members of the putative LGBT community allows us to prise open debates on sex work and problematizes widely-held assumptions that sex work represents a paid violation of intimacy in which men exploit women. Here we are insisting on a plural perspective, wherein people sell sex in contingent ways that may, at times, not look or feel anything like the type of gendered sex work which preoccupies the imaginations of the public and policy makers in the urban West. Indeed, UK government's focus on female worker-male client sex work means that there is a lack of knowledge of other forms of sex work, as well as a practical lack of support for those selling sex in other contexts and ways.

It is in this sense that further work on the diversity of sex markets will help identify how forms of intimacy, monetary and resource exchange intertwine to define and shape the pleasures and perils of sex work in different spaces. For, as van der Veen (2000) suggests (following Gibson-Graham 1996), sex work in fact comprises many class processes: for example, some workers may be involved in processes of capitalist class relations by working in corporate venues, while others may be self-employed, determining the terms of the prostitute/client relation. Yet others may be held in a feudal-type class relation with a pimp, or work collectively through a communal process of producing, appropriating and distributing surplus labour (van der Veen 2000: 134–7). It is hence impossible to make generalized claims that sex work is always exploitative, or that all sex workers are depressed, psychologically damaged or destitute. Indeed, we conclude by arguing that a nuanced understanding of participation in the sex industry requires an awareness that it has different consequences dependent on the specific relationality between bodies engaging in different forms of sex working. As well as the motivations for engaging in sex work, routes of entry and the place specificities of where sex work is undertaken. Given the sheer variety of sex working, any attempt at generalization about LGBT-identified sex workers is always bound to fail. Existing work on the geography of sex work underlines that there may be important ways in which the visibility, surveillance, ambience and management of venues or spaces encourages particular types of sex working (Hubbard 1999). Appropriately nuanced work that considers both the place in which sex work occurs, and the sexual identities of those involved, is therefore vital if we are to grasp the contingent vulnerabilities of sex work.

References

Aggleton, P. (1999). *Men Who Sell Sex: International Perspectives on Male Prostitution*. London: UCL Press.

Ashford, C. (2009). 'Male sex work and the Internet effect: time to re-evaluate the criminal law?', *Journal of Criminal Law*, 73(3): 258–80.

210 *New Sociologies of Sex Work*

Belza, M.J., Llácer, A., Mora, R., Morales, M., Castilla, J. and de la Fuente, L. (2000). 'Socio-demographic characteristics and HIV risk-behaviour patterns of Male Sex Workers in Madrid, Spain', *AIDS Care*, 13, 677–82.

Bernstein, E. (2007a). 'Sex work for the middle classes', *Sexualities*, 10, 473–88.

Bernstein, E. (2007b).*Temporarily Yours*. Chicago: Chicago University Press.

Brewis, J. and Linsted, S. (2000). *Sex, Work and Sex Work: Eroticizing Organisations*. London: Routledge.

Brighton & Hove (2005). *Housing Needs Survey 2005* [online], available at: http://www.brighton-hove.gov.uk/downloads/bhcc/Final_Report.pdf [accessed 6 May 2010].

Brooks-Gordon, B. (2006). *The Price of Sex: Prostitution, Policy and Society*. Cullompton: Willian.

Browne, K. (2007). 'A party with politics?: (Re)making LGBTQ Pride spaces in Dublin and Brighton', *Social and Cultural Geography*, 8(1): 63–8.

Browne, K. and Davis, P. (2008). *Housing: Count Me In Too Additional Analysis Report* [online], available at: http://www.spectrum-lgbt.org/cmiToo/downloads/CMIT_Housing_Report_April_08.pdf [accessed 6 May 2010].

Browne, K. and Lim, J. (2008). *General Health: Count Me In Too Additional Analysis Report* [online], available at: http://www.spectrum-lgbt.org/cmiToo/downloads/CMIT_General_Health_July08.pdf [accessed 6 May 2010].

Browne, K. and Lim, J. (forthcoming). 'Trans in the Gay City', *Gender, Place and Culture*, 17(5).

Browne, K., Lim J. and Brown G. (2007).*Geographies of Sexualities: Theories, Practices and Politics*. Aldershot: Ashgate.

Butler, J. (1990). *Gender Trouble: Feminism and the Subversion of Identity*. New York: Routledge.

Church, S., Henderson, M., Barnard, M. and Hart, G. (2001). 'Violence by clients towards female prostitutes in different work settings: questionnaire survey', *British Medical Journal*, 322, 524–5.

Connell, J. (2009). 'The personal safety of male prostitutes', in D. Canter, M. Ioannou and D. Young (eds) *Safer Sex in the City*. Farnham: Ashgate, 79–100.

Connell, J. and Hart, G. (2003). 'An overview of male sex work in Edinburgh and Glasgow: The male sex worker perspective'. London: Medical Research Council Social and Public Health Sciences Unit, Occasional Paper 8.

Cull, M., Platzer, H. and Balloch, S. (2006*).Out On My Own: Understanding the Experiences and Needs of Homeless Lesbian, Gay, Bisexual and Transgender Youth* [online], available at: http://www.spectrum-lgbt.org/downloads/reports/Out_On_My_Own___full_report.pdf [accessed 12 January 2010].

Davis, P. and Feldman, R. (1997). 'Prostitute Men Now', in G. Scrambler and A. Scrambler (eds) *Re-thinking Prostitution: Purchasing Sex in the 1990s*. London: Routledge, 29–56.

Gaffney, J. (2007). 'A Co-ordinated Prostitution Strategy and Response to Paying the Price – But What About the Men?', *Community Safety Journal*, 6, 27–33.

Gaffney, J. and Beverley, K. (2001). 'Contextualising the Construction and Social Organisation of the Commercial Male Sex Industry in London at the Beginning of the 21st Century', *Feminist Review*, 67(1): 133–41.

Hall, T.M. (2007). 'Rent-boys, barflies, and kept men: men involved in sex with men for compensation in Prague', *Sexualities*, 10: 457–72.

Harris, J. and Robinson, B. (2006). *Tipping the Iceberg: a Pan Sussex Study of Young People at Risk of Sexual Exploitation*. London: Barnados.

Hart, A., Maddison, E. and Wolff, D. (2007).*Community-University Partnerships in Practice*. Leicester: NIACE.

Hemingway, J. (2006). 'Sexual Learning and the Seaside: Relocating the "Dirty Weekend" and Teenage Girls' Sexuality', *Sex Education: Sexuality, Society and Learning*, 6: 429–43.

Hickson, F., Weatherburn, P., Hows, J. and Davis, P. (1994). 'Selling Safer Sex: Male Masseurs and Escorts in the UK', in P. Aggleton, P. Davies and G. Hart (eds) *AIDS: Foundations for the Future*. London: Taylor & Francis, 197–209.

Home Office (2004). *Paying the Price: A Consultation Paper on Prostitution*. London: HMSO.

Home Office (2006a). *A Co-ordinated Prostitution Strategy*. London: HMSO.

Home Office (2006b). *Regulatory Impact Assessment: A Coordinated Strategy for Prostitution*. London: HMSO.

Hubbard, P. (1999). *Sex and the City: Geographies of Prostitution in the Urban West*. Aldershot: Ashgate.

Hubbard, P. and Whowell, M. (2008). 'Revisiting the Red Light District: Still Neglected, Immoral and Marginal?', *Geoforum*, 39(5): 1743–55.

Jeffreys, S. (2008). *The Industrial Vagina*. London: Routledge.

Lim, J. and Browne, K. (2009). 'Senses of Gender', Sociological Research Online, 14(1) [online], available at: http://www.socresonline.org.uk/14/1/6.html [accessed 6 May 2010].

Mai, N. (2009). *Migrant Workers in the UK Sex Industry*. London: London Metropolitan University, Institute for the Study of European Transformation.

Nagle, J. (1997). *Whores and Other Feminists*. London: Routledge.

O'Neill, M. (2001). *Prostitution and Feminism: Towards a Politics of Feeling*. Cambridge: Polity.

Potter, M. (2004). *Response to Home Office Consultation on Prostitution*. Brighton: Oasis Project.

Sanders, T. (2005). *Sex Work: A Risky Business*. Cullompton: Willan.

Sanders, T. (2008). 'Male Sexual Scripts: Intimacy, Sexuality and Pleasure in the Purchase of Commercial Sex', *Sociology*, 42: 400–17.

Sanders, T. (2008). *Paying for Pleasure: Men Who Buy Sex*. Cullompton: Willian.

Sanders, T. and Campbell, R. (2007). 'Designing Out Violence, Building In Respect: Violence, Safety and Sex Work Policy', *British Journal of Sociology*, 58: 1–19.

Scott, J., Minichiello, V., Marino, R., Harvey, G., Jamieson, M. and Browne, J. (2005). 'Understanding the New Context of the Male Sex Work Industry', *Journal of Interpersonal Violence*, 20: 320–42.

Shields, R. (1991). *Places on the Margin*. London: Routledge.

van der Veen, M. (2000). 'Beyond Slavery and Capitalism: Producing Class Difference in the Sex Industry', in K. Gibson-Graham, S. Resnick and R.D. Wolff (eds) *Class and Its Others*. Minneapolis: University of Minnesota Press, 121–41.

Ward, H. and Day, S. (2006). 'What Happens to Women Who Sell Sex?', *Sexually Transmitted Infections*, 82: 413–17.

Webb, D. and Wright, D. (2001).*Count Me In*. Brighton: Brighton and Hove Council.

West, D.J. and de Villiers, B. (1992). *Male Prostitution: Gay Sex Services in London*. London: Duckworth Press.

Wilcox, A. and Christmann, K. (2006). *Sex for Sale: A Qualitative Study of Male Sex Work*. Huddersfield: University of Huddersfield.

Wilcox, A. and Christmann, K. (2008). 'Getting Paid for Sex is My Kick: Qualitative Study of Male Sex Workers', in G. Letherby, K. Williams, P. Birch and M. Kain (eds) *Sex as Crime*. Cullompton: Willan, 118–36.

Wolkowitz, C. (2006). *Bodies at Work*. London: Sage.

Zatz, N. (1997). 'Sex Work/Sex Act: Law, Labor and Desire in Constructions of Prostitution', *Signs*, 22(2): 277–308.

Zelizer, V. (2005). *The Purchase of Intimacy*. Princeton: Princeton University Press.

Chapter 14

Repackaging Sex: Class, Crass, and the Good Vibrations Model of Sexual Retail

Lynn Comella

In 1977, sex educator and therapist Joani Blank opened the Good Vibrations retail store in San Francisco, ushering in a new dawn of sex toy retailing.[1] In founding Good Vibrations, Blank created a different kind of sex toy store, a place where customers could touch, feel, and hold sex toys and talk openly and without embarrassment about sex with knowledgeable and well-trained staff. Her goal was to provide 'especially but not exclusively women' access to a 'clean and well-lit' sex toy store, one that stood in contrast to the prevailing stereotype of adult businesses as inherently 'seedy' and sexist places that catered primarily to men.

The Good Vibrations model of retailing – an educationally-based and quasi-therapeutic approach to selling sex toys – has since become a prototype for other women-owned and oriented sex toy businesses in the United States (US) and in other countries, too. The businesses that have followed in Good Vibrations footsteps have adopted Good Vibrations' unique blend of sexual education, customer comfort, quality product mix, and grassroots feminist politics, helping to establish what Babeland proprietor Claire Cavanah describes as the 'alternative sex vending movement.' In the US this includes businesses such as Babeland in Seattle and New York, Smitten Kitten in Minneapolis, Early to Bed in Chicago, Self Serve in Albuquerque, and Sugar in Baltimore, among others; in London there is Sh! Women's Erotic Emporium; and in Toronto Canada there is Good for Her and Come as You Are. According to Carol Queen, longtime staff sexologist at Good Vibrations, every company that has followed the Good Vibrations model 'shares a certain politics of sexuality' and has brought a degree of 'sensible talk [about sex] wherever they go'.[2]

---

1   Good Vibrations was not the first business in the United States dedicated to women's sexual pleasure and health. Eve's Garden was founded by Dell Williams in New York City in 1974 but operated initially as a mail order company, only later opening a brick and mortar store.

2   Not all women-run or women-oriented sex toy businesses subscribe to the model of sex toy retailing that I discuss in this chapter. A case in point is Ann Summers, a highly successful retailer in the UK, with both brick and mortar stores and a popular home party plan. While Ann Summers differs from more traditional adult retailers, it has not adopted

214 *New Sociologies of Sex Work*

Female sexuality is increasingly mediated through the market, making venues such as feminist sex toy businesses important cultural sites for examining the proliferation and administration of sexual discourses (see Foucault 1977). This chapter draws on over a decade's worth of research on the history and retail culture of sex positive feminist sex toy businesses in the United States to outline the underlying philosophies and retail strategies that comprise the Good Vibrations model of retail. This research includes six months of fieldwork at Babeland in New York City, where I was trained to work on the sales floor as a staff 'sex educator', and over seventy in-depth interviews with sex positive retailers, sales staff, marketing managers, and sex toy manufacturers from across the United States.

My research can be situated within the broader tradition of ethnographic studies of cultural production, which seeks to 'make concrete the universe in which designated "cultural producers" (TV writers, broadcast journalists, filmmakers, etc.) do what they do' (Henderson 2003). There is a growing, interdisciplinary body of scholarship that examines the processes by which advertisers, marketers, and retailers become 'brokers and mediators of preexisting hierarchies of representation' (Davilla 2001: 7). These studies map 'the particular power relations, the context, within which both the identity and the effects of any particular practices are determined' (Grossberg 1993).

Retail culture, like other forms of popular culture, is produced by social actors – storeowners, managers, marketers, and sales staff – who cultivate particular kinds of shopping environments, retail experiences, and consumer identities (see Porter Benson 1986). Through the design of their retail spaces, the kinds of inventory they carry, the strategic display of merchandise, and their direct appeals to consumers on the basis of gender, race, class, sexual orientation and cultural taste, retailers communicate – indeed help produce – a range of cultural knowledge about social identity, desire, consumption, and the interplay between these spheres.[3]

The success and proliferation of Good Vibrations model of retailing offers an interesting case study for examining how dominant sexual codes and conventions can be repackaged – indeed *regendered* – with an eye toward wooing the female consumer. Since the 1970s, sex positive retailers have mobilized a complicated set of discourses about sexual taste and respectability in a concerted effort to transform sex toy stores from taboo and illicit establishments into more respectable and legitimate cultural forms. They have done so, importantly, by painting a stark contrast between their retail businesses and the image of 'sleazy' adult stores

---

the same emphasis on feminist sexual politics and sex education as the retailers in my study. For an interesting discussion of Ann Summers parties, see Merl Storr (2003).

3   While sex positive retailers and sales staff perform a type of 'sexualized work,' I argue that this form of sexualized labour differs from more traditional notions of 'sex work.' Selling sexual products is a very different kind of endeavor, with a different set of stakes, than selling sexual services, such as lap dances or specific sexual acts, the latter of which involves putting one's body on the line in qualitatively different ways.

geared primarily toward men. A focus on the design of their retail spaces, the kinds of products they sell, the type of customer service they offer, and positioning their businesses as sexual resource centers rather than porn palaces are key elements in the alternative sex vending movement.

Marking the distinctions between 'crass' and 'class' and sexual 'safety' versus 'sleaze' is hardly a value-free endeavor; rather, such claims are inscribed with social judgements and hierarchies of sexual taste that are both highly gendered and class-specific, helping to produce, among other things, commercially viable representations of sexuality and desire. By routinely invoking ideas about tastefulness and respectability, sex-positive retailers have also gained a measure of cultural legitimacy – not to mention a market share – previously denied to their 'lowbrow' counterparts. Indeed, this has been instrumental to the growth and mainstreaming of the women's market – a consumer demographic that, at least in the US context, is considered by many industry analysts to be the hottest growth market in the adult entertainment industry today (see Comella 2008 and 2009, Attwood 2005). At the same time, sex-positive entrepreneurs are positioned, and sometimes caught, between new sexual possibilities for women and familiar markers of class distinction, the conventional logic of boutique retail culture and the counter-logic of sexual access and openness, an awareness of sexual diversity and the constraints of gender essentialism.

In what follows I discuss the genesis and circulation of the Good Vibrations model, with its emphasis on sex positivity and the dissemination of sexual information. I then turn my attention to the discourses of distinction that are mobilized by sex positive retailers to differentiate their businesses from their more conventional counterparts. These discourses of distinction – 'safety' versus 'sleaze' and 'crass' versus 'class' – ultimately produce social hierarchies of cultural value and taste that have far reaching effects, from producing commercially viable versions of 'respectable' sexuality to reassuring nervous landlords and community members that sex positive businesses are not 'dirty bookstores' but legitimate and valued resource centers geared toward sexual education and health.

The Proliferation of the Good Vibrations Model

Joani Blank founded Good Vibrations as a sex educator and therapist who recognized the benefits that came from people having access to sexual information and products. Before opening Good Vibrations, Blank was hired by therapist Lonnie Barbach to help screen candidates for Barbach's pre-orgasmic women's groups at University of California, San Francisco (UCSF). Barbach had developed an approach to treating women with orgasmic difficulties that eventually became the basis for her book, *For Yourself: The Fulfillment of Female Sexuality* (1975).

What Blank learned during her time working at UCSF formed the basis of the Good Vibrations model. One of the first things therapists did when they began treating people was to provide them with basic information about sexual anatomy, the sexual response cycle, and 'normal' human sexual variation. This educational component became such a standardized part of therapeutic practice that the counseling program at UCSF decided to hold mandatory education sessions once a month for groups of people who were interested in seeking treatment. What the counseling staff quickly realized was that a surprising number of people never returned for additional counseling. The general information they received at the introductory session was apparently enough to 'fix' them. 'The facts that would come up again and again [in these sessions]', Blank explained, 'and the information that would come up over and over again, mostly had to do with the same kinds of questions teenagers ask, "Is what I experience normal?"' For men, these concerns often focused on what Blank described as the 'old bugaboo' of penis size or the occasional difficulty most men have maintaining an erection. In the case of women, the most common concern was that something was wrong with them because they couldn't achieve orgasm during intercourse or they 'needed' clitoral stimulation or they felt that masturbation was an activity exclusively reserved for men. Once people realized that their experiences were in fact normal, the perceived need for subsequent counseling apparently vanished.

For Blank, opening a sex toy store was a way to reach a potentially wider audience, including people who may have never entertained the idea of visiting a sex therapist. It was also a way to provide women access to vibrators. According to former Good Vibrations employee Cathy Winks: 'In creating Good Vibrations, [Blank] was responding to the need that was being expressed in the pre-orgasmic women's groups and the workshops that she led [and that was] "Well yeah, you say vibrators are so great and I would be happy to buy them but I just cannot find a place where I am comfortable doing it and I don't want to go into an adult store."' Former Good Vibrations employee Anne Semans made a similar point:

> I think in the beginning Joani was really motivated by the very basic idea that was part of the whole feminist consciousness-raising of the seventies that wanted women to learn about clitoral orgasms. And certainly for ninety per cent of us that went into the store, that's what was going on: we walked away with our little vibrators.

Blank combined a quasi-therapeutic, educational approach to selling sex toys with elements of seventies feminist consciousness-raising. By mid-to-late 1980s, Good Vibrations had developed a national reputation as a resource centre for sexual information and a leader in the alternative sex vending movement. Good Vibrations thrived in San Francisco's sex positive, queer Mecca. The company's sex positive mission, one promulgated by Blank and her employees, permeated its store and catalogues, and former staff members, such as Susie Bright – who went on to help launch *On Our Backs Magazine* and write a number of best-selling sex books – became ambassadors for Good Vibrations' unique brand of sex positive retailing.

Sex positivity is a cornerstone of the Good Vibrations model. It is a way of conceptualizing and talking about sexuality that draws on a particular constellation of sexual values and norms – or counter-norms as the case may be (e.g. 'anything goes' as long as it is between consenting adults). As a discourse and, one might argue, a *sexual ethic*, sex positivity seeks to intervene in a culture overwhelmingly shaped by sex negativity, which is the idea that sex is a dangerous, destructive and negative force (Rubin 1993). Sex positivity includes the idea that the more encouragement and support people have around their sexuality, the better; that everyone deserves access to accurate information about sex; that people should not be embarrassed or ashamed for wanting more sexual pleasure and enjoyment in their lives. These ideas function as an ideological matrix that informs virtually every aspect of the Good Vibrations model, from marketing and advertising to product selection and customer service.

Blank's non-competitive ethos, combined with a commitment to seeing stores like Good Vibrations establish themselves in cities across the country, led to a short-lived internship program in the early 1990s. Claire Cavanah, who would go on to open Babeland with business partner Rachel Venning, and Kim Airs, who started Grand Opening in Boston, each paid a small fee to come to Good Vibrations and learn the nuts-and-bolts of the Good Vibrations model of sexual retail. They worked on the sales floor alongside Good Vibrations sales staff, reviewed the company's financial records, attended staff meetings, visited the company's mail order operations, and received a copy of the business's vendor lists, which Cavanah later described as a 'gold mine.'

By the time their internships ended, Cavanah and Airs had all the information they needed to return to their respective cities and open sex positive businesses of their own. Since then, former employees of both Babeland and Grand Opening have opened sex toy stores of their own – Sugar in Baltimore and Self Serve in Albuquerque respectively – further propagating the Good Vibrations model and its message of sex positivity.

Good Vibrations and the businesses that followed in its footsteps generated, and indeed helped popularize an alternative set of representational strategies and retail norms that challenged many taken-for-granted ideas about what sex toys stores could be and who they were for. To accomplish this, they employ an alternative 'sexual vernacular' (Patton 1991) that pivots on highly gendered notions about sexual 'respectability', 'safety', and 'cleanliness'.[4] In the process, they also produce certain 'truths' about female sexuality and desire, which have become powerful organizing principles for their businesses, a point I return to later.

---

4   I borrow the idea of 'sexual vernaculars' from Cindy Patton (1991). According to Patton, sexual performances, identities, and networks are constructed in and as sexual languages or vernaculars. Rather than being universal, sexual vernaculars are intimately connected to specific communities and subcultures of people who have their own ways of speaking about sex, and organizing sexual knowledge and meanings.

The 'Clean and Well Lit' Sex Store

Creating a retail environment that is both 'comfortable' and 'safe' is a defining feature of the Good Vibrations model. These elements ultimately reflect the type of audience that Good Vibrations and its sister stores were initially hoping to attract: the sexually reserved yet curious woman who might have never imagined venturing into one of 'those places.' Good Vibrations wanted to be a store that, according to Carol Queen, 'could be safe enough for anybody.'

Many staff members I spoke with who worked at Good Vibrations in the 1990s invoked the stereotype of the 'Marin housewife' to describe their target demographic.[5] The description of the 'Marin housewife' as the idealized Good Vibrations' customer is a very particular construction of the female consumer, one rooted firmly in race (whiteness) and class (middle to upper-middle). According to Roma Estevez, the 'Marin housewife' is a middle to upper-middle class, presumably white, suburban woman 'who is not very sexually adventurous; who maybe doesn't have an orgasm or who doesn't reliably have an orgasm; who doesn't talk about sex with her friends or husband or mom; who is straight, of course; and who is interested [in sex] but really needs a lot of encouragement and hand holding.'

During the years she worked as the manager of Good Vibrations, Cathy Winks routinely reminded her staff that they needed to think of the Good Vibrations customer as the suburban lady who heard from a friend at church that there was a sex toy store in the city that was 'really nice for women.' 'What is going to make this woman feel safe walking into a sex toy store for the very first time?' Winks frequently asked her staff. 'What kind of music will be playing? How will people be dressed? How will this customer be treated?' Winks encouraged Good Vibrations' sales staff to be attentive to these details in order to ensure that the store continued to be a 'comfortable' and 'safe' space for even the most shy or sexually inhibited woman.

Anne Semans, who worked at Good Vibrations for thirteen years, also emphasized this point. 'There was a real tendency', she told me, 'to forget that suburban housewives made up eighty per cent of our mail order and that we couldn't just assume that everyone was going to be comfortable with a certain terminology or a certain attitude or cleverness.' 'We really strove to make [Good Vibrations] a warm, welcoming place', explained Roma Estevez, 'because sexuality is so frightening, for a lack of a better word, in our society.'

While Good Vibrations desired, quite genuinely, to be a store that 'could be safe enough for anybody' – women and men of various backgrounds and sexual orientations – what this meant in practice was that it *especially* wanted to be a

---

5   Marin County is located in the North San Francisco Bay Area. According to the 2000 US Census, 84 per cent of the 247,000 people residing in Marin County were white with a median household income of $71,000, making it at the time the 14th highest income county per median income and the 5th highest by personal per capita income in the US.

safe and welcoming space for a particular subset of female consumers – suburban, and presumably heterosexual, housewives who were thought to need more hand holding and encouragement around their sexuality than other women. In this regard, the emphasis placed on sexual safety, cleanliness and comfort, takes on extremely class-specific and racially coded dimensions, which are often entirely overshadowed by the emphasis that Good Vibrations and its sister stores place on gender.

The idea that sexuality can be 'frightening' is something these businesses work hard to counteract in the hope of making their stores accessible to people who might otherwise never consider going into a sex store. 'This is very important to us', Carol Queen explained, 'because it means that more and more people who haven't had access to comfortable or correct information will get it from us.' By striving to make their stores 'warm' and 'welcoming', and 'clean and well lit', sex positive businesses communicate to their customers that sex – and by extension sex toy stores – do not, according to Kim Airs, the former owner of Grand Opening in Boston, 'have to be uncomfortable, shameful, or dirty to get something that you want.' 'We tried to make it so that you were inviting people into your living room', Cathy Winks remarked. 'When you read the old articles about the early stores, it was about the armchair and the rug and the plants and how it was so cozy. And that is what we were making a conscious effort to create – a really safe, cozy space for people.'

Designing a sex toy store that resembles a safe and cozy living room is a radical departure from the stereotype of an adult store as a dimly lit and unwelcoming space. But this was precisely what Good Vibrations was striving to do, especially early on. By choosing aesthetic markers that closely mirrored the layout and design of the home, Good Vibrations was effectively domesticating, and some might argue, sanitizing a highly sexualized public setting by anchoring it in the familiarity and emotional comfort of the home.

The businesses in my study have invested a great deal of time and energy, not to mention money, creating retail spaces that encourage sexual curiosity while minimizing feelings of emotional or psychological discomfort. Their goal is to be inviting rather than off-putting. 'One of the things that I have noticed', Alicia Relles, the former Director of Purchasing at Babeland, explained, 'is that there is a safety when you walk into Babeland. There is a corner for books and magazines. Half the people go right over there, and there is a safety in that':

> I like the way that [Babeland] is structured and that there are points in the store that allow people to have different vantage points of things and to distance themselves from objects that may be scary or intimidating. The dildos are presented in a way that is about colour and presentation versus that this is actually a dick. The things that are highlighted in the store are very much about colour and aesthetic and are not so screamingly phallic. You are not confronted with certain images or even if you are, it is done in a different way.

220 *New Sociologies of Sex Work*

As Relles' quote suggests, ideas about sexual 'comfort' and 'safety' are linked to the desire to 'protect' unsuspecting customers from products that might be 'screamingly phallic' or otherwise shocking or 'scary'. Ideas about what constitutes sexual comfort and safety are therefore built into the very design and layout of stores. Sh! Women's Erotic Emporium in London takes the idea of ensuring the comfort of its female shoppers one-step further with a policy of welcoming men only when accompanied by a woman. According to its website:

> Back in 1992 [when the business was founded], we felt this was absolutely necessary to create a comfortable, welcoming place for women... Until a woman in a sex shop is not seen as available or asking for attention [from men], we will carry on putting our money where our mouth is and ask for guys to come accompanied to Sh! (Sh! 2010).

Although most retailers, regardless of the products they are selling, endeavour to create environments where people feel comfortable, many people I talked to during the course of my research felt that the idea of comfort assumes added symbolic weight for Good Vibrations and its sister stores because these businesses deal specifically with sex. By striving to make their stores 'welcoming' and 'safe', they are attempting to establish a different set of retail norms and aesthetic markers than they imagine customers would encounter if they were to visit a more traditional adult business. These revamped norms are also a strategic attempt to challenge ideas about sex negativity – and women's sexual availability to men – that many retailers say permeate the culture at large, including certain segments of the sex industry. Carol Queen explains:

> I assume that you have been in some traditional adult bookstore type sex spaces, and there is just something about the way that they are put together that doesn't seem...friendly. You sure can tell why all these guys stuck their noses in Good Vibrations and said, "I don't really like those places myself." Of course they don't! They are not really very likable as sex spaces and in some ways the ways that they are unlikable sort of support cultural sex negativity. Why would you want to shop for this kind of stuff in a clean and nice environment? Who would think those terms? *Well women thought in those terms.* That's who! [emphasis mine]

Queen's remarks suggest that the representational strategies and aesthetic norms that have evolved alongside the Good Vibrations model work to not only distance Good Vibrations from more traditional adult stores, but they are also a byproduct of gendered discourses of sexual taste. Laura Weide, who had stints working at both Good Vibrations and Babeland, acknowledged that the 'alternative aesthetic' that many women-owned sex toy stores adopted 'sort of assumes a gendered contrast'. Women-oriented sex stores consistently rely on elements of style and 'tastefulness', such as painting the walls lavender, hanging original art, and using

Repackaging Sex 221

warm lighting, to give their businesses a 'non-threatening' and more 'feminine touch.' Within these retail contexts, ideas about female sexuality become virtually indistinguishable from the 'safe' and 'non-threatening' codes of middle class sexual respectability.

Respectability is an ideologically dense discursive terrain, a concept imbued with value judgements and moral prescriptions. Beverley Skeggs (1997) argues that respectability invariably contains judgements about class, race, gender, and sexuality, and that different groups have different access to the mechanisms for generating and displaying respectability. Respectability is a key element in defining what it means to belong and to be seen as worthy. To be respectable is to also embody moral authority.

Having recourse to claims of sexual respectability has allowed Good Vibrations and its sister stores to differentiate themselves from more conventional adult businesses, giving them a degree of 'moral authority' in the sexual marketplace. This has helped to legitimize them in the eyes of anxious landlords and neighbourhood associations concerned about the implications of having one of 'those businesses' and the 'seedier' elements they purportedly attract – salacious men, sex workers, drug addicts and dealers – in their buildings and neighbourhoods.

Retailer Aileen Journey told me that she learned to be 'pretty vague' when she was looking for a commercial space in Northampton, Massachusetts for her store, Intimacies, because she did not want her business to be associated the stereotypical adult store. 'If I say, "sex store" people immediately think of a dirty, sleazy [place] and I didn't want them to get the wrong idea'. Proprietor Jacq Jones had a similar experience when she was opening Sugar in Baltimore. According to her, there was a bit of a "hubba-loo" with the local community council, because many council members did not have a reference point for the type of business she was opening. At their meeting, Jones distributed Sugar's mission statement, described the store, and detailed who would comprise its customer base. She also referenced Good Vibrations and Babeland which, according to her, went a long way to allay the community council's concerns; not only were a number of people familiar with those businesses, but they understood the fundamental difference between an educationally-oriented sex toy store and a stereotypically 'sleazy' one.

Such distinctions are not simply a linguistic slight of hand, but have concrete ramifications when it comes to leasing commercial space, negotiating restrictive zoning ordinances, and reassuring nervous community members that these are not 'sleazy' enterprises but instead, as proprietor Jacq Jones of Sugar put it, 'a place that [is] going to be a safe space for women' (2007). In today's sexual marketplace, 'women' has become a code word for a safe and respectable model of sexual retail; in turn, safety and respectability have become synonymous with a commercially viable version of female sexuality.

'Crass' versus 'Class'

The very idea of creating a sexual 'boutique' is laden with connotations about gender, sexual respectability, and cultural taste. During the course of my fieldwork, proprietors, sales staff, and customers frequently – and often without reflection – used the terms 'classy' and 'tasteful' to describe the difference between women-oriented sex toy stores and 'regular' sex toy stores. 'I enjoyed your store', one woman wrote in an email to Babeland, 'because it was not trashy at all'. Such comments suggest that is difficult to separate discourses about sexual comfort, safety, and cleanliness from gendered and classed ideas about sexual taste and a larger, ideologically complicated project of 'sexual uplift.' As Roma Estevez explains:

> Good Vibrations shoots for a more 'classy' feeling in the store and in the personality of the catalogues and the web site. I think originally that was probably a really good idea and a really good stance to take to differentiate us from the sleazy sex toy shop that had a lot of metal in it and a lot of cheesy packages. So, I think originally it was really smart and it really worked.

Laura Kipnis provides one of the clearest articulations of the complicated relationship between sexuality, class, and taste culture. In the essay 'Disgust and Desire: *Hustler Magazine*', Kipnis argues that Larry Flynt and *Hustler Magazine* disrupted the taken-for-granted codes and conventions associated with the genre of men's magazines such as *Playboy* and *Penthouse* – magazines that reflect a sexual sensibility largely defined through middle class standards of sexual decorum, civility, 'sophistication', and taste (1996). *Hustler* defiantly addresses itself to a working class audience and from its inception was 'determined to violate all the taboos observed by its more classy men's-rag brethren' (Kipnis: 130). It introduced penises – a sight verboten in other men's magazines – and included images of pregnant women, fat women, middle-aged women, hermaphrodites, amputees, and a pre-operative transsexual – images that were clearly intended to shock as well as titillate. The 'improper' and even 'gross' sexual body of *Hustler* assumes its social and political significance in contrast to the 'proper', 'polite', and 'contained' body depicted in *Playboy* and *Penthouse*. In violating the representational conventions of men's magazines, Kipnis contends that *Hustler* also transgresses the socially acceptable limits of sexual tastefulness. Kipnis reminds us that what is considered sexually 'gross' and 'repulsive', or 'tasteful' and 'acceptable', are matters of class distinction.

Kipnis' analysis of *Hustler Magazine* and its more 'tasteful' – and therefore more socially acceptable – counterparts offers an instructive parallel for thinking about the kinds of discourses that storeowners and staff routinely invoke to describe the differences between their businesses and more conventional adult businesses. These 'discourses of distinction' – 'classy' versus 'crass' and 'tasteful' versus 'tacky' – are not simply descriptive terms but generative ones that produce social

Repackaging Sex 223

hierarchies of sexual taste that ultimately function to legitimize certain cultural forms while delegitimizing others.

Indeed, a large part of the commercial success that Good Vibrations and its sister stores have had is a result of mobilizing social distinctions of various kinds, which has not only generated broad consumer appeal but has also garnered a degree of social legitimacy not readily bestowed upon their 'lowbrow' counterparts. The effects of this are manifold, but perhaps most indicative of the increased social status conferred on many of these sex positive businesses is the degree to which they have been able to successfully navigate otherwise restrictive zoning ordinances.

A case in point involves Good Vibrations' second retail location in Berkeley, California. The store's opening in 1994 was temporarily delayed when its zoning permit was rescinded less than a week before its scheduled opening. According to newspaper accounts, a resident had complained to City Council officials that Good Vibrations had been issued a permit as a gift shop and bookstore rather than an adult business, the latter of which would have resulted in a number of restrictions making it impossible for the business to operate in its current location (Caulfield 1995). Employees and supporters of Good Vibrations rallied, arguing that the business was not a dirty bookstore that appealed to 'prurient interests', but a sexual resource center and as such, a valued and respected business. The store's permit was eventually reinstated but only after Good Vibrations marshalled the symbolic resources and community support needed to convince the City that it did not fit the stereotype of a 'sleazy' adult business. Thus, Good Vibrations' ability to differentiate itself from what Carol Queen describes as the 'more lurid [retail] environments or less educationally-oriented or [less] clean and well lit' establishments provided it with a buffer zone of protection and a degree of moral authority not necessarily available to its less 'reputable' and 'lowbrow' counterparts.

In addition to being arbiters of class distinction, discourses about sexual taste are also predicated on appeals to gender and sexual differences. Candida Royalle, who has created a popular line of vibrators, Natural Contours, in addition to running her adult film company, Femme Productions, offered one of the strongest expressions – and indeed naturalizations – of the relationship between gender, class, and sexual taste in describing the appeal of her products to women:

> I always say that women love sex, they just want it done well. They want to look at it done well. One of the biggest words that women would use when they would write me letter thanking me for my work is the word "class." They would say, "Thank you. Finally, something with class." Women don't want low-class stuff that makes them feel even more ashamed of their sexuality and of themselves for looking at it. And I think it is the same thing with these [vibrators]. They wanted something with class. And that is, I think, how you get to women. You give them something with class, with quality, with some kind of artistry, and

they will respond much better than the same old, cheesy kind of approach you can take with men.

In Royalle's opinion, bringing the markers of 'quality' and 'class' to the sexual marketplace is not only how you 'get to women', but also how you rescue sex, porn, and sex toys from their stereotypical crass and 'lowbrow' status. For Royalle, the project of 'sexual uplift' is intimately connected to the larger project of sex positivity. As she explains:

> Women have such a legacy of shame about our sexuality. And by doing it this way there is nothing dirty or shameful about these products. It is not going to make you feel dirty or shameful and in fact it will reinforce feelings of positive self-acceptance of their sexuality. I think that has been very important and that is what [women] have needed.

Royalle describes an extremely fixed and essentialized version of 'what women want' when it comes to sex and sex toys – understandings that, significantly, have broader reaching implications for shaping consumer demands, tastes, and definitions of 'respectable' female sexuality. While these ideas certainly hold true for some women, including those who have written to Royalle expressing their gratitude, it would be a mistake to assume that she speaks for, or that her products speak to, all women. The 'truth' that Royalle presents about female sexuality is at best a partial truth, one that she has been able to parlay, with great success, into her business ventures. Yet there are a number of women for whom ideas about sexual 'comfort', 'safety', and 'respectability' translate into a kind of sexual sterility that is anything but sexy or appealing. Even someone like Cathy Winks, who spent ten years working at Good Vibrations, admitted that she found Good Vibrations to be almost 'counter-erotic' the first time she visited the store as a customer in the early eighties. 'I get the safe atmosphere that they are trying to create', she commented, 'But it is almost oppressively counter-erotic, which is how I experienced it on my first visit there'.

Some women actively embrace the sense of cultural transgression, taboo, and anonymity they experience when they venture into a sex store that has not attempted to sanitize sex or mimic the retail aesthetics of The Gap. One woman I spoke with, a white, middle-class lesbian who enjoys shopping at more conventional adult stores with her girlfriend, explained that women-oriented sex stores 'could be selling anything.' For her, the gendered recoding of these spaces effectively *de-sexualizes* them to the extent that 'they could be a jewellery store' – and thus for her, rather boring. The codes of 'feminine respectability' and 'classy' retailing that Good Vibrations and its sister stores cultivate to distinguish themselves from 'regular' sex toy stores – distinctions that clearly have appeal for many people, myself included – do not always nor necessarily lend themselves to the kinds of sexually transgressive or class inclusive experiences that some people actively seek when shopping for sexual products.

Conclusion

Dennis Hall has describes Good Vibrations as a 'player in an expanding effort to socially sanitize an interest in and use of a variety of sexual goods, especially apparatus, among middle class consumers' (2000: 1). Over the past three decades, Good Vibrations and its sister stores have created a distinct commercial identity, one that employs the 'codes and warrants of middle-class American culture so to legitimate itself and the sexual behaviors implied by the consumption of its products' (Hall 2000: 2). Good Vibrations and its sister stores sell much more than sex toys: they sell sexual information, identities, and a mission of sex positivity designed to combat a politics of sexual shame. In other words, Good Vibrations and its sister stores sell a transformation of sexual consciousness that is 'made intelligible by the sanitizing codes' (Hall: 5) of middle-class feminine propriety and respectability.

The Good Vibrations model is imbued with cultural values and assumptions about gender, sexual taste, and respectability that are produced in opposition to the stereotype of conventional adult business as inherently 'crass' and sexist. These dimensions of difference are mobilized by retailers in an effort to salvage sex toy stores from their pejoratively dirty, 'lowbrow' and male-oriented status thereby giving sex positive retailers a degree of moral authority and social standing not necessary bestowed on more conventional adult businesses As I have argued throughout this chapter, the project of sexual uplift advanced by sex positive retailers is an ideologically dense and complicated one not easily reducible to gender alone. Not only does the Good Vibrations model produce an alternative set of retail strategies and norms designed to appeal 'especially but not exclusively' to women, but it also, and perhaps unwittingly, constructs certain truths about female and male sexuality and desire that organize these businesses in absolutely fundamental ways.

References

Attwood, F. (2005). 'Fashion and passion: Marketing sex to women', *Sexualities*, 8(4): 392–406.

Barbach, L. (1975). *For Yourself: The Fulfillment of Female Sexuality*. New York: Signet.

Caulfield, B. (1995). 'New business raises "adult oriented" issue', *Berkeley Voice*, 16 February.

Comella, L. (2008). 'It's sexy. It's big business. And it's not just for men', *Contexts Magazine*, 7(3): 61–3.

Comella, L. (2009). 'Remaking the sex industry: The adult expo as a microcosm', in R. Weitzer (ed.) *Sex for Sale: Prostitution, Pornography, and the Sex Industry*, 2nd edition. New York: Routledge, 285–306.

Davila, A. (2001). *Latinos, Inc: The Marketing and Making of a People*. Berkeley: University of California Press.

Foucault, M. (1977). *The History of Sexuality*, Vol. 1. New York: Vintage Books.

Grossberg, L. (1993). 'Can cultural studies find happiness in communication?', *Journal of Communication*, 43(4): 89–97.

Hall, D. (2000). 'Good Vibrations: Eros and instrumental knowledge', *Journal of Popular Culture*, 34(1): 1–7.

Henderson, L. (2003). *Sexuality, Cultural Production, and Foucault*. Paper presented at the Sexuality after Foucault Conference, University of Manchester, UK.

Kipnis, L. (1996). *Bound and Gagged: Pornography and the Politics of Fantasy in America*. Durham, NC: Duke University Press.

Porter Benson, S. (1986). *Counter Cultures: Saleswomen, Managers, and Customers in American Department Stores, 1890–1940*. Urbana and Chicago: University of Illinois Press.

Rubin, G. (1993). 'Thinking sex: Notes for a radical theory of the politics of sexuality', in H. Abelove et al. (eds) *The Lesbian and Gay Studies Reader*. New York and London: Routledge, 3–44.

Sh! Women's Erotic Emporium (2010). 'First and only women's sex store in the UK' [online], available at: http://www.shwomenstore.com/newsdesk/About+Sh%21/First+%252526+only+women%27s+sex+store+in+the+UK.html [accessed 25 March 2010].

Skeggs, B. (1997). *Formations of Class and Gender: Becoming Respectable*. London: Sage.

Storr, M. (2003). *Latex and Lingerie: Shopping for Pleasure at Ann Summers*. Oxford: Berg.

Index

ability 158
abuse 24, 29, 33, 134, 205
  see also verbal abuse
academic community 67, 68, 92, 151, 152,
    155, 167
access 59, 60, 77, 78, 81, 86
  and Internet 91-2, 94, 95, 100-101
accomodation 75-6, 77, 141, 203, 204, 207
  emergency 75, 76
acting 144
activists 169, 170, 175, 178
actors 84, 86, 138, 147, 158, 160, 172, 173,
    177, 214
addiction 48, 200, 206
  see also alcohol; drug use
adult entertainment 59, 112, 185n., 215
adult stores 213, 214-15, 219, 220ff., 224,
    225
  see also Good Vibrations; sex toys
    retail
advertising 91, 100, 138, 139, 141, 197,
    217
advice services 75-6, 78, 81
aesthetic markers 219, 220
aesthetics 147, 219, 220, 224
affection 113, 147
Africa 152
agencies, tango 141-2, 143, 145
agency 4, 12, 47, 48, 110, 170
agents *see* cabaret agents; *see also*
    agencies, tango
Agustin, L.M. 1, 84, 149, 150
Airs, Kim 217, 219
Albuquerque 213, 217
alcohol 151, 153, 158, 182, 187, 188, 191,
    200, 204, 207
alcoholism 157
amateurs 11, 13-14, 15, 19, 20
ambivalence 141, 177
AMMAR 6, 168-71, 173, 175-9

challenges to 171-2, 174-5
ideology of 170
objectives 169, 171
strategies 168-9, 171, 175-9
success of 178, 179
anger 66, 69
Ann Summers 213n., 214n.
anonymity 60, 128, 224; *see also* visual
    anonymity
'anti-work' 7, 182, 186, 187ff., 189, 190-92
anxiety 64-5, 67, 68, 70
architecture 124
Argentina 6, 139ff., 167-80
  decriminalization 176
  labour history 178
  law 174, 175, 176, 178
  police harassment 173, 174-5, 176
  sex worker organizing 167-8ff.
    see also AMMAR
  and stigma 173-4
  see also Buenos Aires; tango tourism;
    taxi dancers
arts project 77
Ashford, C. 197, 198
Association for Moral and Social Hygiene
    (AMSH) 12, 16, 18
attitudes 27, 46
authenticity 114, 117
autonomy 190
Avila, E. *see* Hondagneu Soleto, P. and
Avila, E.
awareness 26, 29, 42, 48, 51

Babeland 213, 217, 219, 221, 222
Bain, P. *see* Taylor, P. and Bain, P.
Bales, K. 138
Baltimore 213, 217, 221
Bangkok 113, 115
Bar Council 32
Barbach, Lonnie 215

bargaining 190
bars 124, 127, 169
   see also go-go bars
Barton, B. 183, 185, 186, 187, 189
behaviour 12, 13, 17, 46, 49, 51, 62, 66,
      112, 116, 182, 186, 187, 191
   of sex researchers 64
Berkeley, California 223
Bhattacharyya, G. 118
Bimbi, D.S. and Parsons, J.T. 91
Bindel, J. 182
bisexuals 197, 200, 201, 202
   see also LGTB communities
Bishop, R. and Robinson, L.S. 112
Blackpool 25
Blank, Joani 213, 215, 216, 217
Blue Room, The 77, 81, 82
Blunkett, David 25
bodies 116, 117, 118, 183
   'foreign' 128
   and intimacy 144, 146
   reading of 117
   see also bodywork
bodywork 138, 171, 173
   and emotional labour 143, 144, 146
Booth, Mrs Bramwell 19
Borden, Mary 13
Boston 217
Bott, E. 182, 183, 187
Brain, Chief Constable Tim 33
Brennan, D. 130, 138
Brewis, J. and Linstead, S. 3, 203
Bright, Susie 216
Brighton & Hove 7, 198ff.
   as gay capital 198-9
   housing costs 204
   see also LGTB communities
Britain *see* United Kingdom
Brooks-Gordon, B. 91
brothels 26, 29, 60, 77, 101, 124, 145
Browne, K. 200, 205
Browne, K. and Davis, P. 200, 204
Browne, K. and Lim, J. 200
Bryman, A. 93, 94
Buenos Aires 6, 138, 139, 140, 141, 143,
      145, 176; *see also* tango tourism;
      taxi dancers

cabaret agents 151, 152, 156, 157, 158,
      159, 160
cabaret dancers 6, 112, 149-63
   ages of 158-9
   debts of 159-60
   demand for 158-9
   finding work 158
   interviews with 151
   and law 153, 160
   migratory projects 160
   mobility 150-51, 152, 157, 158
   pay of 155
   permits 150, 152-3, 156
   recruitment 153, 160
   sexual services 153, 157
   work 153
      conditions of 157, 158, 159, 160,
         161 duration of 150, 155-7,
         158, 161
      periods 150, 153-7, 158, 161
cabaret owners 151, 152, 153, 158
cabaret shows
   Thailand 112-13
   see also cabaret dancers; Switzerland
Cabrera, Sandra 169, 175
call centres 143, 144
campaigns 26
Campbell, M. *see* Sanders, T. and
Campbell, M.
Campbell, R. 30, 62; *see also* Sanders, T.
   and
Campbell, R.
Canada 150, 182, 213
capitalism 139, 147, 170, 209
Cardiff 79
care, local authority 200
care chain 147
careers 151, 187, 191
Caribbean 129, 130
Carpenter, B.J. 31
Catholic Church 175
Cavanah, Claire 213, 217
Chakrabarti, Shami 32
Central de Trabajadores Argentinos (CTA)
      170, 171
charges *see* fees; money
Chesterton, Mrs Cecil 12, 13, 14, 15, 17
Chi, R. 114

Index

Chicago 213
childcare 169
children 3, 25, 27, 29, 50, 111, 112, 138,
    154, 169, 172, 173, 176, 177, 178
Chimenti, M. 157
China 2
choice 17, 33, 34, 98, 155, 168, 170, 186,
    199
Christchurch 46
Christchurch School of Medicine 40
cinemas 14, 16, 20
circulation 149-50, 154-5, 158
    see also migration; mobility
citizenship 128, 173, 199
class 11, 50, 111, 114, 119, 170, 178, 209,
    215, 218, 221, 222, 224, 225
cleanliness 217, 219, 222
clients 30, 31, 33, 40, 45, 46, 49, 59, 82,
    83, 130, 131, 142, 146, 153, 209
    see also 'dodgy punters'; gringo
    clients; men who pay for sex
clothes 139
CMC methods 92, 94, 95, 97, 100, 101,
    102
cocaine 188, 190
codes 183, 214, 225
codes of behaviour 49, 51, 188, 189, 192
coercion 23, 27, 29, 33
Cohen, C. 117, 118
collective action 172
collective migratory projects 160
collective techniques 183
Collinson, D. 184
Colombians 125, 126, 127, 132, 133
Colosi, R. 7, 181, 182, 184, 186, 188, 189
comfort 213, 218, 219, 220, 222, 225
Comley, P. 93, 94
commentators 12, 13, 14, 17, 19, 44, 197
commerce 129, 146
commercial sex *see* sex, sale of; sex work
commodification 30, 112, 117, 118, 147
'common prostitute' 4, 16-17, 18, 19, 20
communication 2, 91, 92, 95, 100, 102,
    144, 172
    see also CMC methods
communities 26, 27, 28, 30, 40, 43, 75, 77,
    132, 154, 173, 178, 197ff.
companions 145

competition 156
computer-mediated-communication *see*
    CMC methods
condoms 42, 78, 81, 84, 85, 133
confidentiality 98
Confiteria Ideal 137, 141
Connell, J. 197
consent 42, 168
consultation 23, 25, 26
    and bias 27, 28-9, 34
    lack of 24, 27ff., 35
consumerism 14, 20, 117, 147, 214, 215,
    218, 223
context 3, 4, 12, 61, 76, 94, 97, 152, 168,
    171, 198, 199, 214
control 93, 114, 183, 188, 190
conventions 214, 221, 222
Coomber, R. 100
Coordinated Prostitution Strategy, A
    (2006) 25-6
Copp, M. *see* Kleinman, S. and Copp, M.
Córdoba 174, 175, 177, 178
Costa Rica 6, 167
    law 129
    migrant numbers 126
    national identity 123, 128
    reputation of 126
    sex industry 126
    sex workers 128-9
    tourism 129
    see also Gringo Gulch; San José
Count Me In Too 197, 198, 200, 201ff.
country of origin 151, 154, 155, 157
Craske, N. 172
'crass' 215, 222, 224, 225
Cressey, P. 145, 188
Criminal Justice and Police Act (2001) 28
criminality 11, 13, 25, 46, 85, 86, 100, 101,
    124, 127, 133, 169
criminalization 4
    of men who buy sex 23, 27-9, 32, 40
criminology 1, 4
cultural context 3, 4, 5, 12, 19, 20, 114,
    143, 214, 220, 225
cultural forms 223
cultural production 214
cultures 2, 109, 115, 116, 130
curiosity 219

customer-dancer interactions 183, 189, 192
customers, retail 213, 218-19, 224ff.
Cylwik, H. 62, 66
Cyprus 150

Dahinden, J. and Stants, F. 152, 153, 157, 160
dance escorting 145; *see also* taxi dancers
dance halls 14
dance partners 139, 140, 144, 147
dancers 112, 139-40ff., 150, 155, 181
    literature on 183
    see also cabaret dancers; lap-dancers; taxi dancers
danger 5, 17, 18, 59, 64, 70, 71, 84, 217
data 5, 7, 23, 30, 44, 59, 200
    collection 60, 67-8, 70, 75, 76, 151
        via internet 92, 94, 99
Davilla, A. 214
Day, S. 20, 91
De Vaus, D. 92, 93
Deacon, Stuart 18
debates 11, 25, 45
debriefing 62
debt 159-60
deceit 66, 69
decriminalization 5, 39, 43-4ff., 50-51, 176
    benefits of 39, 40, 44, 47, 50
    limitations of 42-3, 47, 48, 51
    opposition to 40
    research on 39, 40, 43ff.
    and violence 42-3
degradation 29, 30
demand 158-9
    in New Zealand 44-5
    tackling 25, 26, 27, 28
demography 139, 142, 168, 178, 215, 218
deportation 125, 127, 134
depression 157
Deshotels, T. and Forsythe, C. 183
design 215, 219
desire 185, 208, 214, 215, 217
detention 176
deviance 4, 11, 14, 19, 60, 62, 100, 117, 185
difference 114, 118, 129, 130, 133
disapproval 98
disciplines 1

discourses 12, 13, 15, 17, 20, 29, 39, 117, 123, 125, 126, 130, 133, 168, 170, 214, 217
    on sexual taste 220, 222, 223
discrimination 173
display, retail 214, 215
disposability 48
distance 145, 146
documentation 170, 172
'dodgy punters' 82, 83, 199
Doezema, J. *see* Kempadoo, K. and Doezema, J.
Dominican Republic 149, 152
Dominicans 125, 126, 127, 132
drinks, sale of 112, 113, 124, 153
drug dealers 79, 83, 100
drug users 33, 46, 47-8, 51, 77, 131, 182, 187, 188-9, 190, 191, 199, 200, 204, 206, 207
dualisms 117
duty of care 76

Earle, S. *see* Sharpe, K. and Earle, S.
Eastern Europe 152
economic factors 2, 13, 14, 15, 17, 19, 29, 76, 111, 155, 169, 177, 186
    in Brighton 204-5
    and migration 160
    in New Zealand 44, 45-6
Edinburgh 83
education 6, 130, 131, 133, 169, 172, 178
    see also sexual education
Egan, D. 59, 182, 183
Ellis, C. 154, 195
    see also Rambo-Ronai, C. and Ellis, C.
Ellis, M. 154
email 67, 92, 93, 94, 95, 100
embarrassment 60, 67, 208, 213
embodied act 80, 86
emoticons 99
emotion management 142n.
emotional labour 142, 143, 145, 146, 183, 186
emotional narratives 61-2, 94
emotions 5, 6, 59, 60, 61, 63-6, 80, 94, 95, 96, 97, 99, 142, 144, 147
    and knowledge 61
    negative 61, 62, 64-6

Index

recognition of 62, 63, 66ff., 71
research on 62
and research process 67-8
see also emotional labour
empirical research 5, 6, 59ff., 76, 91, 92, 109
employees 142, 143, 144, 183, 185, 214, 218, 223
employers 171-2
employment 2, 3, 6, 41, 156, 158, 169, 172, 206, 209
empowerment 7, 41, 51, 97, 198, 203, 206, 208
enforcement 26
entertainment 16, 20, 59, 112-13, 185n.
entrepreneurs 142, 149, 215
Entre Ríos 175, 176
equality 170, 171
eroticism 13
escorts 5, 77, 91, 94, 98, 146
taxi dancers 140
essentialism 111, 215
Estevez, Roma 218, 222
ethics 76, 83, 183
ethnography 6, 7, 109, 138, 184, 185, 186, 214
Europe 149, 150, 152, 156
European Free Trade Association (EFTA) 152, 156
European Union (EU) 152, 156
Evangelical Church 175
Eve's Garden 213n.
eviction 126; *see also* deportation
evidence 23, 24, 30, 31, 33, 34
excitement 19, 186, 191
exotic dancing 59, 145
exotic 'other' 116, 118, 129-30
experiences 97, 98, 199, 214
experts 24, 27, 35
exploitation 170, 206, 208; *see also* sexual exploitation

families 69, 128, 132, 150, 151, 154, 155, 160, 169, 170, 172, 205
fantasy 113
fear 63-4, 65, 70, 71
feelings 5, 46, 49, 61, 62, 66, 67ff., 70, 142, 144, 154, 176, 219

and interviews 94, 96, 97, 98
management of 144
fees 125, 131, 133, 140
female body 6, 15
female consumer 214
female gaze 113-17
female sex tourists 110, 112, 113, 116ff., 147
female sexuality 11, 170, 214, 215, 217, 221, 224
femininity 117, 128
feminism 3, 61, 110, 213, 216
and CMC methods 95-6, 97, 101
and quantitative surveys 92-3, 94
see also radical feminism
feminists 167, 175
researchers 97
retailers 7
fetish workers 77
fieldwork 75, 76, 77, 79, 81, 84, 138, 146, 184, 185, 187, 188, 214, 222
film 114
First World War 13
Fitzroy, Sir Almeric 16
FIZ 152, 153, 157
flappers 11, 13, 15, 19
flirting 145, 147
flow 144
food 76, 134, 169, 204, 207
foreign sex workers 6
in Costa Rica 125, 126ff., 133
research on 125
foreignness 125-8, 129, 131-2, 134, 150
spaces of 126
Forsyth, C.J. and Deshotels, T. 185, 186
Franzi-Fölmi, M. 152, 157
Fraudevaux, D. *see* Sardi, M. and Fraudevaux, D.
freedom 41, 46, 141
friends 134, 155, 158
fun 7, 15, 61, 140, 182, 186-7, 191, 192

Gall, G. 167
gay men
in Brighton 198-9, 205
and sale of sex 201ff., 206, 208
spaces of 197
see also LGTB communities

gay rights 2
  see also gay men; lesbians
Gaydar 197, 198
gaze 113, 140
  female 113-17
  and gender 114, 115, 116
  male 113, 114, 116, 117
  and power 116, 117, 118
  of tourists 114, 117-18
gender 7, 11, 17, 18, 20, 30, 134, 147, 170,
    214, 215, 221, 223, 224
  language of 217
  and LGTB people 197, 198, 200,
    201ff., 209
  and power 110, 111, 113, 117, 183
  roles 13
  sex tourism in Thailand 109-13, 114
  state and 127-8
  and tango dancers 138
geographies 13, 14, 78, 79, 80, 111, 127,
    198, 209; *see also* place
geopolitics 128, 129
gestures 95
Gies, L. 95-6
Giles, Judy 13
globalization 2, 3, 4, 147
Gloucestershire 31
Good Vibrations 7, 213-26
  and class 218, 222-3, 224, 225
  criticism of 224, 225
  customers 213, 218-19, 224ff.
  internships 217
  locations 216, 221, 223
  model of 213, 214-15, 217, 218, 225
  philosophy of 216-17
  research on 213
go-go bars 112, 113, 115, 116
gossip 83, 183, 184, 187
Gould, Arthur 30
Grenz, S. 60
gringo clients 124, 128, 131-2
Gringo Gulch 6
  clients 130, 131
  and foreignness 125-8, 131, 134
  respectability of 123, 124-5, 130
  sex tourism in 125, 124, 128, 129-30
  space of 126, 127, 128, 130-34
  venues 124-5, 126

Grossberg, L. 214
guidebooks 114
guides, tourist 139, 140, 141
Gunn, H. 93
Guy, D.J. 42, 125, 145

Hall, Dennis 225
Hall, Gladys Mary 17
Hall, Lesley 16
Hall, T. 78, 79
Hall, T. and Smith, R. 77, 78, 79, 83
Hammond, Natalie 5, 62
Hampshire 25
harassment 124, 127, 168, 174-5
Hardy, Kate 6, 35, 87, 138, 167, 170, 171
harm minimization 40, 75
Harman, Harriet 28, 30
health *see* healthcare; health and safety;
    public health; sexual health
health and safety 41, 76, 77
healthcare 170, 173, 177
Henderson, L. 214
Herbert, S. 78, 79
Hernández, M. 123, 125
Hester, M. and Westmarland, N. 31
heterosexuals 200, 201
Hewson, C. 103
hierarchies 140, 187-8, 191, 214, 215, 223
Hirschfeld, Magnus 13
history 4, 11, 12, 20
HIV/AIDS 77, 176, 178
Hochschild, A. 142, 143n., 144, 147
Holmes and Marra 184, 189
home 197, 219
Home Office 16, 23, 24-7, 33, 34, 60
  and consultation 27ff.
  lack of research by 30, 31, 34
homelessness 77, 82, 199, 200, 203-5
Hondagneu Soleto, P. and Avila, E. 154
Horwood, Sir William 16, 17
hospitals 146, 155, 173, 177
hostel owners 139
hotels 124, 125, 126, 141
household needs 160, 161, 172
Hove YMCA 199
Hubbard, P. 7, 13, 48, 59, 68, 77, 127, 167,
    209
Hubbard, P. and Sanders, T. 83

Hughes, D. 91
Hugo, G. 149, 154, 161
human rights 39, 40, 41, 43, 43, 47
Human Rights Joint Committee 33, 34
humour 47, 67, 85, 95, 184, 192
Humphreys, M. 67
Hustler Magazine 222

identity 7, 62, 64, 67, 68-9, 70, 117, 133,
    177, 178, 183, 197, 199, 201, 208,
    209, 214
ideology 23, 24, 29-30, 35, 118, 126, 170-
    71, 222, 225
illegality 100, 101, 126, 129, 149, 159
Illingworth, N. 93, 96-7
images 222
immigration control 125, 127, 129, 151,
    156, 157
immigration raids 126-7, 128, 134, 150
immorality 6, 15, 17, 47
inclusivity 102
independent workers 142
India 168
individuals 160, 183
indoor prostitution 39, 40, 41, 43, 45, 85,
    91, 101, 169
inequalities 111
informal economy 2, 140, 141, 171, 172,
    191
information 61, 82, 83, 96, 97-8, 129, 158,
    215, 217
instant messaging 95, 97, 99, 100
intentionality 110
interactions 60, 65, 68, 70, 93, 95, 151
    literature on 183
    visual 117
international relations 129
interdisciplinary approach 1, 214
intermediaries 159, 160
Internet 2, 5, 60, 62, 63, 139
    and access to sex workers 91-2, 94, 95,
        100-101
    female 92, 94, 96-101
    male 96, 98, 99
    see also CMC methods; email; instant
        messaging; interviews; websites
interpretation 117
interviewees 95, 96, 97, 100, 151

interviewers 95, 100, 115, 206, 214
interviews 5, 7, 39, 44, 59, 60, 63, 64, 65,
    68, 75, 82, 138, 151ff., 184, 200,
    214
    CMC methods 92, 94-5, 97, 100ff.
    data comparison 99-100
    face-to-face 94, 95, 96, 97, 98-9, 101,
        102
    and gender 92, 94, 96, 98, 99
    online 92, 95-6ff., 99, 100, 101, 102
    and qualitative research 95, 101
    synchronous methods 95, 100, 102
    telephone 98-9
intimacy 62, 137, 143-4, 183, 197, 208,
    209
    bodily 144-5, 146, 147
    emotional 142, 145, 146
    see also emotional labour

Jeffreys, S. 16, 30, 34, 110, 111, 167, 208
Jenks, C. 117
Jenness, V. 167
Joinson, A. 94, 95, 96
Jones et al. 181, 182
Jones, Jacq 221
journalists 13, 214
Journey, Aileen 221

Kaplan, L. 113, 114
Kempadoo, K. 125, 129, 138, 149, 167
Kempadoo, K. and Doezema, J. 167
kerb-crawlers 25, 26, 27, 28, 29, 60
Kingston, Sarah 4, 87
Kipnis, Laura 222
Kivits, J. 10
Kleinman, S. and Copp, M. 61, 62, 67
knowledge 61, 63, 79, 83, 86, 143, 158,
    214

labour *see* work
labour relations 179
labour rights 168, 178
lady boys 116
LaFont, S. *see* Pruitt, D. and LaFont, S.
Laite, Julia 12, 15, 20
Langton, F.L. 19
language 24, 27, 60, 77, 143, 170, 217n.
lap-dancers 3, 7, 181-96

autonomy of 190
and customers 183, 189, 192
and drugs/alcohol 187, 188-9, 190, 191
and fun 182, 186-7, 191, 192
and humour 184, 192
motivations 185-7
new girls 188, 189, 191, 192
relationships between 186, 191-2
research on 182-3, 184ff., 192
resistance by 182, 183, 189-9, 191, 192
and rules 187, 189-90, 191
and sexual favours 190
and social rituals 187-90, 191, 192
and stigma 182
working conditions 185
see also anti-work; lap-dancing clubs;
    private dances
lap-dancing clubs 181-2, 184-5, 189
rules of 187, 189, 190ff.
Latin America 129-30, 152

law 12, 15-21, 25, 60, 126, 129, 153, 160,
    170, 175, 176
lack of progress in 19-20
reform of 41
see also legislation
Layder, D. 61
legality 96, 97, 98, 125, 129, 150, 160, 174
legalization 41, 176
legislation 2, 4
    Argentina 175-6
    Costa Rica 127
    New Zealand 5, 39ff.
    reform of 41
    UK 4, 12
    changes 26
    review of 23-7
    solicitation 15-17, 19, 20
legitimacy 29, 173, 177, 178, 215, 225
leisure 3, 4, 14, 111, 140, 182, 191
    venues 197, 208
lesbians 197, 200, 201, 224
    and payment for sex 201-2, 208
    see also LGBT communities
LGBT communities 7, 197-212
    complexity of 197, 208
    and domestic violence 205
    and drug use 200, 204, 206, 207

and gender 197, 198, 200, 201ff., 209
and homelessness 199, 200, 203-5
motivations 203-8
and pleasure 203
research on 197-8, 199, 200, 201ff.,
    208
and sale of sex 197, 201ff., 208
spaces of 197
temporalities of 202-3
liberal attitudes 40
Liberty 32
Lifeshare 77, 81
lifestyles 13, 14, 48, 68, 187, 191
Lim, J. and Browne, K. 201n.
    see also Browne, K. and Lim, J.
Lim, L.L. 2, 149
liminality 129, 198
Linstead, S. 184
    see also Brewis, J. and Linstead, S.
listening 83
literature 1, 3, 12, 13, 30, 34, 62, 76, 77,
    83, 91, 94, 97, 110, 114, 138, 183,
    192, 202
    see also research
Liverpool 18, 20
loans 159
London 12, 16, 213, 220
'looking' 113, 116, 118
    see also gaze; watching
love 110, 117, 147

McKenna et al 98
Macklin, A. 150
Macmillan Committee 16-17, 18-19
MacShane, Denis 31
MacTaggart, Fiona 28
magazines 197, 219, 222
Mai, N. 31, 208
maids 3, 33
make-up 14, 15, 19
Malarek, Victor 62
Male Sex Work Outreach Project
    (MSWOP) 77, 78, 81, 82, 84
male sex workers 124
    access to 77, 78, 81, 86
    and internet 96, 98, 99
    advice services for 75-6, 78
    indoor work 91

relationships with 81-2, 85
support for 81
spaces of 79-82
in Thailand 110, 111, 116-17
see also taxi dancers
management 41, 42, 92, 101, 102, 143, 145, 146, 149, 183, 209
resistance to 182, 184
see also emotion management
managers 125, 143, 183, 184, 185, 190, 214
Manchester 76, 77ff.
Gay Village 78, 79-80, 82, 84, 85, 86
Industry Street area 75, 78, 80, 81, 82, 84, 85
Manderson, L. 112, 113
manners 147
Maoz, D. 116
marginalization 174, 208
market 150, 214, 215
marketers 214
marriage 66, 69
masculinity 128
massage parlours 29, 31, 91, 113, 124
material practices 123, 126, 130, 134
Mathieu, L. 167, 177
Maxim Institute 40
media 46, 60, 125, 127, 174, 214
Mehta, R. and Sivadas, E. 93, 94
Melrose, M. 60, 61
men 4, 5, 16, 34, 62, 63, 65-6, 98, 109, 124, 126, 130, 131, 199, 202, 215, 220
American 132
clients 6, 23ff., 30, 62; *see also* men who pay for sex
criminalization of 23, 24, 26, 27-9, 32
gaze of 113, 114, 116, 117
and sexual problems 216
stereotypes of 64, 68, 70, 119, 147
western 109-10, 114
see also male sex workers; taxi dancers
men who pay for sex
fear of 63-4, 65, 70
relationships of 62-3, 65, 66, 67, 69, 70
UK research project 59-60ff.
men's magazines 222

mental health problems 157, 199, 200, 207, 208
methodology 4, 5, 63, 151, 184
difficulties 60, 67-8
outreach work 76, 77
Metropolitan Police Act (1839) 15-16
middle class 124, 178, 183, 218, 221, 222, 224, 225
migrant sex workers 124, 125-6, 133, 134
circulation of 149-50, 152, 153-60
factors influencing 161
mobility of 150, 152, 157, 158
migration 6, 31, 77, 198, 204
circular 149-50ff., 154-5, 157
European 149-50, 152
theory of 150
see also migrant sex workers; mobility
milongas 139, 140, 146
minors 41
misogyny 61, 68
Mitter, S. 172
mobile services 77; *see also* outreach work
mobility 4, 5-6, 128, 149-50, 152, 157, 158
modernity 117
money 125, 128, 131, 132, 133, 139, 140, 141, 159, 160, 185, 186, 187, 191, 203, 204, 207
Monto, M. 30, 60, 62
'moral economy' 128
morality 4, 6, 11, 12, 13ff., 19, 46, 127, 128, 134, 169, 221, 225
double standards in 170
of professional prostitutes 17
Moran-Ellis, J. 69
Morokvasic, M. 149, 154
mothers 154, 176
motivation 7, 44, 62, 96, 101, 113, 183, 185ff., 203-8
Mulholland, K. 183, 191
murder 175
music 183

Nagel, J. 129, 197
nation 113, 123, 128, 129, 134
national identity 123, 128, 132, 133, 134
nationality 131, 132, 133, 134
National Vigilance Association 16

negotiation 42, 49, 76, 81, 83, 84, 91, 125, 153, 183, 190, 205, 208
Netherlands 26
neutrality 20, 46, 61, 67, 71, 96, 189
Neville-Rolfe, Mrs 14
New Labour 23, 24-7
New York 213, 214
New Zealand 4, 5
   decriminalization in 39, 50-51, 176
   police 45-6, 49, 50, 51
   street sex workers 39
      numbers of 44
      violence against 48-50, 51
New Zealand Prostitutes Collective (NZPC) 40
newsgroups 100
newspapers *see* press
NGOs 151, 152, 157
Nicaraguans 125, 126, 132, 133
nightclubs 127, 145, 146, 149, 159, 169
   see also cabaret dancers
normality 45, 69, 117
norms 217, 220, 225
Northampton, Mass. 221

Oasis 199, 200
objectivity 61, 66
objects 114, 117, 118, 150
O'Connell Davidson, J. 60, 61, 111, 118, 138
office work 182, 189, 192
O'Neill, M. 1, 40, 60, 91
'one-off' experiences 203, 208
Operation Pentameter 31
Operation Pentameter 2 31
Opperman, M. 111, 112
oral sex 133
organizations 12, 16, 19, 24
   see also sex worker organizations
orgasm, female 215, 216, 218
Oso Casas, L. 149, 150, 160
'other' 11, 13, 69, 114, 116, 117, 133, 147
   eroticized 112
   exoticised 112, 118, 129-30
   and race 113, 118
Out On My Own 198, 199, 200, 201ff., 206
outreach work 5, 75ff., 86-7, 91, 199
   complexity of 76, 84, 86

   data collection 76
   definition of 75-6, 77
   risk management 84-6
   and social networks 76, 82-4, 85, 86
   spaces of 79-82, 85
outreach workers 82
   consistency of 81, 82, 84, 86
   emotions of 80
   professional 75, 76, 79, 84
   and protection 78, 86
   reputation of 85
   and risk management 84-6
   skills of 76, 78, 86
   and spaces of sex work 79-82, 86
   volunteers 75, 76, 78, 82
   walking by 78-9, 80
owners 139

Parsons, J.T. *see* Bimbi, D.S. And Parsons, J.T.
participant observation 75, 76, 79, 85, 138, 151, 184
participants 63, 65, 67, 69, 199, 203
   access to 77, 78, 81, 86
      by internet 91-2, 94, 95, 100-101
   control of 93
   emotions of 97
   recruitment of 63, 64, 91, 95, 100
   relationships with 65, 67, 69, 81-2, 85
   and visual anonymity 96, 97, 98
   see also male sex workers; men who pay for sex; participant observation
partners 169
passion 141, 143, 175
passports 128, 129
Patpong 113
patriarchy 30, 170, 201, 208
patrons 153, 158, 159
Pattaya 115, 116
patterns of behaviour 49, 51
pay 155, 159, 169, 185, 202
Paying the Price (2004) 25, 27, 28, 30
peer groups 82, 85
penis 216, 222
perceptions 50, 51
performance 146, 183, 192
permits 150, 152-3, 156
personal expression 143

PhD research 5, 59, 63, 69, 70, 75, 76
Philippines 110
phone sex 3
Phuket 115
physical appearance 130, 158, 184
pimps 32
ping-pong shows 112-13, 115
place 150, 168, 198, 209
    'destination' 149
    'home' 149
places, sexual 111, 112
    see also geographies
pleasure 61, 142, 182, 183, 186, 189, 203,
    208, 217
    see also fun
pluralism 209
police 5, 12, 16, 17, 19, 20, 26, 31, 60, 79,
    80, 81, 85
    in Argentina 173, 174-5, 176
    in Costa Rica 124, 126, 134
    in New Zealand 45-6, 49ff.
    perceptions of 50, 51
Policek, N. 83
Policing and Crime Act (2009) 4, 23ff., 29
    Section 14 23, 24, 26
Policing and Crime Bill (2008) 26, 32, 33
policy 4-5, 11, 167, 209
    debates 20, 29
    and evidence 30, 31, 34-5
    UK review of 23-7
political change 2, 4
politicians 151, 152, 173
politics 60, 117, 126, 167, 168, 170, 213
popular culture 14
porn producers 7
pornography 77, 91
poverty 15, 17, 29
power 3, 49, 110, 111, 113, 116, 117, 169,
    183, 214
    and exotic 'other' 118
    and looking 117
press 13, 126, 127, 128
prevalence 62
prevention 25
Price, K. 183, 187, 189, 192
Prince Hotel 124, 126-7, 134
Pritchard, J. 171
privacy 98

private classes 140
private dances 185, 189, 192
products 213, 214n., 217
professional jobs 155
professionalism 143, 145
profits 101, 113, 126, 134, 156, 169
promiscuity 13, 14, 16, 19, 20
prostitutes 110, 125, 126, 177, 199, 209
    'amateur' 11, 13-14, 15, 19, 20
    definition of 11
    physical appearance of 14-15
    professional 11, 14, 15, 17
        morality of 17
    rights of 20
    see also sex workers
prostitution 1, 3, 170
    in Costa Rica 125, 126
    definitions of 11, 14, 19
    fears of 11, 12, 13, 19-20
    routes out of 25, 198
    and Swiss cabarets 153
    and tango dancing 145-6
    in Thailand 112, 113
    UK research on 12
    see also sex, sale of; sex work
Prostitution Reform Act (PRA) 39, 40-
    41ff., 50-51
    benefits of 40, 44, 50
    limitations of 42-3, 47, 48, 51
protection 48, 81, 86, 142, 146, 220, 223
Pruitt, D. and LaFont, S. 110, 116, 138
Psimmenos, I. 150
psychoanalysis 116
public attitudes 27, 28
public goods 177, 178
public health 40, 41
public nuisance 25n., 39, 40
Public Places (Order) Bill 16
public sex environment (PSE) 78
public spaces 197, 198
public sphere 173
punishment 15, 16, 24, 127
purchasers 23, 24, 28-9
    crack-down on 33
    research on 26, 30
    see also kerb-crawlers; men who pay
        for sex

qualitative research 93, 94, 101, 102, 200, 208

quantitative research 92-3, 94, 97, 101, 102, 200

Queen, Carol 213, 218, 219, 220, 223

queer identity 202, 208, 216

questionnaires 199, 200, 204, 206, 207
  online 92, 93, 101
  see also interviews; surveys

questions 93, 200
  open-ended 94

race 110, 111, 113, 118, 119, 214, 218, 219, 221

racialization 118, 130

radical feminism 23, 30, 34, 40, 44

Rambo-Ronai, C. 183

Rambo-Ronai, C. and Ellis, C. 183, 189

rape 29, 49, 50

reasoning 23

recognition 175, 176

red light areas 60, 76, 78, 84, 112, 113, 115, 124, 130, 131

redistribution 177

re-education programmes 25, 26, 60

referral service 77-8

reflexivity 59, 60, 61-2, 66, 70, 93, 100

regularity 79, 81ff., 85, 86

regulation 40
  informal 81

relationships 62, 63, 65, 66, 67, 69, 70, 154, 182, 186, 191-2
  among female sex workers 132-4
  and male sex workers 81-2, 83, 85
  and respondents 93, 94
  in tango dancing 143-4

Relles, Alicia 219

representation 63, 117, 126, 138, 143, 168, 214, 215, 222

representational strategies 217, 220

reputation 145

research 1, 2, 3-4, 7, 12, 27, 44, 70, 91, 138, 146, 213
  on decriminalization 39, 40, 43ff.
  and emotional stories 61-2, 68
  feminist critique of 93, 97
  on foreign sex workers 125
  on lap-dancing 182-3, 184ff., 192

on LGTB comminities 197-8, 199, 200, 201ff., 208

methodology 5, 7, 60-61

on mobility 149, 150

neglect of 23, 30, 31

objectivity of 5, 30

problems of 59, 60, 61, 62, 64

on purchasers of sex 26, 27

reflexivity in 61

sex tourism 109-13, 119, 129
  female 109, 110-11, 113, 116, 119
  male 109, 110, 111, 113

sex worker organizations, 167-8

strategies 91, 102

see also research participants; sex researchers

research participants
  difficult emotions of 61
  recruitment of 60

researchers 5, 93, 181
  see also sex researchers

resistance 4, 6-7, 47, 51, 167, 172, 175
  by lap-dancers 182, 183, 184, 189-90, 191, 192
  in work places 192
  see also sex worker organizations

respect 190

respectability 13, 15, 17, 18, 20, 214, 217, 221, 224, 225

respondents 42, 64, 93, 94ff., 169, 200, 208
  see also participants

retail spaces 215

retailers 214, 215, 217, 220
  see also sex toys retail

Rio Negro 176

risk 48, 84-6, 98

Rivers-Moore, M. 6, 138, 147

Robinson, L.S. *see* Bishop, R. and Robinson, L.S.

romance tourists 110, 116-17, 138, 147

romantic feelings 144, 146

Royalle, Candida 223-4

rules
  lap dancing 182, 187, 189, 190, 191, 192
  tango 140

rules of conduct 140

Russia 152, 155, 156

Index

sadism 116
sadness 565-6
safe sex 41, 77, 133, 173, 199
safety 64, 76, 81, 82, 85, 128, 146, 215, 217, 218, 219, 220, 221, 222, 225
salaries 159
sales staff 214, 216, 217, 218, 221
Salvation Army 19
San Francisco 213, 216
San José
  foreign spaces in 126
  red light district 130, 131
  sex work areas 123, 124, 130ff.
  sex workers 128, 132-4
    foreign 125
  see also Gringo Gulch
Sanchez Taylor, J. 109, 110, 114, 130, 138
Sanders, Erin 5, 6
Sanders T. 45, 59, 60, 61, 62ff., 77, 83, 91, 92, 98, 101, 182
  see also Hubbard, P. and Sanders, T.
Sanders, T. and Campbell, M. 48
Sanders, T. and Campbell, R. 63, 97
Sanders, T., O'Neill, M. and Pitcher, J. 1
Sandra Cabrera Health Centre 177
Santa Fé 176
Sardi, M. and Froidevaux, D. 149
Sassen, S. 128
saunas 91, 197
scopophilia 114
Seattle 213
self 117
self-esteem 173, 176, 177
Self, Helen 12, 16, 19
self-disclosure 96, 97, 98
self-organization 171; *see also* AMMAR
self-regulation 190, 191
Semans, Anne 216, 218
senses 79, 80, 86, 93
sensuality 143, 144, 185
service providers 199, 200
services 143, 144, 146
Setting the Boundaries (2000) 25
sex, sale of 27, 84, 91, 112
  and cabaret dancers 153, 157
  in LGBT communities 197, 201ff., 208
  others involved in 84, 85, 102
  and tango dancers 145

see also prostitution; sex work
Sex and Exploitation Survey (2008) 27
sex industry 46, 102
  diversity of 1, 3, 4
  legal regulation of 2
  as tourist attraction 115
  see also management; sex work
sex negativity 217, 220
sex positivity 214, 215, 216-17, 219, 223, 224, 225
sex researchers 5, 40, 76, 102, 115
  anger of 66, 69
  anxiety of 64-5, 67, 68, 70
  biography of 61
  and data collection 67-8, 70
  emotional responses 59-60, 61, 63-6ff.
    negative 62, 64-6, 68-9
    recognition of 62, 63, 66ff., 71
  feelings of inadequacy 62, 67
  identity 62, 64, 67, 68-9, 70
  interactions 60, 65, 68, 70
  novice 67, 70, 71
  and objectivity 61
  and sadness 65-6
  safety of 64
  and stress 61
  see also outreach workers
sex retailing *see* sex toys retail
sex shop workers 3
  see also sex retailing
sex slaves 31
sex therapists 215, 216
sex tourism 2, 5-6, 109-13ff., 119
  in Costa Rica 126, 129
    and foreignness 125-8, 129, 131-2
    national aspects 129, 131, 134
    see also Gringo Gulch; San José
  and class 111
  definition of 110, 111, 118
  and gender 109ff., 114ff., 118, 119
  and race 110, 111, 118
  and theory 129, 146
  visual 111-12, 113ff., 116-17
    see also gaze; tango tourism
sex tourists 109ff., 114-15, 139
  in Gringo Gulch 128ff.
  preferential treatment of 129

see also female sex tourists; western
    women
sex toys retail 7, 213-25
    and class 215, 218, 221, 222-3, 225
    environment of 218-20
    growth of 214, 215
    locations 213, 221
    model of 213
    and safety 215, 217, 218ff., 222
    and therapy 7, 213, 216
    traditional type 213, 219, 220ff., 225
    see also Good Vibrations
sex trafficking 23, 26, 28-9, 150, 156, 168
    research on 31
sex work 145, 209, 214n.
    definitions of 3, 167
    dominant myth of 197, 198, 200, 208-9
    structural analysis of 170
sex work organizers 100-101, 102
sex work studies 1, 3
sex worker organizations 6, 167-79
    research on 167-8
    success of 179
    see also AMMAR
sex workers
    accounts by 60
    consultation of 14
    distinctions between 13-14, 130, 134
    freedom of 41, 46
    health of 41, 42
    male 3
    and new technology 2, 91ff.
    recognition as 176, 177
    relationships between 132-4
    rights of 41, 42, 43, 47, 50, 51, 168,
        170, 177
    services for 77
    third world 111
    views of 40
    western 111
    see also foreign sex workers;
        male sex workers; migrant sex
        workers; resistance; sex worker
        organizations; street sex workers
sexism 7, 61, 213, 225
sexual attraction 62
sexual differences 223
sexual education 213, 214, 215-16, 217

sexual exploitation 7, 23, 24, 26, 28, 31,
    101, 110, 111, 152
    challenging 41-2, 49
    and criminalization 32
    definition of 33
    information about 61
    reporting of 33
    surveys 27
sexual harassment 47
sexual health 5, 18, 41, 42, 62, 76, 173,
    199, 215
    research 92, 202
sexual health clinics 60
sexual politics 213, 222
sexual practices 2, 11, 13, 18, 111, 138
    regulation of 12
sexual problems 216
sexual relationships 110, 111, 116, 190
sexual resource centers 215, 223
sexual stories 61
sexual 'uplift' 224, 225
sexual variation 216
sexual-economic exchange research 138,
    146
sexuality 127, 128, 146, 147, 170, 217,
    219, 221
    racialized 130
    stereotypes of 119, 129-30, 225
sexualization 118
Sexually Transmitted Infections (STI) 177
Sh! Women's Erotic Emporium 213, 220
shame 47, 173, 174, 217, 219, 223, 224,
    225
sharing 134
Sharpe, K. 60, 91
Sharpe, K. and Earle, S. 91
shelter 204, 207
shock 222
shops 139
signs 80, 114
Sivadas, E. *see* Mehta, R. and Sivadas, E.
Skeggs, Beverley 221
skills 79, 84, 85, 139, 140, 142-3, 144, 158,
    169, 188
sleaze 146, 214, 215, 221, 222, 223
Smith, Jacqui 33
Smith, R. *see* Hall, T. and Smith, R.
snowball sampling 91

social benefits 170, 178
social bonds 154-5
social care 76, 77, 173
social change 2, 13, 14, 21, 39, 168, 177, 179
social context 61, 168
social distinctions 222-3, 225
social inclusion 178
social movements 167, 177
social networks 76, 82-4, 85, 86, 140, 158
social order 13, 17, 40
social performances 86
social policy 1, 4
social problems 12
social researchers 92, 95
    feminist 92-3, 97
social rituals 183, 187-9, 190, 191, 192
social skills 142, 143
social status 188, 189, 223, 225
socialization 183, 189, 192
society 17, 23, 51
sociology 1, 3-4, 198, 203
solicitation
    UK law on 11, 15-17, 19, 20, 25
solidarity 6, 184, 192
Sosa, Jorgelina 175
South Auckland 43
South East Asia 130
spaces 6, 13, 20, 70, 113, 134, 146, 171, 197, 208
    adult retail 215, 220, 221
    and male sex workers 75, 79ff.
    separation of 126, 128, 130-34
    and sex tourism 109, 111, 112, 116, 126
Spain 150
Spanger, M. 149, 150
specificities 134, 168, 172, 209, 215, 219
Spivey, S. 183
Stants, F. *see* Dahinden, J. and Stants, F.
Stephens, L. 170
stereotypes 30, 31, 46, 47, 48, 68, 69, 70, 101, 111, 119, 147, 201, 213
    national 131-4

stigma 5, 46-8, 49, 51, 59, 60, 63, 70, 97, 98, 170, 172, 173-4, 176, 182, 183, 208
Stoller, R. 114
street environment 76, 78, 79, 80ff.
'street gossip' 83
Street Offences Act (1959) 25
Street Offences Act (1985) 28
Street Offences Committee *see* Macmillan Committee
street prostitution 16, 124
    see also solicitation; street environment; street sex workers
street sex workers 25, 83, 91
    in Argentina 169ff., 179
    in Manchester 76ff.
    in New Zealand 39, 43-4ff.
        demand for 44-5
        impact of decriminalization on 41-3
        and police 45-6, 49, 50, 51
        previous experiences of 49, 50
        research on 43ff.
        violence against 48-50
    and self-organization 172
    views of 40
    see also outreach work
stress 189
strict liability offence 23, 26, 31
    problems of 32-4
    revision of 33
Stringer, Hubert 14
strippers 153, 182, 185, 186
structure 4, 29, 111, 170, 171, 172, 173
students 76
subject 12, 145
subjectivity 69, 71, 93, 177
suburban housewives 218, 219
Sugar 213, 217, 221
suicide 199, 200
supply 44
support servives 199, 200
support workers 5
surveys 5, 27, 60, 92-5, 169
    quantitative 92-3, 94
    online 92, 94-5
    self-completion 92, 93
    see also interviews

Sweden 26, 27, 30, 32, 40
Switzerland 6, 152-60
    immigration policies 151, 156
        cantonal 156, 157
    migration 149, 154-5
    work permits 149, 152-3, 156
    see also cabaret dancers
symbols 99, 114, 117, 134, 178, 223

taboos 60, 61, 71, 222, 224
Tackling Demand For Prostitution: A
    Review (2008) 26, 28, 29, 63
tango agents 141-2
tango clubs 139, 140, 141
'tango feelings' 143-5
tango tourism 6, 137-48
    advertising 139, 141
    businesses 141-2, 143, 145
    companions 139
    guides 139, 140
    and prostitution 145, 146
    rules of 140
    venues 137, 139, 140, 141, 145
    see also body work; tango clubs; taxi
        dancers
taste 214, 220, 222, 223
taxi dancers
    agency 141-2, 143, 144, 145
    and bodywork 143, 144
    and emotional intimacy 143-4, 145,
        146, 147
    female 138, 139, 145-6, 147
    freelance 140-41
    labour of 142-3, 146-7
    male 138, 139, 140ff., 145, 147
Taxi Tango 142, 145, 146
Taylor, P. and Bain, P. 182, 184, 189, 190,
    192
teachers 139, 140, 145, 170
teasing 184
technology 2, 5, 91, 92, 93ff.
telephone interviews 98-9
television 114, 126, 127, 128
temporal dimension 150-51, 153-61
text 94
Thailand 2, 5-6, 109-121, 149, 152
    entertainment venues 112-13
    gendered sex tourism 109-13

and 'other' 113, 114, 116, 117, 118
power relations in 113, 116, 117
western women in 112-13ff., 116, 118
sex workers in 109, 116, 117, 118
    local men 110, 111, 116-17
    local women 114-15, 118
tourist sights 114-16
and voyeurism 112, 113, 116, 117
    see also gaze
therapy 7, 65, 213, 216
Thiévent, R. 6, 150, 153, 158
third parties 83, 85, 101, 102
threats 23, 27, 42, 84, 85
time 145, 172, 202-3
tolerance 40, 43
tourism
    in Thailand 114-16
    visual 111-12
    see also sex tourism; tourism studies;
        tourist industry
tourism studies 116
tourist industry 114, 138
tourists 124, 126, 131, 149
    female 116ff., 145
        see also female sex tourists
    male 124
    and tango 137, 138, 141-2
Town Police Act (1847) 16
trade unions 167, 168, 170, 171-2, 173
    see also AMMAR
training 143, 217
transcription 67
transgender 199, 201
    see also LGBT communities;
        transsexuals
transgression 13, 18
transnationality 6, 123, 129, 132, 154, 155,
    161
transsexuals 112, 197, 201, 222
    see also LGTB communities
travel 3
Truong, T. 112, 138, 149
trust 81, 97-8, 158

Ukraine 152, 155, 157
United Kingdom 2, 39, 40, 91, 209
    fear of prostitutes in 11, 12, 13, 19-20
    lap-dancing clubs 181-2

law 12, 15-21, 23ff.
policy review 23-7
research on men who pay for sex 59ff.
United States 7, 145, 154, 182, 213, 214
universities 64, 70, 85, 155, 198
University of California, San Francisco
(UCSF) 215, 216
unprotected sex, 43
urban spaces 13, 17, 18, 80
Urry, J. 114, 116
users 30, 110

Vagrancy Act (1824) 15
values 215, 217, 221
van der Veen, M. 209
verbal abuse 46-7
verbal skills 142, 143
vibrators 216, 223
victims 29, 30, 33, 46, 110, 150
Victorian era 12
video conferencing 2
violence 3, 5, 23, 27, 30, 32, 33, 61, 63,
116, 169, 171, 175, 199
domestic 205
non-reporting of 49, 51, 173
redress for 49
reporting 42-3, 49
research on 62
in New Zealand 42, 48-50
visas 149, 156
visibility 45, 86, 117
visual anonymity 96, 97, 98
voyeurism 112, 113, 116, 117
see also gaze
vulnerabilities 146, 160, 178, 198, 200,
205, 206, 208

wages 155, 159, 169, 185
Walkowitz, Judith 12
watching 114, 116, 117, 118; see also gaze;
voyeurism
webcams 91
websites 60, 77, 94, 138, 170, 171, 197,
200
Weide, Laura 220
Wesely, J.K. 62, 183
West 167, 178
western women 112, 116, 117, 118, 119

gaze of 113ff.
and Thai women 117, 118
Westmarland, N. see Hester, M. and
Westmarland, N.
white people 113, 116, 117, 118, 129, 178,
183, 218n., 224
Whowell, Mary 5, 59, 75n., 76n., 79n.
Wilson, A. 112, 113
Winks, Cathy 216, 218, 219, 224
Wintherbauer, Janni 32
Wolfenden Committee 12, 25
Wolff, J. 113
Wolkowitz, C. 143, 144, 171
women 3, 19, 30, 98, 124, 197, 199, 201,
202
appearance of 14-15
behaviour of 12, 13ff., 17
changing role of 11, 13
distinctions among 4, 11ff., 17, 18, 20
oppression of 170
and sex toy stores 213, 215, 218-19,
220, 223-4
and sexual problems 215-16
stereotypes of 46, 47, 48, 111, 119, 147
in Thailand 114-15, 118
see also female sex tourists; sex
workers;
taxi dancers; western women; young
women
Women of the Underworld 15
Woodthorpe, K. 66, 67
words 93, 94, 95, 99, 100
work 3, 7, 142-3, 146-7, 150-51ff., 168,
197, 207, 208, 209
definition of 182
informal 171, 172
literature 186, 192
motivation 186
strategy 170
see also bodywork; emotional labour;
sex work
work permits 6
workers 172, 177, 179, 183-4
working-class 123, 169, 222
women 50, 177
working conditions 142, 157-8, 159, 160,
183
Wunderlich, F.M. 80

young people 41, 43, 61, 77, 198, 199, 200
young women 13, 14, 20, 43, 124
   in cabaret industry 151, 158-9
   corruption of 11

Zelizer, V. 208
zoning 221, 223

Milton Keynes UK
Ingram Content Group UK Ltd.
UKHW032146110224
437641UK00006B/19